IMPOSTER DOCTORS

IMPOSTER DOCTORS

Patients at Risk

REBEKAH BERNARD, MD

Universal Publishers
Irvine • Boca Raton

Imposter Doctors: Patients at Risk

Universal Publishers, Inc.
Irvine • Boca Raton
USA • 2023
www.Universal-Publishers.com

ISBN: 978-1-62734-443-2 (pbk.)
ISBN: 978-1-62734-444-9 (ebk.)

Typeset by Medlar Publishing Solutions Pvt Ltd, India
Cover design by Ivan Popov

Library of Congress Cataloging-in-Publication Data

Names: Bernard, Rebekah, 1974- author.
Title: Imposter doctors : patients at risk / Rebekah Bernard.
Description: Irvine : Universal-Publishers, 2023. | Includes
bibliographical references.
Identifiers: LCCN 2023008502 (print) | LCCN 2023008503 (ebook) |
ISBN 9781627344432 (paperback) | ISBN 9781627344449 (ebook)
Subjects: LCSH: Patients--Safety measures. | Medical errors--Prevention. |
Physician and patient.
Classification: LCC R729.8 .B475 2023 (print) | LCC R729.8 (ebook) |
DDC 610.28/9--dc23/eng/20230419
LC record available at https://lccn.loc.gov/2023008502
LC ebook record available at https://lccn.loc.gov/2023008503

TABLE OF CONTENTS

LIST OF TABLES

LIST OF FIGURES

INTRODUCTION

When you experience a medical emergency, you expect to be treated by a licensed physician with expertise in your condition. What happens when you look up from your hospital gurney to find that the doctor has been replaced by a non-physician practitioner with just a fraction of the training and experience? This scenario, which is becoming an increasingly frequent reality in American healthcare, was the focus of *Patients at Risk: The Rise of the Nurse Practitioner and Physician Assistant in Healthcare*, the first—and so far, the only book to focus on a silent but deadly patient safety issue that has been virtually ignored by health policy analysts.

Patients at Risk was released in the fall of 2020 to a firestorm of controversy, including condemnation from nurse practitioner and physician assistant advocacy groups, who accused the authors of peddling conspiracy theories and attacking colleagues. Within weeks of its publication, Mary Mundinger, the veritable godmother of nurse practitioner expansion rights, wrote a letter to the *Wall Street Journal* rejecting the book's premise that there is a lack of scientific research on independently practicing non-physicians. Mundinger pointed to research that she published in 2000 as proof, insisting that nurse practitioners in the study were practicing independently.[1]

To respond to these criticisms directly, co-authors Niran Al-Agba and Rebekah Bernard created a podcast series. Its seminal episode, 'There's Something About Mary,' detailed evidence repudiating Mundinger's *Wall Street Journal* argument, including new revelations obtained from the nurse researcher's memoir and YouTube video recordings that prove significant physician involvement and oversight throughout the study.[2]

With a rapid accumulation of new data on non-physician practitioner care, the *Patients at Risk* podcast aired 72 episodes over the next two years featuring physicians, research analysts, healthcare advocates, journalists, nurse practitioners, physician assistants, attorneys, and most importantly, patients. This book, a sequel to *Patients at Risk,* incorporates new information gleaned from these podcast recordings, and is shared in narrative format to engage the reader. But do not be fooled by the anecdotal nature of these stories: they are factual, and they are backed by data.

The goal of this book is simple: to provide insight into the current workings of the healthcare system so that patients can empower themselves to ensure they receive the best healthcare. To be clear, optimal health care can indeed include care provided by non-physician practitioners. Nurse practitioners and physician assistants are critical members of the medical team and studies have shown over and over that when they work closely together with physicians, patients receive outstanding health care. However, when physicians are removed from the equation altogether, all bets are off—and that's exactly what this book will show.

THE SHOWDOWN

On December 17, 2020, television network WGN America featured the book *Patients at Risk: The Rise of the Nurse Practitioner and Physician Assistant in Healthcare* in a news segment entitled, "Families sound alarm on medical transparency after deaths of their children."[3] The book discussed the increasing replacement of physicians by non-physician practitioners—nurse practitioners (NP) and physician assistants (PA)—and centered around the tragic story of Alexus Ochoa, a 19-year-old honor student who died after Mercy Health Systems, a multi-billion-dollar corporation, staffed an Oklahoma emergency department with an online-trained nurse practitioner working all alone.

The American Association of Nurse Practitioners (AANP) was desperate to keep the public from seeing this news piece. The advocacy group worked frantically, issuing a call to action to its 121,000 members, urging them to inundate WGN with phone calls, emails, and social media messages demanding that the station pull the broadcast. An email written by AANP president Sophia Thomas read,

> Dear AANP member,
>
> I have an urgent request. We need your help to contact WGN America, News Nation using Facebook, Twitter, email, and phone to pull an irresponsible news story by reporter Rich McHugh that maligns NP [nurse practitioner] care.
>
> The story is scheduled to air tonight around 7 PM CST. This news piece suggests that NPs are unsafe providers who are unqualified to provide care. The storyline parrots the recent book [Patients at Risk] by Physicians for Patient Protection President Rebekah Bernard and a coauthor.

> This piece has the potential to reach millions of households nationwide. I was interviewed for this story, and the reporter's bias was clear. We have worked together to stop irresponsible journalism before. We need your action immediately today.[4]

The message was followed by contact information for WGN, including the network's phone number, email address, website, and even direct contact information for WGN executives. It included this sample phone message:

> Shame on you, WGN. Pull this irresponsible story from Rich McHugh. You are maligning NPs working on the frontlines of a pandemic. NPs' outstanding safety track record is backed by decades of research. News should be free of bias.

A sample Tweet suggestion read:

> @newsnationnow @RichMcHugh Your news promo on NP care is irresponsible and clearly biased. Pull this story. You should be ashamed of maligning frontline health care workers when patients need more care, not less.[4]

Despite the AANP's aggressive actions, WGN aired the segment, prefacing the report with a mention of the techniques used by the organization.

> Even before the story aired Thursday night on NewsNation, there was significant pressure directed at us by the AANP—The American Association of Nurse Practitioners—not to run the story and alleging that our report unfairly maligns nurse practitioners in America. That is not the case and certainly not our intention, and it's one reason we interviewed the AANP in this story.[3]

After watching the complete segment, it was clear why the AANP wanted the story pulled. Journalist Rich McHugh pulled no punches, challenging Sophia Thomas with some of the toughest questions facing the nurse practitioner profession today. He began with a question that is far more complex than it seems at first light: "Do nurse practitioners practice medicine?"[3]

Nurse practitioners are registered nurses who complete an additional two years of training, which includes a minimum of 500 hours of clinical experience.[5] To be licensed to practice medicine, physicians must complete a minimum of 7 years of training, including 15,000 hours of clinical experience[6] (Table 1). Because of these differences, nurse practitioner advocates often state that rather than practicing medicine, NPs practice 'advanced nursing.'

Table 1. Minimum Years and Clinical Hours of Training by Profession

	College	Graduate Program/ Clinical Hours	Residency/ Clinical Hours	Total/Minimum Clinical Hours
Physician	4 years (BS/BA)	4 years (MD/DO) 6,000 hours	3 years 9,000–10,000 hours	11 years 15,000–16,000 hours
Nurse Practitioner	4 years (BSN or BA/BS direct entry)	2 (MSN) – 3 years (DNP) 500 (MSN) – 1500 (DNP) hours	Zero	6 years 500–1500 hours
Physician Assistant	4 years (BS/BA)	2 years (MS-PAS) 2,000 hours	Zero	6 years 2,000 hours

Thomas took a different tack, answering, "Nurse practitioners practice healthcare."

McHugh's brows furrow. "But I'm confused," he said. "If nurse practitioners are prescribing medicines and treating patients, aren't they practicing medicine?"

Thomas's reply: "I think the definition of medicine is changing."[3]

Indeed, the AANP has worked tirelessly for decades to expand the definition of medicine to incorporate care provided by nurse practitioners. Through strategic alliances and intensive lobbying efforts, nurse practitioners have successfully achieved 'full practice authority,' the right to treat patients without physician oversight, in about half the states of the Union, despite having just a fraction of the training of doctors.

McHugh asked Sophia Thomas if the AANP's goal is for nurse practitioners to have full practice authority—"basically the ability to run their own practices in every state in America."

Thomas answered in the affirmative, noting that this goal is supported by organizations like the Federal Trade Commission, the National Academy of Medicine, and the National Governors Association. "They all also recommend nurse practitioners have full practice authority because they know and understand that NP practice and clinical outcomes are equal to our physician colleagues and NPs improve access to care," she said.[3]

While this messaging of 'equal outcomes' is a core AANP talking point, it fails to include an important caveat: studies comparing nurse practitioner care to physician care have always evaluated low-risk patients with known diagnoses. Further, these studies have invariably involved some degree of physician supervision.

Just as the definition of medicine is being stretched, research findings are being extrapolated to the point of illogic, with advocates arguing that if nurse practitioners can treat simple medical problems with physician assistance, they should have similar outcomes with complex patients and no physician oversight.

Advocates also fail to mention that the last large-scale analysis evaluating NP outcomes was published more than 20 years ago, and well before the rapid growth of nurse practitioner training programs pumping out poorly prepared graduates. Rich McHugh asked Sophia Thomas about the rise of such programs. "Would you agree that there is an issue with online diploma mills with regard to nursing schools right now?"

Thomas: "I think that there is an issue with—," she paused. "There are a few non-accredited programs out there, and AANP doesn't support programs that are not accredited."

McHugh: "If I understand you correctly, you're saying it's an issue but it's not that big of an issue."

Thomas tells McHugh that nurse practitioners need to graduate from an accredited program of nursing. "They are expected to meet certain core competencies and things like that," she said. "AANP has an issue with these programs that don't enforce these core competencies—meet the certain standards that are set forth by the educators." However, Thomas did not underline any planned actions by the AANP to close such programs.[3]

As part of the news story, Rich McHugh interviewed the family of Alexus Ochoa, who died after receiving improper treatment by a nurse practitioner working alone in an emergency department. Alexus's mother Amy told McHugh that the nurse practitioner who treated Alexus introduced herself as a doctor, saying, "I am the attending physician." It wasn't until after Alexus's death that the Ochoa family learned the truth.[3]

Regarding this lack of transparency, McHugh asked Thomas if she had any issue with nurse practitioners inappropriately referring to themselves as a doctor. Thomas responded adamantly: "Doctor is an academic term. Doctor doesn't mean physician and the physician world doesn't own the term doctor."[3]

When its efforts to cancel the WGN news segment failed, the American Association of Nurse Practitioners mounted a public relations campaign against the network, issuing a press release condemning the report. The AANP accused WGN of bias, stating that the news organization "chose to decline interviews with nationally recognized experts whose views diverged with the outlet's preferred and biased narrative"—even though the segment included extensive comments from the AANP's president.[7]

The press release also named the authors of *Patients at Risk*, stating, "WGN's coverage, at best, misrepresents the NP profession and parrots the conspiracy theories and misstatements of Rebekah Bernard, MD and Niran Al-Agba, MD, physicians who derive direct economic benefit from limiting patient access to NP delivered health care."[7] The news release failed to clarify how the two primary care physicians with full solo practices could benefit from limiting nurse practitioner care—especially since both would be more likely to financially gain from hiring or remotely supervising nurse practitioners.

In the press release, the AANP insisted that 'decades of evidence-based research' have demonstrated nurse practitioner safety (true, when managing low-risk patients under physician supervision) and stated that "not one of the 22 states, District of Columbia or two U.S. territories that authorize Full Practice Authority for NPs has ever reversed course" (also true, despite a lack of any randomized, controlled studies evaluating the care by unsupervised nurse practitioners in these states).

The AANP's efforts to downplay WGN's report about patient safety were largely successful. Two years after this exposé, no meaningful action has been taken to limit independent practice by nurse practitioners nor to improve standards at training programs. On the contrary, nurse practitioners—and physician assistants—are replacing physicians more than ever, with no end in sight. The employment of non-physicians is projected to grow by 40% for nurse practitioners and by 28% for physician assistants in the next ten years.[8,9] At the same time, the employment of physicians and surgeons is projected to grow by only 3%.[10]

As predicted in *Patients at Risk*, the likelihood of being treated by a non-physician practitioner rather than a physician continues to increase, with dangerous repercussions. In fact, in just the few years since the book was published, enough new information has come to light on the subject to warrant this entirely new publication.

For example, the COVID-19 era has witnessed the rise—and fall—of nurse practitioner-staffed telehealth startups for various medical conditions, including mental illness. Rather than hiring psychiatrists to treat patients with serious psychiatric problems, these for-profit companies elected to employ less expensive and far less trained nurse practitioners, with dire consequences, including flooding the market with prescriptions for stimulant drugs like Adderall, causing addiction and death.

Despite the ongoing coronavirus pandemic and monkeypox outbreak, U.S. hospitals and clinics, increasingly owned by private equity for-profit companies, have slashed physician staffing, and replaced physicians with nurse practitioners and physician assistants as a form of cost-cutting. Citing narrowing profit margins due to the pandemic, these medical facilities increased the ratio of non-physician practitioners to unsafe levels, which has led to patient deaths.

Even premier academic organizations have embraced the trend of replacing physicians. In the last two years, Johns Hopkins University began to promote the use of nurse practitioners instead of gastroenterologists to perform colonoscopies, and the University of Pennsylvania studied using radiology technicians rather than radiologists to interpret chest x-rays on critically ill patients in the intensive care unit.

In recent years, there has been a significant increase in the number of nurse practitioners and physician assistants choosing to hang their own shingles, opening urgent care clinics, and eschewing primary care in favor of cash-based practices. Companies like *Collaborating Docs* and *The Elite NP* seem eager to help, potentially profiting from connecting non-physicians with doctors who may supervise in name only, and selling online courses about non-FDA approved and potentially risky anti-aging hormones, unnecessary intravenous infusions, and cosmetic treatments. In many cases, patients are not being informed about the credentials of these physician replacements, and few safeguards are in place to ensure patient safety.

But the pendulum may be starting to swing. The last two years have also seen the publication of multiple academic papers expressing concern about the state of nursing education. In 2021, academic nurse researchers exposed serious deficits in the educational experiences of family nurse practitioners, and in 2022, concluded unequivocally that nurse practitioners should not work in emergency departments without strict physician supervision. 2021 also saw a correction added to one of the most influential papers used to promote nurse practitioner independence, noting a previously undisclosed conflict of interest by lead author Mary Mundinger.

Legal interpretations of non-physician practice liability are also beginning to shift. Case law has traditionally held that nurse practitioners and physician assistants cannot be held to the standard of care of a physician in a malpractice trial. Plaintiff's attorneys are challenging the court to consider the standard of care, not for a particular clinician, but rather, the standard care that any patient should expect to receive in a comparable situation. In August 2022, the North Carolina Supreme Court overturned a ninety-year-old legal precedent that protected nurse practitioners from liability, citing an evolution in nursing responsibilities.

Importantly, data is beginning to accumulate showing concern about the effectiveness and cost of care provided by non-physician practitioners. A 2022 landmark review by Hattiesburg Clinic showed that independent nurse practitioners and physician assistants had poorer outcomes at a higher cost than physicians, increasing healthcare expenditures by an estimated $28.5 million per year. This finding led to a transformation of the clinic's practice model, and a return to physician-led care teams. There is also evidence that patients are becoming more aware of the differences in training and beginning to demand physician-led care.

But it's not all positive news. Despite evidence that physician-led care is best for patients, in 2021 the healthcare executives responsible for the creation of the retail pharmacy urgent care chain *MinuteClinic* launched a new primary care chain—staffed entirely by nurse practitioners. Based in Minneapolis, The Good Clinic has six locations in the area, and plans to expand primarily in states that allow nurses independent practice.

Private equity for-profit organizations have also begun to creep into healthcare markets outside of the U.S. In 2021, an investigative report revealed that the United Kingdom's largest chain of primary care clinics had systematically replaced physician general practitioners with physician assistants to save money. This policy change occurred when Operose Health, a private equity company owned by U.S. healthcare conglomerate Centene, purchased clinics that provide care to 600,000 National Health System patients.

IMPOSTER DOCTORS

Advocates for non-physician practice insist that there is no need for concern because nurse practitioners and physician assistants are just as good—or better—than physicians. They are wrong. Not only does the claim make no logical sense—is there any field of study in which similar skills can be gained with just 5% of the training? There is no scientific evidence to support such an audacious assertion. When asked to defend their position, organizations like the AANP often use impressive-sounding statements like this one:

> Since the NP role was established in 1965, research has consistently demonstrated the excellent outcomes and high quality of care provided by NPs ... Furthermore, NP care is comparable in quality to that of their physician colleagues, demonstrated by numerous studies that conclude no statistically significant difference across outcome measures.[11]

However, none of the studies cited by the AANP to support this bold claim include care provided by independent nurse practitioners managing typical patients; instead, they involve care teams of NPs and physicians working together and the management of straight-forward problems in low-risk patients. The truth is this: Despite over 50 years of scientific analysis of the care provided by non-physicians, there is no conclusive evidence that non-physician practitioners can provide safe and effective medical care without physician oversight. In fact, recent studies have shown the opposite: that the replacement of physicians puts patients at risk for worse outcomes at higher costs.

The assertion of being 'just as good or better' than physicians is aggressively promoted in marketing materials, media appearances, and in legislative committee hearings. Due to the fact that patient lives depend on these discussions, it is important to be clear and to label these claims for what they are: a deliberate effort to deceive the public. Organizations that advocate these mistruths knowingly sacrifice patient health and lives in the service of advancing corporate profit and political power.

Following the ethical principle of non-maleficence, or, 'do no harm,' some physicians are speaking out about these dangers to patients. This is not to say that physicians don't make mistakes themselves—in fact, the understanding of personal fallibility is one of the reasons that physicians are so concerned about the future. If errors can occur despite years of physician training, then how much more danger do medical professionals with less training pose?

An additional concern of these doctors is this: will there be a physician to care for them—or for their loved ones—in a time of medical need? While some physicians do not speak out due to the legitimate fear of job loss and cyberbullying, many others are either unaware of the extent of the problem, have been misled by non-physician claims, or are complicit with efforts to undermine the medical profession. Physicians must wake up and act before it is too late, because the truth is, we are all patients—or one day, we will be.

While *Patients at Risk* lay the groundwork for patients to better understand the dangers of physician replacements, *Imposter Doctors* provides more ammunition for patients to advocate for their own medical care. The only cure for today's healthcare crisis is for patients to become informed about who is providing their care. They must know the difference in training and education, and demand answers from those who would deprive them of physician-led care.

CHAPTER 1

THE PHYSICIAN SHORTAGE: A MANUFACTURED CRISIS

Seven-year-old Betty was the light of her family's life. "Betty was life, and she was happiness. We used to call her 'Wonder Betty' because even though she was autistic, she was making amazing progress," said her father Jeremy Wattenbarger during a *Patients at Risk* podcast recording.[12] "We were starting to see things in her that we were told were never to be expected. She was becoming verbal. She started riding her bicycle and running and interacting with other children."

When Betty suddenly developed a fever, Jeremy called her pediatrician who was unavailable but suggested that Betty be evaluated at a local pediatric urgent care. That seemed reasonable to Jeremy, who assumed that an urgent care would be like an emergency department. "In fact, this one advertised that they had the same capabilities as an emergency room and everything they needed to diagnose and take care of her," he said.

Photos taken of Betty in the urgent care waiting room showed a child that appeared quite unwell. Her expression is listless, her eyes sunken, and her lips dry, cracked, and tinged blue.[12] Indeed, measurements of Betty's vital signs showed concern that she wasn't getting enough oxygen, with a pulse oximetry reading between 88–94% (normal over 95%).

Jeremy said that he and his wife assumed that the clinician in the white coat who came to evaluate Betty was a physician. They were wrong. In fact, there was no physician on-site at the urgent care that day. Instead, Betty was treated by pediatric nurse practitioner Madeline Broemson, who diagnosed the child with influenza, a viral infection, and discharged her home. Jeremy remembered, "She told us that Betty just had the flu; that her lungs were clear, and everything was fine."

But Betty was not fine. She slept throughout the day, and the next morning, Betty would not wake up. As Jeremy attempted to rouse his daughter, he noticed black fluid—blood, he realized—coming from her mouth. Despite rushing Betty to the emergency department, it was too late. The light of Jeremy's life had been extinguished.

Autopsies showed that Betty did indeed have influenza, but she also had streptococcal pneumonia and evidence that the bacterial infection had spread into her bloodstream, causing sepsis. Jeremy and his wife questioned how their child could have declined so quickly, and whether earlier treatment could have saved her life. As they sought answers, it was only then that they discovered that Betty had been treated not by a physician, but by a nurse practitioner.

The Wattenbargers were shocked. "She did not identify herself as an APN [advanced practice nurse]," said Jeremy. "She did not wear a name tag or a badge or any other type of identification." Additionally, there was no signage to indicate that a physician was not on the premises, said Jeremy, who later discovered that Broemson's supervising physician Michael Cowan, DO was out of the country at the time that Betty was evaluated. Although Cowan had assigned a proxy to oversee Broemson while he was away, there was no evidence that the nurse practitioner sought any physician advice about Betty's care.

Jeremy Wattenbarger is now on a crusade to ensure that no one else loses a child. "Had we known Betty was going to see an advanced practice nurse and not a physician, we would have realized that she may not have had the skills to see Betty based on the way she looked that day, and we would have taken her to the emergency room," he said, noting that one of the points of confusion was the use of the word 'provider,' which he assumed was the same as a physician.[12]

NAME CHANGE: THE 'PROVIDER' IS IN

Originally used to refer to healthcare delivery agencies like hospitals, group practices, and insurance networks, the title 'provider' has been embraced by administrators and insurance payers as a way of grouping any clinician with a prescription pad. Non-physician advocates have been particularly enthusiastic about the title, with position papers by the AANP encouraging use of the term. Citing a recommendation from the Institute of Medicine calling for nurse practitioners to be "full partners with physicians and other healthcare professionals," the group encouraged policymakers to use the terms 'healthcare provider' and 'advanced practice provider,' while strongly rejecting the terms 'midlevel' or 'physician extender.'[13]

Writing in the *American Journal of Medicine*, Laura Kendall, MD argues that the word 'provider' is intended to create a false equivalence between physicians and non-physician practitioners—"a targeted method of obscuring the hierarchy of training and expertise, confusing the public, and quietly removing physicians as the captains of the healthcare team as a cost-cutting measure."[14]

Jeremy Wattenbarger agrees. "When most people hear the word provider, they hear 'doctor,' but it's not. Until this started, I didn't even know what a provider was." Jeremy says he has learned to ask, 'what kind of provider?' and chooses to wait to see a physician, noting that this has become increasingly difficult in his area. Describing a new primary care practice that he visited, Jeremy said he was told, "You can see the provider today, but the doctor only comes in once a week."[12]

CREATING A PHYSICIAN SHORTAGE

Indeed, patients are increasingly finding that the doctor is no longer 'in,' but has been replaced by a non-physician practitioner. Although healthcare experts have been warning about a physician shortage for the last twenty years,[15] the profession is increasing at a rate of just 3%, nowhere near enough to fill the projected deficit. Instead, nurse practitioners and physician assistants are being used to fill the gap, with employment rapidly rising and far surpassing the growth rate of physicians. Based on the current number of clinicians and projected growth rates, it is reasonable to expect that the number of non-physician practitioners will eventually surpass the number of practicing physicians (Table 2).

This disproportionate growth of clinicians reflects 30 years of U.S. healthcare policy, as influenced by non-physician lobbyists and corporate strategists. While healthcare companies and government agencies argue that they have no choice but to hire nurse practitioners and physician assistants due to a supposed 'physician shortage,' the truth is far more sinister. They are systematically replacing physicians with lesser-trained clinicians for one simple reason: money.

Nearly every discussion by advocates for non-physician independent practice begins with the phrase, '*because of the looming physician shortage …*,' followed by the proposal that non-physicians be permitted to practice medicine, despite having an estimated 5% of the training of physicians. Where did this shortage come from, and how was it allowed to happen?

Table 2. Total Number of Physicians, Nurse Practitioners, and Physician Assistants in 2022 and Projected 10-Year Growth Rate[15–18]

Type of Clinician	Total Number (2022)	Projected 10-Year Growth Rate
Physician	1,074,000	3%
Nurse Practitioner	355,000	40%
Physician Assistant	158,000	28%

In large part, the physician shortage was created by government policies instituted in the 1990s, when the government actually paid hospitals *not* to train physicians.[19] While medical school graduates receive 6,000 hours of clinical exposure, they cannot practice medicine without completing additional years of postgraduate training, called residency. In 1997, Congress froze residency funding, creating a bottleneck for the production of physicians. Every year, thousands of medical students graduate with an MD (Medical Doctor) or DO (Doctor of Osteopathic Medicine) degree, but because there are not enough residency positions, they are not permitted to practice medicine. Nurse practitioners and physician assistants, by contrast, may practice without additional required training.

Ironically, at the same time that government policies restrict thousands of new physicians from practicing medicine, state legislatures are pressured to allow non-physicians to step in to alleviate this artificially created shortage. The replacement of physicians by non-physicians is therefore a problem created by government policy—and could be solved by commonsense political action.

THE PHYSICIAN SURPLUS MYTH

While the physician shortage is currently accepted as fact, just forty years ago, experts were predicting the exact opposite problem: a physician surplus. A 1980 report produced by the Graduate Medical Education National Advisory Committee warned that the U.S. was training too many physicians, estimating a major surplus by the year 2000. To solve the problem, the committee recommended drastically decreasing class sizes and halting the creation of new programs. Medical schools hastened to comply by freezing or reducing admission rates, and between 1980 and 2005, just 16,000 new MDs graduated per year.[20]

Policy concerns over a physician surplus persisted throughout the 1990s, with the Pew Charitable Trust recommending that existing medical schools be closed to slash physician graduates by another 25%.[21] In 1996, the Institute of Medicine (now the National Academy of Medicine) recommended a moratorium on medical schools and freezing of class sizes, stating that "the United States has an oversupply of physicians." The organization also advised a reduction in first-year residency positions to restrict the entry of foreign medical graduates.[19]

The next year, a consortium of medical organizations agreed that further steps should be taken to limit the number of physicians, recommending a decrease in funding for residency training (the mandatory 1–3 minimum years that graduates must complete to be licensed to practice medicine).[22] That same year, the 1997 Balanced Budget Act capped residency training funds, which would remain frozen for the next twenty-five years.[23]

There was such urgency in the 1990s to slow the production of physicians that the government began paying hospitals not to train doctors. In 1997, the Clinton administration instituted a pilot program in New York State that paid teaching hospitals $400 million over six years to reduce the number of resident physician slots. A news article about the program quoted Bruce C. Vladeck, Medicare's administrator at the time, as saying that it was time for the government to stop "giving hospitals an incentive to hire more residents," and that Medicare would save money by no longer paying for unnecessary physicians. The article noted that hospitals across the country were 'bombarding' the government with requests for the same financial deal.[17]

Too many physicians, but not enough non-physician practitioners?

The initial 1980 report predicting a physician surplus noted that the use of nurse practitioners and physician assistants was likely to exacerbate the problem, and recommended curbing the growth of these professions. With the expectation that non-physician practitioner numbers would double by 1990, the committee wrote that the growth rate "aggravates the impending physician surplus and poses a public policy dilemma," and recommended holding levels of nurse practitioners, nurse midwives, and physician assistants stable at current numbers.[24] Despite these recommendations, in the next twenty years, the number of nurse practitioners quadrupled, and the number of physician assistants doubled (Table 3).[25,26]

As policies were instituted to decrease the number of physician graduates, government agencies took active steps to increase nurse practitioners and physician assistants. For example, at the same time as his administration was paying hospitals to stop training physicians, President Bill Clinton designated the first funding program for graduate nurse education, allocating $200 million in 1994 to train nurse practitioners.[27] Fifteen years later,

Table 3. Trends in the Nurse Practitioner and Physician Assistant Workforce

Year	Number of Nurse Practitioners	Number of Physician Assistants
1980	24,000	29,000
1990	30,000	23,000
2000	80,000	57,000
2010	140,000	87,000
2020	290,000	125,000

President Barack Obama signed the Affordable Care Act (2010), legislation that expanded funding to nurse practitioner and physician assistant training programs, without increasing residency training for physicians.[28]

Ironically, organizations sounding alarm bells on the dangers of too many physicians simultaneously advocated for the growth of non-physician practitioners. For example, the Pew Charitable Trust, which recommended cutting medical school admissions in 1995, later advocated that nurse practitioners "step in where doctors are scarce" and encouraged an expansion of independent nurse practice.[29] Perhaps the loudest mixed messaging has come from the Institute of Medicine, a nonprofit public policy advisory group founded in 1970, which has loudly insisted for the last twenty years that the U.S. should cut physician production and focus instead on expanding the role of nurse practitioners.

Although the Institute of Medicine advised cutting medical school numbers to decrease the supply of physicians, just a year later, the group recommended increasing the number of nurse practitioners by redirecting physician training funds toward clinical training for nurse practitioners.[30] As recently as 2014, the Institute continued to argue against a consensus of other voices that there was "no credible data" to support the idea of a physician shortage, and discouraged additional funding for physician residency programs, stating that increasing federal funding would be "irresponsible without evidence." The group instead advised "innovative approaches to health care delivery"[31]—including the replacement of physicians by nurse practitioners, as outlined in the Institute's magnum opus, the *Future of Nursing* (2010) report.

The *Future of Nursing* report was published through a $4.2 million grant from the Robert Wood Johnson Foundation, an organization that has aggressively advocated for an expanded role for nurse practitioners. The report was commissioned to provide "national recommendations for action on the future of nursing,"[32] which included scope expansion for nurse practitioners, and a call for nurses to be full partners with physicians.

To achieve this goal, the Institute asked Congress to expand Medicare to cover nurse practitioner services "just as physician services are now covered," recommended requiring insurance companies to pay nurse practitioners directly, and asked that hospitals be mandated to give nurse practitioners medical staff privileges. To prepare nurses for these expanded roles, the Institute advocated for funding to implement and support nurse practitioner residency programs.[33] In response to the Future of Nursing report, in 2019 the U.S. Government Accountability Office recommended diverting physician residency funds toward funding nurse practitioner and physician assistant 'residency' programs, stating, "while increasing physician supply is one way to reduce physician shortages, some experts have also suggested increasing the number of non-physician providers."[34]

THE PHYSICIAN SHORTAGE

While the Institute of Medicine was a notable exception, by 2006, most experts were no longer predicting a physician surplus, but a shortage. Analysts attributed the surplus prediction error to calculation models that failed to consider increased economic expansion and increased population growth.[35]

In retrospect, the physician shortage could have been predicted by comparing the U.S. physician supply to that of similar nations. While the United States had one of the highest numbers of physicians per population in the 1960s, that ratio rapidly declined in the following two decades, and by 1980, the U.S. had fewer physicians per capita than western European nations.[36] With policies enacted to curb a predicted physician surplus, the U.S. physician supply continued to drop below comparable countries, and by 2018, the U.S. had 2.6 physicians per 10,000 compared to an average of 3.6 in similar nations.[37] Canada ranked just ahead of the U.S., having followed a similar physician-reduction tactic as the United States in the 1990s.[38] The U.S. also lagged behind other nations in the production of physicians, with an increase of just 14% between 2000 and 2018, compared to an average of 34% in Western Europe.[37]

Policy analysts continue to decry a physician shortfall today, with anticipated shortages across all medical specialties, but especially in primary care.[39] While medical schools have responded by gradually increasing enrollment by 30%, residency slots increased by just 1% due to a lack of program funding.[40] This created an entirely new problem: unmatched medical school graduates, saddled with hundreds of thousands of dollars of debt, but unable to practice medicine.

The match

Although medical students will have received 6,000 hours of clinical experience by the time they graduate, they are required to complete additional postgraduate training to receive a license to practice medicine. Every state in the country requires at least one year of residency training for U.S. citizens, with some states requiring two or three years, and most states requiring three years for graduates of foreign medical schools. A lack of postgraduate residency training positions creates a bottleneck for medical students who wish to pursue any type of medicine, including primary care.

The *match* is a computer algorithm that determines where medical students will continue into residency training, based on ranking lists submitted by applicants and training programs. According to the National Resident Matching Program, there are more than enough residency slots to accommodate all graduating U.S. medical students, with 1.82 residency positions per graduate. However, after factoring applicants who trained at medical schools outside the country, including U.S. citizens, there are in reality just 0.85 positions per applicant. This leaves thousands of aspiring physicians unmatched and unable to continue the journey of becoming licensed to practice medicine.[41]

Failing to match is devastating for medical students. While a minority are fortunate enough to scramble into an open position, the remainder must seek work outside of medicine while they wait to re-apply the following year. This process is not only a time-consuming and costly endeavor, but takes a psychological toll, with reports of depression and even suicide among unmatched applicants.[42]

Alethea Poste, MD is a physician who failed to match for several years after graduation. Although she attended medical school in Mexico, Poste transferred into New York Medical College's 5th Pathway Program, an additional fifth year of medical school for international graduates, where she excelled in all her rotations and received very strong letters of recommendation. Despite applying for 20 primary care programs, Poste did not match. "I called all over the country, looking for any place that would take me to work doing anything in the medical field, but no one would take me," she said in an interview. "After five years of undergraduate studies, five years of medical school, and over $200,000 in debt, I was devastated."[43]

On top of everything, Poste learned that she was pregnant with her first child. "I had no health insurance and no income. I felt like a failure. If it were not for my husband, my faith, and the joy of having my son, I don't think I would have made it through that year." Poste got a job working minimum wage at a research lab at New York Medical College. Her husband was a Ph.D. student working at two Universities. "We lived off of $20,000 that year and were on welfare," said Poste, who remembers feeling "embarrassed by my failure, depressed, and helpless."

The next year, she reapplied for residency positions, but once again failed to match. "I cried for days," she said. "I told myself if I didn't match again, I would start a new career path." Fortunately, her tenacity paid off. On her third attempt, Poste matched at a Family Medicine program, where she was ultimately awarded "Resident of the Year" all three years—an unprecedented achievement at her program. "Today, I am a successful Family medicine physician," she said. "I'll never forget how difficult it was for me to get where I am today, and I am grateful every day."[43]

While providing additional funding for residency training would immediately alleviate a physician shortage, Congress has failed to act, despite the introduction of multiple bills addressing the issue. Legislation proposed by U.S. Senator Bill Nelson (D-FL) in 2007 and again in 2009 did not pass committee hearings, with critics arguing that the bill targeted non-primary care training. The bill was reintroduced nearly every year since 2011, with the most recent legislation sponsored by Senator Robert Menendez (D-NJ) in 2021.[44]

While Congress did allocate funding for 1,000 residency positions (200 per year) as part of the Consolidated Appropriations Act of 2021, critics note that the slots are tied up in Medicare red tape including overly complicated and burdensome compliance rules that they believe exceed legislative intent.[45] The most current version of the bill, the Resident Physician Shortage Reduction Act of 2021, which would fund 14,000 residency positions over seven years, is the tenth attempt to lift the 1997 freeze on residency positions. The bill has the bipartisan support of over two hundred House members and a third of Senators, but as of February 2023, Congress had not yet taken any legislative funding action.[46]

Without proper funding for residency slots, medical school graduates must reapply and pray for the opportunity to fill the physician shortage. Meanwhile, nurse practitioners and physician assistants are ready and willing to step in, with legislators working to make it easier for them. For example, California became the first state to require that all physicians complete three full years of residency training to receive a medical license.[47] While this law change was instituted in the name of patient safety, just a year later, California granted nurse practitioners the right to practice without physician supervision after three years of practice. In other words, California has determined that nurse practitioners may practice independently after about 5,000 hours of experience, while physicians must complete 15,000 hours for the same privilege.[48]

Following California's lead, in 2022 Virginia politician and nurse practitioner Dawn M. Adams introduced legislation reducing the requirement for nurse practitioner independence from five years of practice to two years.[49] At the same time, Adams introduced HB 243, which increased the requirement for physicians to practice medicine from 12 months after medical school to 36 months.[50]

FULL CIRCLE: ANOTHER PHYSICIAN SURPLUS?

The increasing dependence on non-physician practitioners has had a negative downstream effect on the hiring of physicians, and may be creating a newly manufactured physician 'surplus.' Consider the field of emergency medicine. In a podcast episode of *Patients at Risk*, residency director Thomas Cook, MD said that until recently, he has never seen a time in his career in which emergency physicians were not in high demand. "I've had 200 residents over 20 years, and when people ask me the question, *'Do your graduates get jobs?'* the answer has been, 'Yes, it's a no-brainer,'" he said. "It has been a feast for us for the 30 years of the specialty in which there's been very, very high demand and not enough supply."

But according to Cook, that trend suddenly began to change. "Five years ago, analysts said, 'In the next 10 years, supply will exceed demand.' And then just recently, another paper comes out and says, 'whoops, we're already there. Supply is meeting demand,'" he said. "And so, we're in a place we've never been in our lives."[51]

The reason is multifactorial: increased hiring of nurse practitioners and physician assistants to work in emergency departments, decreased patient volume during COVID-19, and the creation of corporate-sponsored residency programs. For-profit hospital company HCA Healthcare entered the medical training business in 2015 to become the largest sponsor of graduate medical education in the U.S. The company's goal is simple: to "train and retain" physicians to work at HCA hospitals across the country.[52] This flood of new corporate programs has created a sudden surplus of emergency physicians, who are now struggling to find jobs or have no option other than to choose employment at a corporate entity, which often requires them to supervise multiple non-physician practitioners.

Some for-profit companies are thrilled about a surplus of emergency physicians potentially driving down wages. A slide deck presented by American Physician Partners (APP), an emergency department staffing firm, informed investors that, an "Expected oversupply of ER docs will keep costs low," due to "employer-friendly compensation rates."[53]

Physician trainees are becoming more aware of these market forces and turning away from emergency medicine as a specialty choice. With a 17% decrease in applicants, emergency medicine failed to fill an unprecedented 200 positions in 2022.[54]

Is the field of emergency medicine an outlier, or is it a canary in the coal mine for the medical profession? While some medical specialties feel insulated from replacement by non-physician practitioners, even the final frontier of surgery is facing encroachment. In response to a shortage of surgeons in the United Kingdom, there is a plan to train nurses to become "surgical care practitioners," allowing them to operate on hernias and skin cancer. According to reports, while surgeons complete 16 years of training, surgical care practitioners will have completed a three-year nursing degree, followed by a two-year surgical training course.[55]

Can't happen in the U.S.? Think again. In 2020, Stephen DeVries became one of the first physician assistants to be credentialed to surgically procure hearts and lungs for transplantation independently at the University of Wisconsin, a procedure that physicians train for seven years after medical school to be permitted to perform.[56]

A manufactured physician shortage has led to a double crisis: (1) a lack of fully trained and qualified physicians, (2) and an increase of 'imposter doctors,' non-physicians hired by hospitals and corporations to increase patient access and more importantly, to make money.

CHAPTER 2

A TALE OF TWO PROFESSIONS

Despite the vast difference in the type of education and number of hours of training, advocates for independent nurse practice insist that they are as equally prepared as physicians to care for patients. One way to find out if this is true is to talk to someone who has been a nurse, a nurse practitioner, and a physician—someone like Toni Manougian, who described her professional journey in a podcast episode of *Patients at Risk*.[57]

Toni Manougian began her career as a registered nurse. "At the time, we went into nursing school to be nurses—we were there to take care of patients at the bedside," she said. Manougian chose a diploma program rather than a bachelor's degree program because it offered a strong clinical focus. "We were very much in charge of our patients and accountable for what we did, starting from the introductory first semester. After that, we were held accountable to the standard of care for excellence in nursing." Manougian noted that her program emphasized bedside care over nursing theory. "We had classes probably two days a week, but then the other three days we were at the bedside a full eight hours, not including the preparation it took to get ready to understand our patients."

After earning her nursing certificate, Manougian began work as a bedside nurse in a critical care burn unit. "I loved what I did, but I just always wanted to know more and learn more." Although Manougian dreamed of becoming a physician, she said she was encouraged to enter advanced practice nursing rather than medicine by her nursing colleagues. Discouraging nurses from pursuing a career in medicine is not unusual, according to Cheryl Ferguson, MD. As a registered nurse, Ferguson enrolled in a master's degree program to become a nurse practitioner, but decided to withdraw after the first semester to pursue medical school instead. "When I told my faculty advisor of my plan to become a physician, she was furious. She grabbed my arm, pushed me out the door, and slammed it behind me," Ferguson recalled.[58]

At the time that Toni Manougian was considering furthering her nursing education, her options were limited to becoming a nurse anesthetist, a nurse educator, or a clinical nurse specialist. "I wanted to remain a clinician, and I thought that a clinical nurse specialist would be the best option for me. And so, after twelve or fifteen years as a bedside critical care nurse, I entered an advanced nursing program." Since she had earned her registered nurse degree through a diploma program, Manougian first had to complete a bachelor's degree in nursing. She says she was surprised to find that her bachelor's program contained far more theoretical information than practical nursing know-how. "We had courses on nursing theory and the critical thinking aspect was very much non-clinical in focus," she said. "To me, it did not add any layer of excellence to understanding how to take care of patients as a nurse."[57]

After completing her bachelor's degree, Manougian enrolled in an accelerated master's program designed for experienced nurses, earning her MSN from Columbia University as a clinical nurse specialist. However, Manougian began to have concerns about the quality of her education. "My nurse specialist training focused primarily on educating staff nurses rather than patient care." Further, she found that some of her clinical courses had nothing to do with the actual care of critically ill patients. "My desire was not only to educate staff but also to take excellent care of patients and to learn more about medicine." She noted that the coursework lacked the clinical focus she was seeking. "It was mostly theoretical information: how to talk about nursing theory, how to lead staff, and how to design staffing patterns. I was disappointed because that was not what I wanted."

Manougian said she was disappointed to learn that programs allowed students to take shortcuts in clinical training. While nurse practitioners must complete 500 clinical hours of practice in the role, she discovered that her school permitted students to simply apply work hours from their day jobs. "Because I was a practicing nurse at the time, I could just put clinical experience as work I was already doing at the bedside, and my nursing colleagues could become my preceptors," she said. The term 'preceptor' is meant to refer to an experienced nurse practitioner or physician that provides an opportunity for nurse practitioner students to practice treating patients under their strict supervision. Manougian said that it was wrong for students to apply work hours to the clinical requirements for nurse practitioner training since these hours did not involve practicing skills required in the role, but that it was allowed by the program and commonly done by students.

Still seeking a further opportunity to expand her clinical knowledge, Manougian enrolled in a new university-based critical care nurse practitioner program. "Working in critical care was always my focus. So, I thought, 'Aha! I finally found it, this is going to be it for me.'" But it wasn't long before Manougian discovered that this preparation was not much better than her last program. "I was disappointed because, within the first semester, I realized the program was not going to provide what

I wanted for my future. It just did not get to the thrust of medicine and the depth of understanding of how to take care of patients."

Manougian said that she was seeking an understanding of why physicians made the decisions they did. "I wanted to have that information and that knowledge," she said, but instead, she found her training superficial and lacking the foundation needed for understanding clinical medicine. "I knew that courses in nursing theory weren't going to get me there," she said. "There was a little pharmacology, but it was heavily based on outpatient management rather than critical care because, at the time, the nursing boards were all generic. We did have some classes in ventilator management and some ICU-type things, but it was not what I was looking for. I decided that as soon as I could, I would start to figure out how to get into medical school."

One particular element of her training especially worried Manougian—an emphasis by her instructors that after her nurse practitioner training, she would be just as good—or better—than a critical care physician. "From day one, we were told that we were going to be the leaders in health care. And we were as good as the doctors, if not better," she said. "We did not need to be accountable the way physician assistants were—instead, we could work independently." Manougian recalled feeling perplexed. "I was wide-eyed, sitting there in the chair thinking, 'how can this possibly be?' I came to this program because I didn't understand what the doctors were doing. And now on day one, you're telling me that I'm just as good as the physicians?"

Manougian said that after hearing this mantra repeated so often, she started to believe it. "In the beginning, I kind of bought into it and my family will tell you that I used to spout that stuff." Everything changed when she began treating patients. "When the ball was really in my court, I thought, 'okay, I'm the one putting my name on this prescription. I'm going to be accountable for this. Do I have the belief that I'm doing the right thing for the patients?' And I didn't think I was well prepared enough with that kind of training. There's no way you can come out of an 18-month online program and be prepared to care for critically ill patients."

Disillusioned, Manougian considered dropping out of the nurse practitioner program. Her husband, an internist/ endocrinologist, advised her to finish the program and start the process of applying to medical school. "It was a very hard journey to figure out what to do. I was in my late 30s with two kids—how do I get into medical school? No one was advising me. I didn't have a college program helping me. I was just basically knocking on the doors of deans of medical schools asking what to do and how to get in."

Despite having taken science classes in nursing school, Manougian had to take all of the required pre-medical courses, including two semesters of organic chemistry and physics. "Nursing school did not prepare me for that kind of basic science—no way. The sciences I took in nursing school were courses like 'statistics for nurses,' and 'math for nurses.' Pre-med classes were more intense because you have to be ready to take the MCAT [Medical College Admission Test] and then use organic chemistry and genetics in your basic sciences in medical school."

Manougian said it took her about two years to get into medical school. "I had to take and retake the MCAT, but I did it because it's what I really wanted to do." Once she got accepted to medical school, she discovered that her nursing background did not add any extra advantage to her basic science coursework. "Some of my classmates would ask, 'You don't have to take all the classes because you were a nurse, right?' But the truth was that I did have to take the same classes because that type of pathophysiology, histology—it's not covered in nursing school." She did find her nursing background helpful in feeling more comfortable talking to patients and performing nursing skills. "I could go in and talk to a family member, start an IV, put an [arterial] line, I could do those things very well. But the basic sciences, we don't have that in nursing school. And honestly, you really do need that foundation to practice medicine."[57]

Robin Rose, MD, a physician who also previously trained as a nurse practitioner echoed Manougian's sentiment in a separate podcast episode.[59] A self-proclaimed '60s kid,' Rose traveled through India before settling in rural Tennessee where she took a job as a nurse's aide in a county hospital earning $2.10 per hour. Eager to continue in the health field, she completed an Emergency Medical Technician degree and then enrolled in an RN program. Rose studied nursing while her husband, a medical student, studied medicine. "I started typing class notes for my husband's medical school class, so I could really see the difference between the level of science we were studying," she said.

During those years, nurses could gain a pediatric nurse practitioner certificate as an undergraduate, but Rose decided to expand her knowledge by entering a Family Nurse Practitioner master's program at the University of Missouri. "This was in the '80s, and the program was fairly rigorous. Compared to medical school, it was not. The biochemistry in nurse practitioner school was very simple. The anatomy and physiology were ridiculously simple." When her husband began his family medicine residency, Rose saw the gap between her knowledge base and his widen, and decided that she wanted to have that level of training. "I went back, and I did organic chemistry and physics and cried over physics homework—I'm not a good math person, but I got accepted at the University of Arizona College of Medicine."

Once she started medical school, Rose saw even greater holes in her knowledge. "I'm really glad that I persisted because the basic sciences in medical school were not easy—and I'm not that stupid! So, if it was the same science, if I knew it already, it wouldn't have been so hard." Rose joked that regarding the depths of basic science, "In nursing and in the nurse practitioner program, we did the abstract or the first paragraph of a chapter. In med school, we did the whole chapter. And in residency, we did five of those chapters in five different books."[59]

Besides the differences in coursework intensity, Toni Manougian said that another factor that separates physicians is the amount of effort that doctors have to put into their education and training. While some nurse practitioner programs boast 100% acceptance rates to potential students,[60] the average medical school acceptance rate is 7%.[61] "In medicine, nothing is handed to us," said Manougian. "We need to fight to get a seat in medical school, we need to earn that place, and then we need to continue to earn our rankings so that we can get a good residency, and then take our exams. It isn't just about passing those exams, but it's to be well enough prepared that you can get the best residency you can." Since Manougian wanted to be an anesthesiologist and needed to stay in the New York City area for her family, she had to work to stay at the top of her class. "You had to be pretty much on top of your game to get a seat there. It wasn't handed to you."[57]

Manougian notes that this commitment to excellence throughout the educational process is reflected in the practice of medicine. "I think it trickles down to my daily care. What I see in daily practice is that people will call me as I'm on my way out the door at night and ask me a question or ask me to speak to a patient's family. And yeah, you take your coat off, and you just go do what you have to do. Your shift isn't over until it's over, that is built into the integrity that develops when you have to struggle to get your seat and maintain your seat and have that level of commitment. It's reflective in everything you do as a physician."

Looking back on her experience as a critical care nurse practitioner compared to her knowledge as a critical care physician, Manougian is deeply concerned about a trend toward independent nurse practice. "In no way was I qualified to care for critically ill patients without physician supervision, and I was an experienced critical care nurse for over a decade before I even tried to do this education as a nurse practitioner," she said. "I'm speaking for myself. No, I was not well prepared." Manougian explained the reasoning: training as a nurse practitioner is based on algorithms, rather than a deep understanding of medicine. "What you saw before, you repeated, or you tried to understand based on experiences that you had seen before," she said. "But you don't have the background in medicine to understand what to do when differences occur or when something is not routine." Manougian believes that medical care can't just be 'okay.' "Every patient deserves to have the best. And if you don't understand medicine, then you are just practicing based on what you did before. But every day is different, every patient is different."[57]

Research from the United Kingdom has shown that having more physicians on duty in the hospital is associated with lower mortality rates[62] and that more intensive care physicians reduce length of stay and lower hospital and ICU mortality.[63] Despite this evidence, most intensive care units in the U.S. provide little to no physician intensive care coverage,[64] and many are replacing physicians with nurse practitioners, often without a background in critical care.

Having worked both as a critical care nurse practitioner and a critical care physician, Manougian says that this is a dangerous practice. While intensive care physicians will have received a minimum of about 20,000 clinical hours during medical school, internship, residency, and critical care fellowship before they are permitted to care for seriously ill patients, hospitals are hiring nurse practitioners to treat these same patients after just 500 hours of training. Manougian notes that it is more than just the difference in clinical hours, but also in the training setting, pointing out that nurse practitioners with training in out-patient care are being hired to work in in-patient critical care settings. "You can be certified as a family nurse practitioner and have a job in a critical care unit, and yet your nursing education in your NP training was in primary care on stable patients, not critically ill patients. I don't know how that relates to an ICU environment."

Manougian believes that her decision to go to medical school was worth the effort. "I would not be as well-prepared, and I just would not love what I do as much." But she also believes that her registered nurse background did help prepare her for her journey. "I think that excellence in clinical care was instilled in me in my diploma program as a nurse." Unfortunately, Manougian is seeing changes in nursing education that are moving students away from an emphasis on bedside nursing care. "I'm not seeing that same type of really compassionate care and drive for excellence in a lot of the fast-track programs that we see for nurses today." She says she is disheartened to see young people and even second-career students choosing nursing solely because they want to be nurse practitioners. "I see people coming to the bedside, and they're in and out. As soon as they graduate, they're already in an NP program. And it's a disservice to the bedside nurses who have put decades into that profession, that they're somehow not valued enough."

Manougian believes that increased salaries and career advancement for nurse practitioners over staff nurses who have spent years at the bedside are contributing to the demise of the nursing profession. "I think it's a real shame. It's a shame for the patients. And for me as a working physician, I need to rely on bedside nurses. If I know that a nurse has the experience and they tell me something, I'm listening. It's a whole different ball of wax when it's a new grad with very limited experience, and as a future patient one day, I want that experienced nurse who loves what they're doing."

As a physician, Manougian says that she values working with nurse practitioners, physician assistants, and nurse anesthetists. "I have worked with many over the years, and I enjoy working with them. I just do not envision them being the leaders of healthcare or having independent practice."

Manougian does believe that non-physicians can play an important role in routine day-to-day care, following algorithms and protocols. "But there's just so much more to medicine. So independent practice, no. Working alongside us and within teams? Absolutely. Do they have value? Of course. I think we also really need to value our bedside nurses. I don't think that there would be such a drive into nurse practitioner schools if our bedside nurses were happy and valued and respected."[57]

NURSE PRACTITIONERS SPEAK OUT

Some practicing nurse practitioners express concern about being urged to treat patients without physician supervision. In a *Patients at Risk* podcast episode, Shannon Keaney, a nurse practitioner who received her master's degree from Georgetown University, said that despite having a strong nursing background and excellent training, she does not feel prepared to practice independently.[65] Keaney began her career as a certified nursing assistant working in a nursing home. She earned her degree as a licensed practical nurse and then became a registered nurse, working at the bedside in critical care for 10 years. She then enrolled in a two-year master's level program to become a family nurse practitioner.

Like Toni Manougian, Keaney is particularly concerned about nurse practitioners who skip nursing experience or rush through nurse practitioner training. She said that not only did she have extensive nursing experience, but she also made sure to attend a reputable nurse practitioner program. "I attended a brick-and-mortar school, which usually means a university that you attend on campus or an established distance learning program through a university." Keaney noted that there is a difference between 100% online programs and distance learning. "I had to attend campus as well as online. Some of our classes were via Zoom, where we spoke with our professors and interacted with our classmates for lectures, but we would also have to attend university on campus for exams."

Keaney compared her experience to that of other students she has worked with. "I attended some clinical rotations with these students [of online programs], and alarm bells went off. Students are basically attending clinicals, but they're not being supervised to make sure that they're actually showing up. They're not being followed closely at all." In some cases, Keaney said she has heard precepting physicians complain that they haven't even heard from the nursing school, "It's embarrassing when you hear a physician preceptor express concern that the NP profession is going in this direction. It's being said that nurse practitioners can just go online and get a degree now." She was also shocked to rotate with students who admitted to her that they were permitted to take open-book tests in which they could look up information during the examination. "I was mortified because I know that my university held us to very high standards. My nursing school was quite rigorous. Just to think that to be a provider, you can just go online and take exams with open books? We're supposed to be about patient safety. How can we do this?"

While Keaney contemplated attending medical school, she ultimately decided that it wasn't realistic. "I was getting ready to sit for my MCAT and I had turned 40. I just decided, I didn't want to do it. Point blank. I didn't want to finish when I was close to 50 years old." Instead, she decided to become a nurse practitioner. "I felt that being an NP was the closest thing I could get to being able to practice medicine, per se," but notes that she always wants to work closely with a supervising physician. "I'm not offended at having to be supervised," she said. "I have not had the training after graduating from a two-year program to be alone. I would never put myself or the patients in that position. There's just no way. I'll admit that and I'm an astute clinician who was a critical care nurse for 10 years." Keaney said that she doesn't find any shame in admitting that she needs supervision. "I don't think that belittles my cognitive abilities. NPs are great. I've given great care to patients. It's just that we have a limit to our training."

Keaney firmly believes that nurse practitioners should not be practicing independently. "As an ICU nurse, you see things that have gone wrong in primary care. You see how severely sick patients can be," she said. "My experience has taught me that human beings are complicated, and that there's an intense amount of education that you must receive to autonomously care for these patients." Keaney says that this applies to primary care, as well. "When you are the eyes and ears and are supposed to be focusing on prevention, you have to be able to catch things that are wrong. I am aware of what I don't know," she said. "I'm aware and I just cannot advocate for NPs to be autonomous. I can't."

Shannon Keaney's opinion on independent practice is informed by her observations of the decline of nurse education in recent years. "I cannot understand how the nurse practitioner community thinks that it's okay to have diploma mills putting out nurse practitioners, ready to step out and practice right out of school," she said. "Some of them haven't even been nurses for long and they think it's okay to care for patients unsupervised in a primary care setting. It's [about] patient safety; there's no way that I am ready for that, and I can't anticipate that I would be ready for that in five years. I just don't see how patients gain anything from independent practice."

Unfortunately, Keaney believes that nurse practitioners are being forced to practice in situations that they are not prepared for. "I have seen this happen in medicine," she said. "They are utilizing nurse practitioners more, and quite frankly, it's to save money." She said that hospitals are doing the same with nurses, replacing registered nurses (RNs) with lesser-trained licensed practical nurses (LPNs). Keaney compares the training of nurse practitioners and physicians to that of LPNs and RNs. "When you have a registered nurse who has at least four years of school and compare that to an LPN who has one year of training, there is a difference," she said. "I don't care if the LPN says, 'I can do whatever an RN can do,' the training is not the same." Keaney notes that she received much more training to become a registered nurse than she had as a licensed practical nurse, which is why she was able to work in critical care. "It's the same thing as nurse practitioners or PAs in comparison to physicians," she said. "It's not that I want us to feel that we're inadequate. It's a different level of training. Nurse practitioners were never meant to replace physicians and shouldn't be used as such. We are, in essence, physician extenders."

This isn't a popular opinion among nurse practitioner leadership, but Keaney feels she needs to speak out. "I think nurse practitioners are worth more than how we are presenting ourselves. We have value. We don't have to try to equal or supersede the education of the physician," she said. "We are intelligent beings and we have so much to offer patients. The nursing model is great, it truly is, but promoting independence is going in a bad direction. We're offending physicians, we're offending PAs—this is not good. We all need to work together to take care of patients."

She is especially compelled to call out what she terms 'diploma mills' that pump out poorly trained nurse practitioners. "Our leadership groups should be focused on the fact that we're putting out mediocre nurse practitioners from these diploma mills, but it's all about money at this point." Keaney is concerned about the Doctor of Nursing Practice or DNP degree, which has been encouraged by nurse practitioner leadership. "Online DNPs are not at the standard where a nurse should be graduating and calling themselves a doctor, but there is a big push to do this," she said, noting that she feels that the degree has become a political tool intended to undermine PAs and physicians. "The nursing community feels that there's a lot more power to be gained by having more doctorally prepared nurses," she said.

Keaney also believes that an emphasis on advanced degrees has a major financial downside. "Although there are some benefits, ultimately, the push for nurses to all have bachelor's degrees [rather than an associate's] has increased nursing debt with no increase in pay. Same for nurse practitioners; nurses are pushed to get their doctorate—I am already over

$200,000 in debt for my student loans. I'm not doing a DNP. If I do go back, it's going to be for my Ph.D. because I want to do in-depth research, which is just nonexistent in some of these diploma mill schools."

While Keaney believes that physicians should lead medicine, she doesn't want to see the system return to a patriarchal hierarchy. "I believe in the team approach and to have a team, you have to have a leader. If you look at the law, the leader is usually the judge, and then you have the lawyers, then you have paralegals. The paralegals don't lead. The same as in medicine, it goes by years of education; it's a given." She also points out that part of the problem is corporate leadership and the mistreatment of bedside nurses. "It shouldn't be an MBA leading either. That's another reason why nurses are leaving in droves," she said.

Keaney says that nurse practitioner leadership is following the wrong path. It has taken bravery for her to speak out. "It's difficult for nurse practitioners to have a voice because NP leaders will take it personally, and I'm going to be ostracized for sure. They say I practice advanced nursing, but I'm really practicing medicine—diagnosing and treating diseases. You can call it what you want, but regardless, you are responsible for the care of these patients. You cannot go to school, take open book tests, and think that you're going to put on a long white coat and care for these patients adequately."

Keaney also points the blame at physicians who fail to properly supervise. "In my state, a nurse practitioner or PA can own a practice, but they must have a supervising physician. However, the supervising physician may only be present four times a year. I find it concerning that that is allowed. If we're going to require NP supervision, we need to look at it from the angle that physicians are making a rather nice income supervising some of these clinics. They are going to have to step it up as well."[65]

Another nurse practitioner who agrees with Keaney's sentiments is Patrice Little, the founder of *NP Student Magazine*, an educational resource for nurse practitioner students.[66] Little shared her journey to becoming a nurse practitioner in a *Patients at Risk* podcast. "I studied biology as premed in college, and then taught high school science for a short period before entering an accelerated BSN program," said Little. She practiced nursing briefly in an acute care setting, and then transitioned into case management, which involved admission and discharge planning for patients rather than direct nursing care. "From there, I segued into a nurse practitioner program that was hybrid, which means that it's mainly online, but there are times when you meet in person."

Little said that she was excited about the program. "I felt it was rigorous, in the sense that we got the information that we needed, but I felt like it happened very quickly." So quickly, in fact, that Little said that even though she graduated and passed her board exam, the information didn't stick. "I say that because when I got my first NP gig, I was sent home the same day—they told me not to come back." She recalled that she was simply overwhelmed on her first day by her lack of knowledge and confidence. "When you start any type of practice or discipline, it's part of the learning curve to check in with people just for validation, but I was interrupting my colleagues with just about every patient I had." She said that she realized she wasn't yet ready to care for patients. "I had to be honest with myself. I wasn't fully equipped like I thought I was."

Little was devastated. "I had invested so much—time away from my husband and my daughter and a lot of money." She was also surprised by her poor performance, because not only had she passed her classes and her nurse practitioner certification exam, but she had also received excellent evaluations from her physician preceptors. "My preceptors were amazing, so I can't fault them. They did the best that they could. It's just I needed more time and more exposure. It's repetition. When it comes to this type of practice, the more you do it, the more it sticks. That's really what's key." She also notes that like many other nurse practitioner students, she was working full-time as a case manager while attending her training. "These types of factors interfere with the learning capacity. If you have all these things going on and you're trying to learn how to practice medicine, it's not going to stick." Little pointed out that this is why many nurse practitioner students graduate with a 4.0 grade point average, pass their board exams the first time, and yet find themselves unprepared to practice. "Often students take board exam prep classes, so they master how to take the test, but they don't know the material. Passing a certification exam is not saying that you'll be a great practitioner, it's just saying you have the minimum competency to go out there and practice." Despite passing her exam and supposedly having that minimum competency, Little said that she was unprepared to care for patients without constant support from a more seasoned clinician.

This experience opened Little's eyes to the deficits in modern nurse practitioner education. "I actually wrote my scholarly project on how to convince legislators to allow nurse practitioner independent practice to increase access to care," she said. "But the deeper I got into it, the more concerned I became." Little says that as she interacted with different people—physicians, other nurse practitioners, and members of the general public—she found it difficult to advocate for full practice authority for nurse practitioners. "First of all, I learned that not every nurse practitioner wants independent practice. Some people like me prefer having a collaborative physician because of the gaps in our knowledge and training."

Little points out that she is not the first person to call attention to deficits in nurse practitioner education. "If you look in the literature for the past few years, it's been identified. The pathophysiology, pharmacology, and advanced physical assessment, which are part of the core education—it's not as strong as it once was, and the reason is that the education has changed." Little says that when nurse practitioner programs were first developed, students received their training from physicians. "We have to look back to when it originally started with Dr. Loretta Ford and Dr. Henry Silver, and the whole intent was to close the primary care gap—that's the same reason we exist today. But we do not have that same type of standardized training. Now it's more of a hit or miss." For example, Little said that getting a qualified preceptor during training is just the luck of the draw. "By chance I may get a good preceptor for my pediatrics rotation, or for my geriatrics rotation; that's where the concern is."

Little said that the biggest worry that she and other like-minded nurse practitioner colleagues have about independent practice is patient safety. "What about the patients? On top of that, as a minority, I have to think about the care of different communities." In her training, Little received about 630 hours of clinical experience, more than the required 500 hours, but she believes that nurse practitioners need not only hundreds of hours, but thousands of hours of hands-on care. "The more hours of exposure to variations, complexity, and complications of particular conditions, the better," she said.

She also thinks that nurse practitioner training needs more emphasis on critical thinking skills, pointing to her pre-med training in college. "I keep going back to that in my mind, even though it was a long time ago. It was the type of thinking like, 'why is this leaf considered poison ivy and not such and such, even though it looks just like another leaf? What makes it different?' And then you're like, 'oh, okay, well, let me turn to look behind the leaf.' And that's probably why it's different."[66]

Comparing the study of botany to the study of medicine makes sense, said Niran Al-Agba, who participated in the podcast with Patrice Little. "This is like talking about differential diagnosis. When you're looking at a leaf, it's not just 1,000 leaves we're trying to pick from, right? Maybe it's got five points, and those five-pointed leaves fall into five categories. Then of five categories, when you turn them over, they're deciduous, or you see veins on the back and they're not random; they look like a Christmas tree. Okay, so then that's three leaves that fit into that same group. Then one is deadly and two are not, and one smells like this or tastes like that. There are these little things—these branch points. You need thousands of hours of study and practice—really 15,000 hours at a minimum—to be able to figure out that leaf. [Then]—bam—because you know the different branch points by heart."

Using an example from medicine, she points to a patient with sinusitis. "It could be simple sinus infection, but it could be a foreign body, it could be allergies, it could be Pott's puffy tumor," she said. "You could just go on and on about the different things on that differential. And to be honest, if you haven't seen all of those things, how do you know that it's not?"[66]

Patrice Little agrees that lack of experience is a patient safety issue and worries about new nurse practitioner graduates who are starting their own practices from day one. "I've been a practicing NP since 2014, and I have spent hours with my collaborative physician," she said, noting that the physician personally trained her when she started to practice. "This is someone who knows how I think and is comfortable with giving me feedback." Because her supervising physician has worked closely with her for years, Little said that he trusts her to come to him if she is unsure about the care of a patient.

Rather than developing relationships, Little said that many nurse practitioners are using online services that connect them with a collaborating physician. "You have no rapport with that person. They don't know how you think. They don't know how you practice. They don't have a comfort level." She believes that this type of perfunctory supervision is more likely to lead to patient harm. "We know that in medicine, there are times things can be missed. So, we need to be intentional with how we approach care. If we know that there's a gap, we need to address it." She notes that treating patients blindly, with a 'fake it 'til you make it' attitude is dangerous. "What about that one patient? What if you make a misdiagnosis or omit care and that patient ends up succumbing all because you didn't know?"

It's for this reason that Little wrote a proposal to the president and dean of her nurse practitioner program, encouraging more standardization in nurse practitioner education. "Preceptors must be dedicated to the role. They need to know what the expectations are. It's not enough just to give them a form or a checklist. They need to have a conversation." Even with standardized training, Little said that students still need more time and experience, including thousands more hours of exposure before beginning to practice. "There's an assumption from employers when they hire you that you already know what you're doing, and [that]'s not true now."[66]

THE APPRENTICE MODEL OF MEDICINE AND THE FLEXNER REPORT

When considering the deficits in nurse practitioner education, John Lafferty, MD sees comparisons to the problems that medical education faced before 1910. "It might surprise the public and even some doctors to learn that at the turn of the century, the educated public viewed most physicians as charlatans, hucksters, and quacks—and for good reason," he said in a podcast episode for *Patients at Risk*. The turning point, according to Lafferty, was the publication of the Flexner Report, a scathing indictment of medical education that launched major reforms for physician training. Lafferty is a retired North Carolina obstetrician-gynecologist who has studied the Flexner Report. "I have a distinct memory of the first day of medical school—and I went to med school a long, long time ago," he recalled. "The first thing they told us was, 'We are lucky to have you, and you are lucky to be here at this marvelous time in history, thanks to the Flexner Report.'" It wasn't until Lafferty reached the end of his career that he finally dedicated the time to read the entire 300-page report, but when he did, he was astounded by the parallels between the pre-Flexner practice of medicine and current concerns about nurse practitioner training.[67]

While the earliest medical education in the U.S. was limited to the wealthiest individuals who could afford to travel to universities in Europe, shortly after the Civil War, medical education transitioned toward proprietary medical schools, private schools created by one or more physicians. "There were no standards or regulations in these programs," said Lafferty. "They would generally have a series of lectures in the morning, and a series of lectures in the afternoon. It would go for a year or two, and there were generally few if any exams." At the end of a designated period, graduates received an MD degree and set out to practice.

Concerned about the quality of medical education at these proprietary schools, the Carnegie Foundation hired Abraham Flexner, an educator and graduate of Johns Hopkins University.* Flexner traveled across the country by train for two years, visiting medical schools. Of the 155 programs in existence, Flexner determined that only twenty were of adequate quality. "The 'good' schools required students to have attended at least some college, including science courses, while many other medical schools didn't even require a high school diploma," said Lafferty. "The good schools were tied to a university and associated with a teaching hospital. They had a faculty dedicated exclusively to teaching."

Based on Flexner's assessment, the number of medical schools was reduced from 155 to 66. Requirements for admission increased and education programs became standardized. "What happened as a result of this was that the quality of physicians went way up, but the total number of physicians declined," said Lafferty. The demand for medical care grew exponentially after World War 2, especially as medical schools researched and developed drugs and therapies. "These treatments worked, and for the

---

*Author's note: After reading the entire Flexner report, I was horrified at the section on Black physicians (and Flexner's thoughts on Black people in general). While I was previously aware that Flexner expressed racist viewpoints, reading his actual words, which likely express the feelings of most Americans in 1910, was chilling. I encourage anyone who is skeptical of the idea of systemic racism in medicine to read pages 179–182 of the report.

first time, when you went to a physician, you probably had a pretty good chance of actually being helped rather than hurt."

With the increase in demand for medical services, physicians looked for ways to expand their reach, creating the nurse practitioner and physician assistant professions in 1965. These early training programs had high standards. "In the beginning, these programs were brick and mortar. They were generally nurses with at least five years of experience. They were probably the best of the best. Same for the PAs—they were veteran medics that had been to Vietnam," said Lafferty. "But within 15 years, these two new professions began to ask for increasing practice autonomy, and the problems proliferated. There are now over 400 nurse practitioner programs and 250 PA programs, bringing us full circle to the problems we had with medical education in 1910."

Based on his experience precepting non-physician practitioners, Lafferty believes that these professions are overdue for a Flexner Report of their own. "While the physician assistant students I precepted were expected to receive 200 hours of clinical experience in women's health, most of them spent only about 30 hours with me," he said. "And since we had some patients who didn't want them to participate, their actual face-to-face time with patients during their entire women's health experience was often under 15 hours." During the rest of their hourly requirement, students attended online lectures. "That sounds an awful lot like the proprietary medical school of the 19th century," he said.

Lafferty empathizes with nurse practitioner and physician assistant students who are receiving short shrift when it comes to clinical experience and notes that Flexner addressed the same issues with medical students. "On page 15, [Flexner] writes, 'A heavy sympathy for the American youth who too often to the prey of commercial advertising methods is steered into the practice of medicine with almost no opportunity to learn the difference between an efficient medical school and a hopelessly inadequate one.'"[67]

CHAPTER 3

DIPLOMA MILLS AND FACEBOOK CONSULTS

As demand for non-physician practitioners has increased, there has been a proliferation of training programs, which is affecting the quality of some graduates. In a *Patients at Risk* podcast episode, Thomas Cook, MD discussed the impact of these so-called diploma mills on the healthcare system. A fundamental problem with nurse practitioner schools today is the quality of applicants that are being accepted, said Cook, pointing to a *US News and World Report* article about the number of nurse practitioner programs with 100% acceptance rates. "They were sort of bragging about it, ironically," he said, noting that he found the very idea implausible. "My immediate thought was, 'well, do they accept all applicants to become nuclear engineers and to police academies and to become airline pilots and all sorts of other things?'"[51] Cook said that when he began to investigate the schools listed, he discovered that the headline was accurate, noting that one nurse practitioner program affiliated with Purdue University had 500 applicants, and all were accepted.[68]

In addition to accepting all applicants, some schools will pass inadequately prepared students. Toni Manougan experienced this when she worked as an adjunct faculty member at an Ivy League nurse practitioner program. "I was asked to pass one particular student whose work was very substandard," she said. "I didn't want to, because I thought her work was not up to a master's level of nursing, but I was told by the administration at that school that I had no choice."[57]

Due to the decline in educational quality, Thomas Cook believes that independent practice by non-physicians is dangerous. "In about half of the states that allow independent nurse practice, all you need is to graduate from school," said Cook. "This is a two-year curriculum; it might be entirely online. There's no way to validate what clinical experience they've had. They don't take the [United States Medical Licensing] exams 1, 2, 3; they don't take the MCAT. They don't have to compete with all those other undergraduate students to get into medical school. And oh, by the way, symptoms, attributing her shortness of breath to anxiety rather than a medical emergency caused by the procedure. "What is different is the ability to identify that something has gone wrong, [then] assess the patient, and know what steps to take to remedy the situation," she said. "That requires knowledge of anatomy, physiology, and pharmacology." It is for this reason that Anegawa believes that superficial training is inadequate for medical practitioners. "There is a gap or disconnect that can't be remedied by just trying to kind of teach someone in a patchwork way without that deep fund of knowledge that physicians receive through a decade-plus of supervised training."[85]

LACK OF PRECEPTORS

Preceptors are clinicians that offer training opportunities in their office or clinic. Ideally, a preceptor should allow students to evaluate patients by taking a medical history and performing a physical examination, followed by a presentation in which the student describes their findings and suggests a diagnosis and plan of action. The preceptor then evaluates the patient personally and provides feedback to the student on what was done correctly and areas for improvement. Providing quality preceptorship requires time and effort. While some preceptors are volunteers, others may receive financial remuneration, since teaching interferes with time seeing patients and negatively impacts revenue.

With an increase in students needing preceptors, it has become more difficult to find willing clinicians, and in many cases schools are requiring students to find their own preceptors. Rayne Thoman said she experienced difficulty finding a qualified preceptor for her psychiatric nurse practitioner clinical experience. "They sent me to clinicals with a physician assistant working in an emergency room, and then human resources called and said, 'You can't be there.' I found out that New York state regulations do not even allow nurse practitioners to complete clinical hours with a physician assistant."[78]

As a graduate psychiatric nurse practitioner, Rayne Thoman would have been considered qualified to care for patients across the lifespan, including children with mental illness. However, Thoman noted that her school offered just 100 hours in pediatrics out of a total of 540 required clinical hours. Despite this minimal criteria, Thoman observed that some of the students graduated from her program with zero hours in child psychiatry because it was so difficult to find preceptorship in pediatrics.[78] Despite a lack of training and experience, nurse practitioners may find themselves hired by companies to prescribe potentially dangerous psychotropic medications to children, and academic centers are encouraging psychiatric nurse practitioners to take a more active role in the care of children.[86]

Pediatrician Niran Al-Agba finds this worrisome, noting that despite her years of primary care experience, which has involved a significant amount of mental health care, she is uncomfortable prescribing certain psychiatric medications to children. "I just had a fourth-year medical student working with me and she said she had no idea how much psychiatry we do in pediatrics," said Al-Agba. "I would say it's probably 25% of every pediatrician's work, but there are certain lines I won't cross. There are only one or two antidepressants I'm comfortable using. I won't use any of the others without psychiatric consultation."[78]

For Rayne Thoman, the reality of her educational deficiencies struck her when she began rotating with a psychiatrist, and was unable to understand much of what he said to her. "I realized I should have more of a foundation, but we didn't learn anything in school." With this epiphany, Thoman decided to withdraw from the program. "When the exam room door closes and you're alone with the patient, I just don't feel comfortable faking." Thoman said that when she told her peers that she was quitting, they encouraged her to finish the program. "They told me to just finish because of the money that I could earn," she said. "And that's why people stay—and also because they are so deep in debt at that point. Ok, but how am I going to sleep at night? What if I hurt somebody?"[78]

Concerned about the quality of education, Thoman reported her program to the New York Department of Education and the Commission on Collegiate Nursing Education, but said her complaints went unanswered. It was at this point that she decided to take matters into her own hands by speaking out about deficiencies in nurse practitioner training. "This is not something I feel comfortable keeping quiet about," she said. "Talking amongst ourselves isn't working. Calling these people, emailing, filing complaints—we have been doing this for years."

Thoman began posting on social media, including sharing screenshots from other nurse practitioner students. "When you start talking to people all over the country, you learn that they are seeing the same problems and reporting it, too. There's this movement to send complaints but nothing happens." Thoman said that students are discouraged from talking about their concerns openly. "We're not supposed to talk about it outside of medicine, but we have some serious problems and the people in power are not doing anything about this," said Thoman, referring to instructions from the American Association of Nurse Practitioners to remain silent about concerns over nurse practitioner education and independent practice.[87] She believes that concerns are being suppressed for political and financial reasons. "Something is going on here because it's actively being quieted. They tell us to just keep it in nursing—well, nursing isn't fixing itself."

One of the reasons that Thoman is so adamant about exposing these deficiencies is patient safety. "If people don't know this is happening, how can they protect themselves?" She believes that allowing improperly trained clinicians to practice is harmful to society—"because, at the end of the day, we are all human beings. Take my nurse hat off—I'm a person. This affects us all."[78]

ESTABLISHMENT DENIAL

Rayne Thoman says that she began her mission to expose poor quality nurse practitioner programs because of denial of the problem. "That's kind of how this got started. You've got people saying, 'that's not true.'" Thoman's response: "There is ample evidence this is going on. People post about this every single day on social media, discussing poor quality schools or the fact that they don't know what they are doing." In some cases, she believes that those who deny the problem genuinely don't know what's going on, but she also thinks that there are forces actively working to suppress the information. "There are some that seem to want to almost brainwash everybody, keep it silenced, or [claim] that [it's] not happening, but there's evidence." Thoman points to screenshots of nurse practitioner students discussing the easiest online programs, noting that this is a source of great debate. She says that some students appreciate schools with lower acceptance standards because otherwise, they would not get in. "Just because the program is on some level challenging to that individual doesn't mean they're going to be safe and competent once they graduate."[78]

Thoman is also concerned that students are increasingly entering into psychiatric nurse practitioner training without any experience in psychiatric nursing. She believes that this increase is partly due to supply and demand: a decrease in jobs for family nurse practitioners and increased hiring in the mental health field. "When I started there were six people in my class, but a year later, nurses with no psych experience began flocking to it. Word got out how easy this is, and you can make a lot of money. You see it on the internet: "What's the easiest, fastest way I can do this?" Although some students will argue that they have gained psychiatry experience while working in primary care or at a hospital, Thoman believes that mental health nurse practitioners need experience working as a nurse in psychiatry first. "It's a foundation. You're supposed to have nursing experience, but these schools just let them in, and they make a lot of money."[78]

Social media influencer Dardy NP has also seen this surge in psychiatric nurse practitioner students. In his YouTube series 'Life of a Psych NP,' the video blogger discussed concerns over the field becoming oversaturated because so many students are flocking to the profession—and because schools are increasingly accepting students without any previous nursing experience.[88] Despite concerns about having too many graduates, the Human Resources and Services Administration says that the demand for psychiatric nurse practitioners remains high and is predicted to increase by the year 2030.[89]

Rayne Thoman says that you can see the decreased quality of nurse practitioner education in social media posts asking for clinical advice, which she shared on a YouTube video recording with the co-authors of *Patients at Risk*, which featured screenshot of the posts.[78] "It's so bad, and you see it every single day. It's not like looking for a needle in a haystack. It's the whole haystack." A common concern that Thoman sees from nurse practitioner students is the quality of education. For example, one commenter stated that their program offered just two hours of learning how to read an EKG, but spent an entire semester writing a thesis on nursing theory.[78]

Misreading an EKG, a tracing of the electrical activity of the heart, can be a matter of life or death in medical practice, and physicians invest serious time studying the subject. For example, Niran Al-Agba recalled spending at least 40 hours practicing EKG reads on her internal medicine rotation alone. "I was there for 12 weeks, and we would sit in the afternoons for about three or four hours at a time and go through hundreds of EKGs to study them."[78]

Other posts that Rayne Thoman has shared include basic questions, often from nurse practitioners already in practice. She has posted screenshots of questions like, "How do I learn to interpret labs?" and "How do I learn what antibiotic goes for which infection?"[90]

"It's almost become the culture at this point," said Thoman. "It's become normal, and I don't think people understand that this is not acceptable."

For example, a post on the Family Nurse Practitioner Networking Group page asked for help learning how to manage hypertension, an essential aspect of primary care. "Hi, does anybody have a good chart, or resource, for BP [blood pressure] meds? Specifically when to use each drug? Like some Calcium channel blockers are better for this condition etc. Thanks in advance! My [pharmacology] class was kind of a bust." One group member responded by suggesting, "I just googled hypertension algorithms the other day and found something." Another nurse practitioner asked their social media audience, "Hey guys! Does anyone have or can you point me in the direction of pearls of prescribing oral steroids? Brand new here and I'm in allergy and [rheumatology]. Tapering is confusing to me. I feel nervous every time I prescribe outside a Medrol dose pak!!"[90]

Steroids are probably one of the most dangerous medications to use without experience. Pediatrician Niran Al-Agba recalled the case of a child who died after receiving long-term steroids for a cough. "Rather than investigating the cause of the cough, the child was just given steroids. It turned out that she had an anterior mediastinal mass that got missed and she died. I was doing chest compressions on her, and I've never forgotten it. It's impacted me and how I practice for the last 20 years." Al-Agba points out that physicians are trained to be very cautious with steroids. "You do not mess around with these. You think about infection because you could kill someone," she said, noting that it's also important to consider what diagnoses could be causing the symptoms. "It's not just, 'they're coughing—give them a Medrol pack.'"[90]

Rayne Thoman also posts disciplinary reports of nurse practitioners who have been sanctioned for improper treatment. She's had commenters disagree with her practice of naming practitioners, but, she says since everyone is licensed, it's all public information. In an era of misinformation, especially on social media, Thoman said, "I want to be abundantly clear how real this is—these are real people." As one example, she points to a case report in which a nurse practitioner misinterpreted thyroid lab results, prescribing thyroid replacement medicine to a patient who already had an overactive thyroid, causing a delay in care and a potentially dangerous medical situation.[90]

Niran Al-Agba said that while some aspects of primary care can be performed by following an algorithm, thyroid disease is an example of a condition that can be more complex than it seems, requiring an understanding of pathophysiology that physicians learn in medical school. "This is an example of algorithm-following that can get nurse practitioners into trouble. It's not just a thyroid that's too fast or too slow. There's the pituitary gland and the hypothalamus; there are all these higher-level functions. Here we are talking about an NP who figures that the patient has a simple hypothyroid problem, but it wasn't simple. You have to think about other factors, but if you don't learn these things, you don't even know to consider them."[90]

Rayne Thoman says that she is sharing these cases to raise awareness and to keep patients safe, and her work is gaining results. One post by a Yale-graduate psychiatric mental health nurse practitioner asking for help on social media garnered the attention of a state Senator. The post read: "18-year-old female with depression starting at age 11, suicide attempt at age 16, reports anxiety and depression worsening since starting college," and continued to describe what sounded like a manic episode, family stressors, and an overdose of the medication lamotrigine, which the nurse practitioner had prescribed at her first visit. The post continued, "I have her down as [rule out] bipolar disorder. She was just discharged from the hospital yesterday. I plan on seeing her within the next week. How would you proceed? I'm thinking lithium, but I'm worried about her [overdosing] on it!"[90] Horrified by this post, Thoman shared it and included the fact that the nurse practitioner involved had no supervising physician because she worked in Washington, a state that allows independent practice. Someone tagged Washington State Senator Patty Kuderer, responding, "This is why practicing medicine without a medical license is dangerous, and if you do it, don't even try to outsource it on Facebook."[90]

Kuderer responded, "I read it and I'm engaged," and asked to be contacted via her government email. However, Niran Al-Agba, a Washington resident, fears that little action will occur. "Washington State is extremely underserved for psychiatric care. A lot of us have done different pilot projects to try to help expand it, but it's being flooded with these psychiatric nurse practitioners who are just throwing medication at people." She pointed out the irony that child and adolescent psychiatrists must complete another 1–2 years of fellowship training after psychiatry residency, consisting of thousands of hours, while psychiatric nurse practitioners are permitted to treat children after completing just 100 hours of experience in pediatrics.[90]

"These children need real help," Al-Agba said, pointing to another case that Thoman shared involving a psychiatric nurse practitioner treating a 10-year-old boy who threatened to shoot students and teachers at his middle school. The psychiatric nurse practitioner asked, "The father wants meds, what should I start him on?" Al-Agba continued, "This is a potential Columbine shooter we're talking about. I don't want to make it sound overly dramatic, but this is a person who threatened to shoot someone at school. It could just be an idle threat, but you've got someone … asking Facebook?" Al-Agba, a pediatrician, noted that this type of behavior is unusual in children. "I know the media makes it seem very common, but when you have a child at this age threatening to shoot someone at school, you need to take it seriously. And that child needs help. They need a psychiatrist; they need to have a full workup to keep themselves and the public safe. This is so frightening that this is going on, being ignored, and someone's asking Facebook how to treat them."[90]

Another post by the same nurse practitioner asked, "12-year-old coming to the ER with signs and symptoms of depression cut her forearm the night before. Boyfriend broke up with her, bullied at school … new to meds … should I start low-dose Zoloft or fluoxetine? Peds is new to my practice … any advice? Thanks."[90]

"This is a child who is cutting herself and at high risk for potential suicide or self-harm—and you're asking Facebook what meds to start?" asked Al-Agba, who adds that mental health problems require more than just medication. "They need an intervention, they need support."[90]

"They need more than Facebook," said Thoman, but with the replacement of psychiatrists by lesser trained nurse practitioners, social media consults are the best that some of these vulnerable patients are able to get. Patients like a seven-year-old girl born to a mother with schizophrenia and methamphetamine addiction. In a post, the psychiatric nurse practitioner describes "the sickest child I have ever seen at her age," with severe flashbacks, inconsolable screaming, and disassociation.

> She was on Risperdal and just [discontinued] due to firm knots in her breasts. Started on Zyprexa 2.5 [mg], increased to 2.5 [twice daily] and clonidine for flashbacks, added Haldol 0.5 mg PRN [as needed]. Trying to admit her tomorrow again. What would you diagnose with? I know PTSD possible, schizophrenia or something else?[90]

In addition to children, psychiatric nurse practitioners are also calling for help on social media to treat pregnant patients, including this post regarding a high-risk patient:

> Hey guys! I know you have all posted wonderful resources for pregnancy/medication safety in the past. I have a 38-year-old pregnant woman with anxiety and depression on escitalopram 10 mg, bupropion 150 mg and wanted to double check meds and provide her with resources. Thanks tribe![90]

Senior citizens are also being shortchanged, with a psychiatric nurse practitioner asking for help in treating an 80-year-old patient with anxiety and insomnia due to the pandemic.

> [Primary care] prescribed Trazodone 50 [mg] & Cymbalta 30mg 2 weeks ago … [Patient] stopped taking meds coz [sic] she feels like a zombie and unable to function during the day … what can I try to help her sleep without feeling drowsy? Can Xanax 1 mg [at bedtime] and Buspar 10 mg [twice daily] do it?? Thoughts???[90]

Xanax (alprazolam) is a sedative medication that carries the risk of addiction. The starting dose is generally 0.25 mg, although this class of medication is generally discouraged, especially in seniors. A dose of 1 mg would likely be extremely sedating and could potentially even be life-threatening in an at-risk individual on other potentiating medications—they may not ever wake up.

Because she has been accused of making up these screenshots, Thoman often includes confirmation that the person posting it is actually a nurse practitioner or a nurse practitioner student, such as a picture of them holding their diploma. "One of the accusations is that these aren't real nurse practitioners or real students—these are just trolls and are making it up to make NPs look bad," she said. "No, these are real people—these are licensed, real people. They're not doctors pretending. Here's the evidence. This is all unfortunately very true."[90]

Speaking out has earned Thoman some admirers—but has also created enemies. Jeny Conrad-Rendon, a nurse practitioner who owns Absolute Health, a concierge primary care clinic in Memphis, TN,[91] took to social media to urge "Professionals who support FPA [full practice authority] for APRNs" to report Thoman for her posts.[92] Members of the PMHNP [Psychiatric Mental Health Nurse Practitioner] Resource Group responded to a press conference that Thoman participated in, opposing independent practice for California nurse practitioners, and discussed plans to retaliate against her. One commenter wrote, "Surely her school and preceptors would like to be aware of her thoughts? I will email them her video and the screenshots of her comments." Another wrote, "I see a libel lawsuit coming her way."[92] But Thoman says she won't stop because she cares about patient safety. "Who is protecting the patients out there who don't know what is going on?"

THE PLOT THICKENS

While Rayne Thoman's posts have been met with incredulity, there may be a perfectly good explanation for the recent surge in naïve questions from new nurse practitioners: some of them may have never even attended nursing school.

While direct entry programs have long allowed students with a bachelor's degree in anything—economics, theater, history—to become a nurse practitioner in as little as 18 months,[93] most students start with a degree in nursing. This degree is typically a bachelor's, however, there are multiple programs that allow registered nurses to earn a bachelor's degree and immediately enter into a master's degree program, with much of the coursework completed online.[94] But what if these students never even completed training for a registered nurse degree?

In January 2023, the U.S. Justice Department announced the results of "Operation Nightingale," a seven-year investigation that exposed a massive nursing diploma scheme in which nursing programs sold false transcripts and credentials to more than 7,600 students in multiple states for $15,000 each.[95] These documents allowed prospective nurses to take the nursing licensure exam and, once passed, to gain employment in healthcare—or to go on to apply to nurse practitioner school.

Authorities began their investigation after identifying low pass rates of the nursing exam from several nursing schools. However, even students who are attending classes are struggling with the basic licensing exam to become registered nurses. According to testing authorities in both the United States and Canada, pass rates for the NCLEX (National Council Licensure Examination) have been declining since the COVID19 pandemic began, dropping from 73% to 69%.[96] Some nursing students and professors are calling for a decrease in testing standards, citing a systemic shortage of nurses. Joseph Oujeil, a nursing professor in Quebec, supports lowering the pass rate to 50% to support students who are trying to balance school with family and work responsibilities. "Many of them are good, hard workers and were shocked they should have to pass the exam another time," he told reporters. Licensing authorities have resisted lowering pass rates, citing patient safety and noting that students have three attempts to pass with resources available for students who need extra preparation.[96]

Maintaining high standards for practicing clinicians is paramount to maintain patient safety. In an article about "Operation Nightingale," U.S. Attorney for the Southern District of Florida Markenzy Lapointe said, "When we take an injured son or daughter to a hospital emergency room, we don't expect—really cannot imagine—that the licensed practical nurse or registered nurse [treating] our child took a shortcut."[95]

CHAPTER 4

THE DEATH OF PRIMARY CARE

Sixteen-year-old-Isaac (name changed) was at his pediatrician's office for an annual physical and vaccination update when he happened to mention that he'd been having occasional left-sided chest pains for about two months. Listening to Isaac's heart, the clinician announced to Isaac's father that he heard a murmur and advised that Isaac be taken directly to the emergency room, 'just to be safe.' Meghan Galer, MD, was on duty at the emergency department when Isaac and his father rushed in. "The patient's father was anxious and stressed, and Isaac was terrified," she said. After obtaining a more detailed history and examining Isaac, Galer concluded that his pain was musculoskeletal 'growing pains,' and that his heart murmur was completely innocent. "The chest pain and the murmur had nothing to do with each other," she said. "Any real pediatrician could have explained this to the patient and his father in maybe three minutes." Galer asked Isaac's father to go back to his car to get the paperwork from the morning clinic visit. "Sure enough, Isaac was never seen by a pediatrician, but by a nurse practitioner," she said. While no physical harm was done to Isaac, Galer noted that he and his father wasted a good part of the day in needless panic and are likely to face a large emergency department bill. "This unnecessary emergency room visit also wasted precious resources," said Galer.[97]

Primary care includes the fields of family medicine, general internal medicine, and pediatrics. High-quality primary care is not easy. It requires balancing the needs of the patient—to be reassured or to feel better from symptoms—with medical priorities like chronic disease management and preventive screenings. Patients are sicker and more complicated than ever, and yet primary care physicians are being asked to do more in less time, sometimes being given minutes to address multiple health conditions while achieving high patient satisfaction scores. In addition, they are tasked with multiple administrative burdens, with studies showing that for every hour spent face-to-face with a patient, primary care doctors spend two hours on computer documentation.[98] Despite these challenges, primary care is being relegated to non-physician practitioners with a fraction of the training, in part due to a deficit of primary care physicians.

Emily O'Rourke, MD, a family physician in Virginia, is worried that the current healthcare system has dumbed down primary care to a dangerous degree. She recalls her earliest exposure to primary care with rural country doctors in Nebraska. "They did everything for their patients, who were often rural people that were afraid to drive in the city. If it wasn't done by their country doctor, it wasn't going to be done at all, and so these doctors delivered babies, did colonoscopies, they saw patients in the hospital, they did it all. That's how I saw primary care and why I wanted to become a primary care physician." But this model of full-spectrum primary care by qualified physicians is changing, especially as thought leaders push for nurse practitioners and physician assistants to take over the role. O'Rourke believes that this is the wrong solution. "Without proper training, you're just trying to mimic things that you've seen other people do, and you're doing it wrong. You may be taking shortcuts, doing things like ordering extra tests, or you may be referring out excessively because you don't know what to do."[99]

The American Academy of Family Physicians says that primary care doctors are specifically trained to offer first contact and continuing care for patients with undiagnosed health problems. While advocates for non-physicians claim that they can provide this same care, current data is generally limited to the evaluation of low-risk patients with established diagnoses, and has always involved some degree of physician oversight. While logic would conclude that more training should result in better outcomes, there is data to support the argument, with physician studies noting fewer adverse outcomes when more knowledgeable and experienced primary care physicians treat patients.[100]

Unfortunately, clinicians with less knowledge may not assess themselves as providing inferior care, as demonstrated by the Dunning-Kruger effect (Figure 2), a syndrome in which people that have a low level of experience overrate their expertise. This false self-confidence is dangerous, as the illusion of competence can lead to failed medical judgment with life-threatening consequences.

Brandon Faza, MD, an emergency physician in Florida, has seen evidence of this. He says that he can tell whether patients are referred to him by primary care physicians or non-physician practitioners. "I highly respect a great primary doc. Their patients are rarely in the ED [emergency department] at all, so when they come, I know it's serious and unavoidable." He contrasts that to new non-physician graduates. "For the past few years, the average nurse practitioner referral is based almost exclusively on lack of knowledge." Faza blames academic institutions for these shortcomings. "It is usually the fault of the very poorly regulated, profit-above-all educational

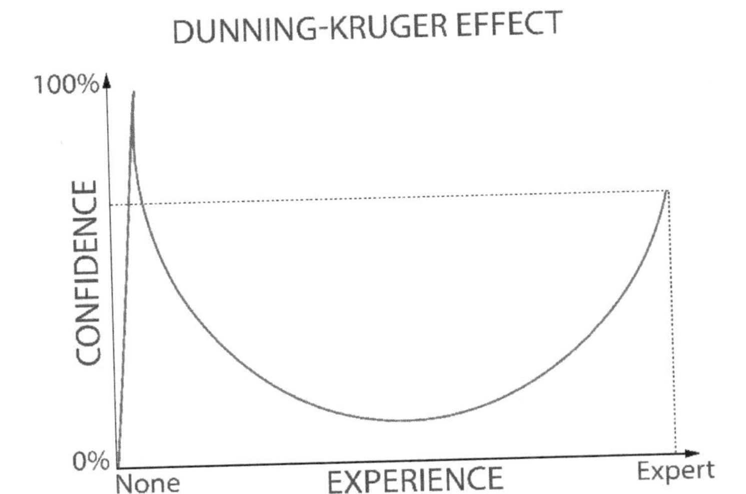

Figure 2. Dunning-Kruger Effect

system," he says, noting that schools often mislead and take advantage of students who believe that they will be qualified to care for patients when they graduate. He also points the finger at nurse practitioner leadership. "In the past few years, they seem to spend more time brainwashing their students and anyone else who will listen that their freshly minted 100% online NPs will be 'better than a doctor' coming straight out of school."[101]

NURSES IN PRIMARY CARE

Mary Mundinger, DrPH (Doctor of Public Health), Dean Emerita and Professor of Health at the Columbia School of Nursing is one such leader calling for an expanded role for nurse practitioners in primary care. A recipient of the Robert Wood Johnson Health Policy Program Fellowship in 1984, Mundinger is a well-respected and influential nurse researcher with multiple publications advocating for nurse practitioners to be "the preferred primary care providers for the 21st century."[102] In her writing, Mundinger is unapologetic about her views on the high value of nurse practitioners, arguing that nurse practitioner care is indistinguishable and even superior to care provided by physicians.[103]

Mary Mundinger is perhaps most important for her 2000 study, 'Primary care outcomes in patients treated by nurse practitioners or physicians: a randomized trial,' a seminal report on nurse practitioner care that has been cited over 1,300 times in the medical literature[104] and used extensively to justify independent nurse practice policy.

"To give her credit, Mundinger forewarned the shortage of primary care physicians," said Niran Al-Agba in a podcast interview about the study. "However, she had her own thoughts about what the proper answer would be: to train more nurses to work in primary care."[2] Mundinger's study, which she called 'the Columbia experience,' was designed to prove once and for all that nurse practitioners could take over the role of primary care. But according to Al-Agba, while the Columbia experience did evaluate specific aspects of primary care: routine physicals and well child-care, pre-diagnosed hypertension, diabetes, and asthma, the study did not come close to replicating a true primary care clinic. Further, Mundinger's research had serious deficits that were not fully revealed upon publication.

Al-Agba, who special ordered an autographed copy of Mundinger's book, "A Path to Nursing Excellence: The Colombia Experience (2014)," pointed out the irony of the theme of Mundinger's work: *activism needs to be based on empirical evidence*. "When you're talking about the gold standard, which would be a randomized, controlled, blinded study, this is the only one that even came close. But when you delve into the details, it isn't an independent study at all."[2]

Cracks in Mundinger's seminal work

Mary Mundinger's study, published in *JAMA* in 2000, has been considered instrumental in informing health policy decisions regarding nurse practitioner scope of practice. According to nurse research experts, the report "clearly determined that nurse practitioners provide high-quality primary care and chronic care management better than or equal to care by physicians."[105] But upon close examination, the study is in no way as decisive as its champions insist. In fact, a *JAMA* editorial that accompanied Mundinger's article pointed out that the research had significant defects, stating that "because the Columbia study leaves so many questions unanswered, its evidence that nurse practitioners and primary care physicians are interchangeable is far from convincing."[106]

Mundinger aggressively defends the study, insisting that nurse practitioners were practicing independently of physicians. Responding to a 2020 Wall Street Journal op-ed that pointed out a lack of evidence for independent practice written by this author,[107] Mundinger wrote, "There is no room for misinformation in any debate about nurse practitioner and physician comparability. Rebekah Bernard argues that 'studies that show equivalence in care between nurse practitioners and physicians are flawed,' and that, 'not a single large-scale study has compared the care provided by nurse practitioners practicing independently without physician supervision.'

Dr. Bernard is wrong on both counts." Mundinger argued that her study was both large, consisting of 1,300 patients, and that nurse practitioners had full admitting and discharge privileges, as well as full prescriptive privileges. The result of the study, according to Mundinger, was that "nurse practitioners could provide the same care and achieve the same health outcomes for patients as care delivered by physicians."[1] However, a close reading of literature produced by Mundinger herself shows serious cracks in this conclusion.

The Colombia experience study evaluated 1,300 mostly Hispanic women in their mid-40s with stable hypertension, diabetes, or asthma over six months and reassessed at two years. Patients were randomized to care by a physician or a nurse practitioner. Outcomes included patient satisfaction, health status (based on a short self-assessment survey of general health), physiologic test results of blood pressure, hemoglobin A1C (a marker of diabetic control), and peak flows (a marker of asthma control). Mundinger concluded that there was no difference in these outcomes between patients treated by nurse practitioners and physicians.[108]

Niran Al-Agba says that these results have limited implications, as the study was not designed to evaluate differences in severe illness and death which occur infrequently in a low-risk population, especially over such a short term. "I'm not sure there are many studies that would find a huge difference because you're not going to see a lot of deaths from high blood pressure in women in their mid-40s," Al-Agba said. Further, she notes that patients in Mundinger's study were not typical primary care patients. "They were what's called 'ambulatory care-sensitive,' which means that they had simple conditions that were previously diagnosed by a physician in an emergency room or urgent care." The study did not include the evaluation, diagnosis, and treatment of undifferentiated patients, meaning patients with medical symptoms that have not yet been diagnosed. Further, Al-Agba said that the study focused on the care of one specific problem at a time, whereas, "In a typical primary care office, physicians will treat patients with multiple different complaints that require a smorgasbord of things to work up."[2]

According to Phil Shaffer, MD, a physician with a background in research analysis, the Mundinger study is similar to most studies of its type, showing that well-trained nurses can follow an algorithm on an already diagnosed patient, but not evaluating how well a nurse practitioner can evaluate the care of a complex patient for the first time. In a podcast episode of *Patients at Risk*, Shaffer explained that a true evaluation of quality care would include an analysis of history-taking and physical exam skills, as well as the formulation of a differential diagnosis and treatment plan. Instead, Shaffer says that most studies hand over patients on a silver platter with a diagnosis and treatment in place.[2]

Emergency physician-turned primary care physician Meghan Galer explains that the treatment of undifferentiated patients with multiple complaints makes primary care one of the most challenging fields of medicine—and is the reason why it is the worst place for someone with minimal training. "What emergency medicine and primary care have in common is that our patients come to us completely undifferentiated. If you don't have that ability to start with a comprehensive unbiased history and physical, and develop that broad differential diagnosis, there's a high likelihood that you're going to miss something and you're going to inappropriately pigeonhole that patient down one path of care without regard for what the actual issue may be."[99]

While the Mundinger study evaluated the care of patients with either diabetes, hypertension, or asthma, a typical primary care physician often manages all three in combination, along with other issues. Primary care has become increasingly complex, especially with the aging of the population and increased rates of chronic disease. Primary care physicians must be excellent diagnosticians and multi-taskers, not just taking care of simple problems and referring everything else to specialists. To achieve this level of care, primary care physicians complete four years of college, four years of medical school, and three years of residency training—a minimum of 15,000 hours of clinical experience—before they are permitted to treat patients independently. Family nurse practitioners receive 1–2-years of post-baccalaureate training which includes a minimum of 500 clinical hours of experience, with most programs requiring from 540 to 825 hours, and an average requirement of 686 clinical hours[109] (Figure 3).

Family medicine residency director Mark Huntington says that this additional training matters. "There's a big difference between the training of a family physician and the training of an advanced practice clinician, and that has to do with really being able to think outside the box," he said in a podcast interview. Huntington notes that because training is abbreviated, nurse practitioners and physician assistants learn how to use algorithms. "For physicians, those basic science years in which we learn how everything works are important because it helps us think outside the box. So, when that algorithm fails us, we know what to do next, we can figure out not just what to do, but why."[79]

This extensive education is especially important in the case of multiple co-morbidities. "For example, if someone has renal failure, we may need to give them more fluid, but if they also have heart failure, we need to give them less fluid. How do you figure it out?" said Huntington. "The algorithm won't help you. That's where a physician's training comes into play. And if you're taking care of sick people, you do need a physician for that."[79]

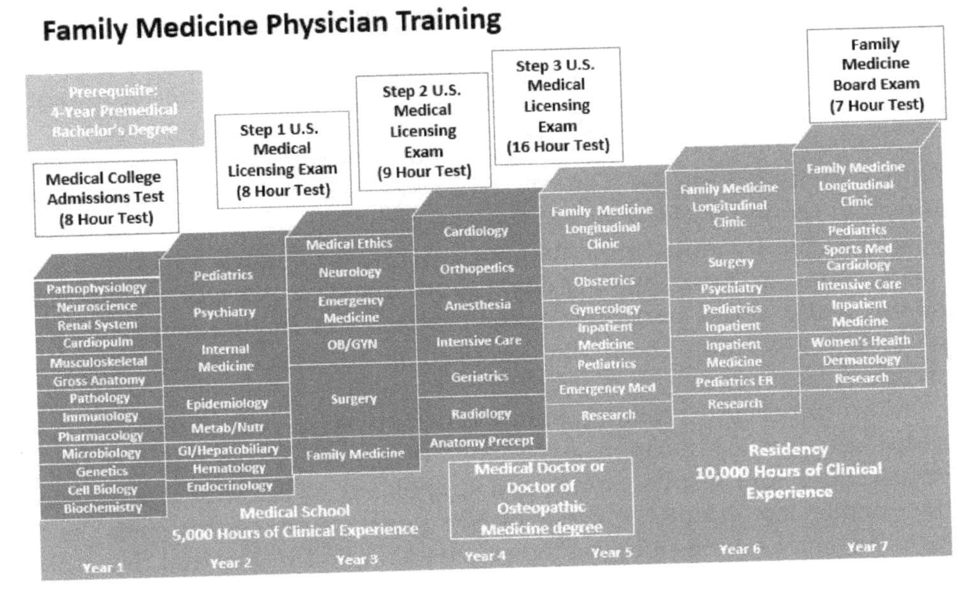

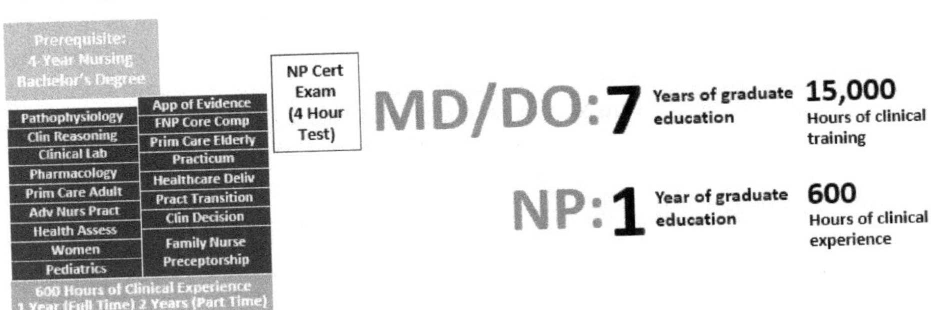

Figure 3. Family Medicine Training—Physicians vs NPs

BIAS AND NONDISCLOSURES

While Mary Mundinger's study has been used to endorse nurse practitioner-led care, a meta-analysis found that it had a high degree of bias. Despite inclusion in 'Nurses as Substitutes for Physicians in Primary Care,' reviewers noted that the study had the highest amount of bias of 18 studies included and that study authors only reported favorable data.[110]

One of the most serious shortcomings of the study is the omission of important details about the training and supervisory relationships of nurse practitioners in the published article. "When you're writing scientific papers, the methods are crucial," said Phil Shaffer in a podcast on the subject. "You are supposed to reveal everything about your methods so that if anybody wants to read it carefully, to understand it clearly or reproduce it, it's all right there. And she did not do that."[2]

Shaffer refers specifically to details about the nurses hand-selected to participate in Mundinger's study. "This was not originally listed in the study, but I found it as I've done more research," Shaffer said. "First, there were four family nurse practitioners and three pediatric nurse practitioners working four hours per day, four to five days per week. So, we're talking really about part-time nurse practitioners in that they weren't working in a full-time clinic that was running eight hours a day, 40 hours a week."[2]

More importantly, Shaffer points out that nurse practitioners in the study had significantly more experience than the average nurse graduate, and therefore results cannot be extrapolated to the way most nurse practitioners are trained. "Three of the seven nurse practitioners had doctorate-level nursing degrees when they enrolled in the trial. In addition, one was the director of the geriatric nursing program, one was the director of the adult nursing program, and one was the director of the pediatric nursing program at Columbia School of Nursing. This is important because we aren't talking about your average nurse practitioner," he insisted. "These were assistant professor level, all appointed to the faculty of the Columbia School of Nursing. We're talking about the top of the top in nursing education." Shaffer notes that the typical nurse practitioner now gets a year and a half to two years of book training, and then 500 hours of clinical training. "By contrast, the NPs in this study were experienced associate professors and higher."[2]

In addition, in the 20 years since Mundinger's paper was published, nurse practitioner education has changed dramatically with the rise of online education and accelerated programs. "The NPs evaluated in this study are not similar to what we have now," said Shaffer. "Today, most nurse practitioners don't get trained on how to evaluate labs and x-rays. They have zero training in x-rays. I'm a radiologist, I pay attention to that, and they get no training at all."[99]

Additional 'residency' training

In her writing, Mary Mundinger often equates medical school to nursing school, even though a registered nurse (RN) degree or Bachelor of Science in Nursing (BSN) are both undergraduate degrees, and a medical degree (MD or DO) is a graduate degree completed after undergraduate training. Mundinger theorized that the Doctor of Nursing Practice (DNP) degree, which she helped to create, would be equivalent to a physician residency, even though nurses can earn a DNP in 1–2 years, while physician residencies last from 3–7 years.

Despite Mundinger's expressed belief that a DNP was equivalent to physician residency training, she still required additional training for the DNPs in her Columbia study before she enrolled them in a trial against physicians. Before beginning the study, nurse practitioners underwent a special 'residency' training in dermatology, radiology, and cardiology, and were mentored by physicians to conduct emergency department evaluations, as well as to admit and co-manage patients. However, this information was not revealed in the original study paper. "We went through this paper with a fine-tooth comb and Mundinger says nothing about how the nurse practitioners were trained," said Phil Shaffer. "There was also no description of the physician trainers nor about the physicians to whom the nurse practitioners were compared in the study."[2] Shaffer discovered the details in a YouTube video in which Mundinger describes the special nurse practitioner training as follows:

> "... they went through the training the medical residents went through for the first nine months, and they learned how to do ER evaluations, they learned how to co-manage patients in the hospital, how to call for help, how to evaluate labs and x-ray findings that they hadn't gotten in their conventional training. In a sense, they would be much more able to be compared to the physicians in the trial."[111]

However, this additional training and mentorship by physicians was not described in Mundinger's original paper. "These NPs got far more training than the usual NP and are in no way representative of NPs as a group," said Shaffer. "In the YouTube video, it was clear that she knew about this additional training when they wrote the paper but made a conscious decision not to reveal it."[2]

Indeed, the Columbia experience did demonstrate to Mundinger that nurse practitioners needed more training. In her YouTube video, she said that the project led her to advocate for a doctorate in nursing which would be more clinical to make it competitive with medicine. However, even Mundinger herself in more recent years has criticized DNP training programs, noting that only 15% of them provide enhanced clinical education.[112]

While nurse practitioners received extra training from physicians before Mundinger's study, they also had access to physicians throughout the study period. New York State required that nurse practitioners work with a collaborating physician, which meant that nurse practitioners could always call for help. How often this may have occurred was not revealed in the study. Moreover, Mundinger's book noted that the nurse practitioners personally selected their collaborating physicians, and stated that the nurse practitioners were well served by the arrangement because a physician would respond immediately if medical assistance was required. For patients requiring hospital admissions, nurse practitioners followed a protocol requiring a physician to see the patient and sign off on orders within 24 hours.[2]

Mundinger did demonstrate that experienced, specially trained nurse practitioners could compare favorably to physicians when managing low-risk, previously diagnosed patients over a 6–24-month period, but these caveats are never mentioned in the study itself, nor in the more than thirteen hundred citations of the work. Further, Mundinger did not include these details in her *Wall Street Journal* rebuttal. Instead, she simply stated that nurse practitioners "provide the same care and achieve the same health outcomes for patients as care delivered by physicians."[1]

Ultimately, the co-authors of *Patients at Risk* stand by the argument that no high-quality scientific evidence has shown the safety and efficacy of nurse practitioner care without physician involvement. While Mary Mundinger's study comes the closest, in the more than twenty years since her work was published, no better-quality research has been released. Additionally, while nearly half the states in the country have allowed independent practice for decades, no randomized, controlled trials have been published on the quality of care being provided by these unsupervised nurse practitioners.

Mary Mundinger's belief that nurse practitioners can provide the same care as a primary care physician indicates a fundamental misunderstanding of the role of primary care, says Niran Al-Agba. "She says things like, 'primary care is much simpler than it used to be. It's not like specialty care; it no longer requires the level of training it once did.' What's interesting is that she goes on to say that referring to specialists is part of the primary care role, but what she's missing is when we're out in small areas, we don't have a lot of specialty backup. We are seeing undifferentiated patients who are coming in off the street with a host of issues that we need to puzzle out or problem solve to put together," said Al-Agba, who works in a rural, underserved area. Al-Agba believes that this miscalculation of the role of primary care has created a disconnect with the reality of a primary care physician's work. "There is this idea that a primary care doc just follows an algorithm. I would argue that that's actually not true. In my experience, we follow fewer algorithms."[2] Studies have confirmed that indeed, primary care physicians refer less often and more appropriately than non-physician practitioners.[113] This is important because unnecessary referrals put pressure on physician specialists who are also in short supply.

THERE'S SOMETHING ABOUT MARY

Mary Mundinger's research on nurse practitioners in primary care has helped to obtain increasing acceptance of the role by insurance payers. Part of the reason may be Mundinger's close relationship with several for-profit healthcare companies, including the medical insurance company United Healthcare Group (UHG), where she served on the board of directors. Analysts note that just a year after Mundinger joined the board, UHG and other major insurance companies changed coverage policy "to not only pay for nurses providing physician care, but also to do so without cutting their reimbursement rates."[114] In media interviews, UHG officials spoke favorably of Mundinger's project of creating nurse practitioner-led clinics.[114]

In addition to her role on the board of directors, Mundinger served on the company's three-member compensation committee, which was tasked with determining the salary and benefits for the company's senior executives, including signing off on a $100 million compensation package for CEO William McGuire in 2000.[115] As a director for UnitedHealth, the eighth best-compensated board in the nation in 2004, Mundinger earned at least $400,000 per year in cash and options,[114] with additional pay for her participation on the compensation committee.[115] Around the same time, Mundinger earned cash and stock options chairing the compensation committee at Cell Therapeutics, a $400 million cancer treatment developer. She also received cash and options serving as the director of Gentiva Health Services, a $315 million home health company.[115]

While the average nurse researcher or nursing professor earns about $100,000 per year,[116] Mundinger's net worth from serving in these directorship positions was estimated to be at least $12.29 million in 2008, after selling an estimated value of $3.79 million over the previous five years of UnitedHealth Group stock.[117] In 2022, Mundinger's net worth was estimated at $15 million.[118]

Corporate scandal

Mary Mundinger's tenure at UHG was not without controversy. On March 18, 2006, the *Wall Street Journal* published a front-page article entitled *'The Perfect Payday,'* discussing "unusually propitious timing of stock option grants to executives" at publicly traded companies including UnitedHealth Group. The article reported that the United States Securities and Exchange Commission (SEC) was investigating accusations of backdating options to increase stock value to executives—reportedly granting options on dates when the company's stock hit its low price for the year.

Following this exposé, the SEC, United States Attorney's Office for the Southern District of New York, and Internal Revenue Service opened investigations into UHG's stock practices, and the U.S. Congress asked the company to provide documents for committee review. Multiple shareholder derivative lawsuits were filed against UHG officers and directors, including Mary Mundinger, alleging a breach of fiduciary obligations of good faith, loyalty, and due care. Multiple retirement and pension fund managers also filed suit against the company for SEC violations and breach of duty, claiming that directors personally profited from backdated stock options, including Mundinger, who allegedly obtained more than $1.6 million through the exercise of stock options since 1997.[119]

In response, UHG formed a special litigation committee (SLC) to investigate shareholder claims and determine whether remedies should be pursued against board members. Ultimately, the committee accepted settlements from top executives, including over $600 million in relinquished stock value from CEO William McGuire and $30 million from General Counsel David Lubben. Regarding accusations against outside director Mary Mundinger, including "Breach of Fiduciary Duty, Abuse of Control, Gross Mismanagement, Waste of Corporate Assets, and Unjust Enrichment," while the SLC expressed "disappointment" in Mundinger's performance, they declined to pursue a settlement, citing "significant obstacles to successful litigation" including substantial cost to the company, "potential distraction of management of the Company from its ongoing business; and the potentially harmful effects on the Company's efforts to recruit new directors."[120]

Conflicts of interest

Besides questionable remuneration practices, critics have other concerns about Mary Mundinger's role with UHG, including a potential conflict with her position as a nurse researcher at Columbia University's School of Nursing. Research support for the expansion of the nurse practitioner role in healthcare would be expected to provide a financial boon to healthcare employers since nurse practitioners earn about half the salary of a primary care physician.[121] Yet none of Mundinger's publications revealed her lucrative positions as director of multiple for-profit corporations with a potential financial interest in expanding the role of nurse practitioners in healthcare. Indeed, UHG is not only the nation's largest health insurer, but also owns Optum, a division that sells clinical healthcare services. The company is the nation's largest nongovernmental employer of nurses and employs 20,000 nurse practitioners, as well as 60,000 physicians.[122] Many of its nurse practitioners provide house calls and work in long-term care settings, especially as part of its Medicare Advantage plan coverage for seniors, with UHG nurse practitioners making nearly 753,000 home visits to members in 2014.[123]

This is a serious flaw, according to Phil Shaffer. "At the time that Mary Mundinger's most important paper was written, she was on the board of directors of United Healthcare. As a board member, it's your fiduciary responsibility to advance all of the interests of the company and not do anything that would harm the company. So that is a powerful motivation." Shaffer notes that these conflicts were not revealed in the original papers or at any time afterward, and were only discovered through extensive outside review.[2] After Shaffer and several colleagues sent a letter to *JAMA*, the journal issued a correction, noting Mundinger's potential conflict of interest—more than 20 years after the original publication.[124]

Shaffer also points out a further conflict of interest: the relationship between United Healthcare and the American Association of Retired Persons (AARP). "I get notices from the AARP, and they are always trying to sell me United Healthcare products," he said.[2] The relationship between United Healthcare and the AARP has earned billions for each company, with the AARP receiving a 4.95% fee for every insurance plan they sell, which includes Medicare supplements and Medicare Advantage plans funded by the federal government. The AARP has worked very closely with nurse practitioner advocates, and received a $10 million grant from the Robert Wood Johnson Foundation in 2007 to create the *Center to Champion Nursing in America.*[125] In addition, the AARP's *Campaign for Action* was formed to enact policy recommendations from the Institute of Medicine's *Future of Nursing Report*, which called for an increase in nurse practitioner scope.[126]

Mary Mundinger served as a project advisory committee member for RAND corporation, a public policy think tank formed in 2005 and funded in part by both the AARP and United Health. The advisory committee's goal: To predict the effects of health policy changes and provide information to policymakers. Featured publications have focused on the impact of health insurance changes including allowing younger patients to buy into Medicare, expanding insurance enrollment, and a public option for healthcare.[127]

THE IMPACT OF CORPORATE INTEGRATION ON PRIMARY CARE

Why are insurance companies interested in an expanded role for nurse practitioners? Part of the reason is profit, but another is a shortage of primary care physicians, as the U.S. has one of the lowest ratios of generalists to specialists among high-income countries, with just 30% of physicians providing primary care.[128]

This deficit flies in the face of the facts: primary care by trained physicians is associated with improved health outcomes,[129] not because of treatment of minor, self-limited conditions like colds, cuts, or scrapes, but because of interventions that reduce overall mortality. According to studies, there are two critical factors involved in decreasing mortality. The first is by reducing cardiovascular risk—heart attacks and strokes—through the management of risk factors like blood pressure, cholesterol, and diabetes. Secondly, comprehensive primary care results in reductions in death from cancer due to screening tests that lead to early detection and treatment.[130]

Most primary care physicians provide these services as part of their routine evaluation of patients. While some patients may present to their regular doctor for an annual physical exam, many only enter into the health care system for evaluation of a minor ailment. It is during these visits that physicians may note an elevated blood pressure and initiate antihypertensive medication, measure a patient's body mass index and discuss healthy weight, or order overdue cancer screening tests. When patients skip their primary care doctor to stop into a drugstore walk-in clinic, they may miss these opportunities. Unfortunately, patients are being siphoned by insurance carriers toward retail clinics staffed by nurse practitioners. One of the reasons is profit from corporate integration.

Corporate integration involves the delivery of healthcare services by multiple providers under the same corporate umbrella. Companies may combine and incorporate services into a larger syndicate, such as mergers between insurance companies and pharmacy chains. While large healthcare conglomerates often argue that they can provide better quality under one roof, studies show that increased market concentration may be associated with reduced quality of care.[131]

According to Marion Mass, MD, the co-founder of Practicing Physicians of America, corporate integration also leads to increased healthcare costs, especially when factoring in drug management by Pharmacy Benefit Managers (PBMs), companies that administrate prescription benefits by acting as intermediaries between the patient and the pharmacy. PBMs make money by earning a processing fee on each prescription they fill, but also by working with insurance companies to create a formulary or list of medications that are covered on a benefit plan. As they select what medications they will cover, PBMs may receive monetary remuneration from drug manufacturers.[132]

Since PBMs have become so profitable, insurance companies are buying and merging with them to increase revenues, a process called horizontal integration. For example, when insurance company Cigna bought PBM giant Express Scripts in 2018 for $67 billion, their revenues tripled. That same year, drugstore chain CVS acquired insurance company Aetna for

$69 billion, with 60% of their income coming from their pharmacy benefit manager.[132]

Before a PBM can collect any fee, someone has to prescribe medication. Along comes vertical integration, in which insurance and pharmacy companies employ medical practitioners to diagnose patients and prescribe medications (Table 5). Hiring non-physicians rather than physicians is a logical choice for two reasons: companies can pay them less, and non-physicians tend to prescribe more medications.[133]

In some cases, vertical integration involves the use of clinicians hired by insurance companies to treat patients. This can be done for cost savings to control healthcare spending, or to make money from government payers. For example, Medicare pays private insurance companies a set fee to manage the medical care of seniors through Medicare Advantage plans, which act like HMOs, requiring patients to see clinicians within a designated network. In some cases, these companies hire nurse practitioners to oversee patient care and to collect healthcare data to submit to Medicare for payment.[134]

Medicare sets payment rates based on the complexity or level of illness of patients being managed. In a lawsuit filed by the federal government, insurance company Cigna was accused of using nurse practitioners to over-diagnose Medicare patients to make them appear sicker and more medically fragile to gain more funding.[134]

The lawsuit, based on a whistleblower complaint, alleged that Cigna submitted fraudulent diagnoses to receive tens of millions of dollars in higher payment from Medicare. These diagnoses were made by nurse practitioners hired by Cigna vendors to perform in-home assessments of patients targeted by the insurance company as being most likely to have higher risk scores. According to the suit, "nurse practitioners spent limited time with the patients and did not conduct a comprehensive physical examination. Instead, they relied largely on the patient's self-assessment and their responses to various basic screening questions." In addition, nurse practitioners typically did not review complete medical records, nor did they order or perform diagnostic testing to confirm diagnoses.[134]

Table 5. Examples of Horizontal and Vertical Integration

Insurer	Pharmacy Benefit Manager (PBM)	Patient Care Services
Aetna (merged with CVS)	CVS Caremark	CVS MinuteClinic
Cigna	Express Scripts	Cigna Collective Care
Humana (merged with Walgreens)	Humana Pharmacy Solution	Partners in Primary Care, Conviva, Kindred at Home
United Healthcare	OptumRx	OptumCare

Another aspect of vertical integration involves hiring clinicians to prescribe medications. "They've discovered that they can create a revenue source by having a brick-and-mortar location to treat patients," said Marion Mass in a *Patients at Risk* podcast episode. She uses CVS as a prime example. "CVS has thousands of little CVS drugstores called MinuteClinics," which hire predominantly nurse practitioners. "So, the standard of care for medicine, according to CVS, which owns an insurance company and a pharmacy benefit manager, is not to use a physician. Instead, they hire a nurse practitioner."[132] On CVS's website, the company downplays the differences between a physician and a nurse practitioner, writing that "physicians and nurse practitioners are more alike than people realize … The biggest difference between the two medical professions is the type of schools they attend."[135]

Mass said that since insurance companies are integrated with pharmacies and retail clinics in shopping centers, they can incentivize patients to utilize their clinics rather than an independent physician. "Since Aetna and CVS are horizontally integrated, they can easily incentivize patients to utilize the retail clinics they own with a co-pay maneuver. They may say, 'Zero-dollar copay if you go to the CVS MinuteClinic first, and 'x' dollar copay if you go to your primary doctor.' So where are most people going to choose to go?"[132]

Indeed, a 2018 study showed that fewer insured patients are seeing primary care physicians, while visits to non-physician practitioners are on the rise. Data from patients with Aetna, Humana, United Healthcare, and Kaiser Permanente insurance showed a reduction of 18% in primary care physician visits between 2012 and 2016, while visits to nurse practitioners and physician assistants increased by 129%. The study authors expressed surprise at the finding that there was essentially no cost savings from seeing a non-physician practitioner (averaging $103 per visit) compared to seeing a physician ($106 per visit).[136] Additionally, when patients bypass their regular physician for the treatment of minor medical complaints, they miss out on opportunities for chronic care management and preventive services.

Mass points out that companies like CVS benefit doubly because nurse practitioners tend to prescribe more drugs. When a patient is prescribed a medication by a MinuteClinic nurse practitioner, they are likely to fill it at that same pharmacy. "You can also train staff to direct patients to other items for sale," said Mass. "'And while you're here at CVS, I think you better make sure that you get this particular brace that we have on aisle 16,'" she said.[132]

Mass also says that Medicare payment updates in 2021 have favored the treatment of seemingly simple problems by nurse practitioners at retail clinics, noting that of the five levels of coding based on medical complexity, lower-level codes received a pay increase while payment for higher-level codes representing more serious conditions decreased. "Insurers incentivize patients to go to the retail clinic, and for most simple problems, the patients may tend to be okay anyway and don't even necessarily need any medical treatment," for example, a runny nose or sprained ankle. Mass said that the company now collects more money for those simple level visits. "But if the patient is more complicated, the nurse practitioner may say, 'Well, this is too much for me to handle. So, I'm sending you to your primary.' Now the primary care doctor, who sees the more complex situation referred from the retail clinic has to spend more time on the patient and collects less money from the insurer." Mass notes that this creates a downward spiral for primary care physicians. "If this is allowed to go on as it is with MinuteClinics—and I call them drive-by clinics, because quite frankly, that's what they feel like to me, well, I think that we're going to lose primary care."[132]

BACK TO BASICS

Some physicians believe that the only way to take primary care back is to return to self-ownership. This is exactly what Meghan Galer did when she resigned from her corporate hospital emergency medicine job to open her own general practice. Galer quit over concerns about patient safety and physician devaluation in the corporate staffing model, noting that she was deeply concerned about liability when supervising non-physicians, because she wasn't given enough time to ensure that non-physician management was appropriate.

Trained as an emergency physician, Galer realized that she had few options in the field other than corporate medicine. Instead, she decided to open her own direct primary care practice. "I'm very upfront with my patients that I'm emergency medicine trained, and I'm going to take a little longer with some things to make sure that I'm doing them properly," she said in a podcast on the topic, noting that she supplements her formal medical training with an intensive review of primary care subjects. Galer says that it's unfortunate that a corporate quagmire has forced patients to ask the question: *Are you better off in a real emergency department with a fake doctor—NP or PA—or with a real emergency doctor practicing in a private office?*[94]

Increasingly, primary care physicians—and even some specialists—are embracing this direct care model, which they say allows them to focus on the physician-patient relationship. Removing third-party payer requirements significantly reduces the administrative and financial burden on physicians, freeing up time to spend with patients. While direct care is generally affordable for most patients, averaging $77 per month, the model can increase the income potential of primary care physicians, who are among the lowest paid in medicine. While primary care physicians face high rates of burnout, direct care often improves physician quality of life by lowering total volume of patients being managed.[137]

CHAPTER 5

PROFITS OVER PATIENTS

Hospitals are increasingly hiring non-physician practitioners in the place of physicians for one simple reason: Profits. There is money to be made in healthcare—and plenty of it. While hospitals in the United States originated as philanthropic organizations, the creation of Medicare in 1965 provided an opportunity for profit, and by 2019, just 19% of hospitals in the U.S. were publicly (government) controlled, while 57% were nonprofit, and 24% for-profit.[138]

The term 'nonprofit' is a misnomer when it comes to healthcare. While for-profit companies distribute gains to investors, nonprofit funds are meant to be re-invested into the company for improvements and growth. This reinvestment may take the form of buying up smaller hospitals to create healthcare conglomerates that eventually become virtual monopolies in a given area. In addition, nonprofit health organizations pay executives generous salaries. While annual CEO pay for nonprofits outside of healthcare averages around $150,000, hospital CEOs receive an average pay of $600,000. Salaries tend to correlate with patient volume, and the top 10 best-paid nonprofit health executives earned more than $7 million each in 2017.[139]

Nonprofit hospitals are expected to serve as a community safety net, providing charitable care to low-income patients, so they also receive favorable tax exemptions. This tax status helps to increase operating revenue and allows further expansion. What happens when the hospital begins to lose money, through demographic changes, mismanagement, or national crises like COVID-19? Generally, the organization starts by slashing expenses, especially staffing, often replacing physicians with less expensive non-physician practitioners. In some cases, when company executives decide that the organization has lost enough money, they just close shop and walk away, abandoning patients and the community.

Case example: Mercy-El Reno Hospital

Mercy is the 7th largest Catholic healthcare system in the U.S. operating 30 hospitals across the southwest. The company has an operating revenue of $5 billion and $3.4 billion in assets.[140] Mercy leaders are compensated generously, with more than 75 top corporate executives earning a combined $50 million in 2020.[141]

In 2010, Mercy entered into a lease agreement to take over management of Parkview Hospital, a small public hospital built in 1954 and owned by the city of El Reno, Oklahoma.[142] As part of its corporate strategy, Mercy systematically replaced hospital physicians with nurse practitioners, resulting in the death of Alexus Ochoa. Travis Dunn was the lead attorney for the family of 19-year-old Alexus, whose tragic misdiagnosis is detailed in *Patients at Risk*. Like most people, Dunn knew very little about the scope of practice of nurse practitioners before he took this case. "We knew that mid-level practitioners were being used to save money, but I didn't know a whole lot about them," Dunn said in a podcast recording. "What I've learned is that a family nurse practitioner may attend, in this case, an online school, with very little practice, and that their scope of practice is shockingly small. You can't treat them as physicians; they have to stay within their scope of practice."[143]

According to Oklahoma state law, scope of practice is determined by an individual nurse practitioner's educational background. "If you go to a family nurse practitioner program, your scope of practice is limited to primary care, and not hospital care," said Dunn, noting that that the hospital chose to hire nurse practitioners to practice outside of their training. "I think [nurse practitioners] probably would prefer to stay within their scope, but when they're granted privileges to do things that are far broader, they're put in a position to fail."

Oklahoma law permits nurse practitioners to work in the same capacity as a physician, but only in the narrow scope that they are trained for, according to Dunn. By hiring a family nurse practitioner to work in an acute care setting, Mercy violated the Oklahoma Nurse Practice Act and put patients at risk. "We approached this case based on 'there's nothing wrong with a family practice nurse practitioner working in an emergency room. She can work on family practice issues,'" Dunn said. "But if you credential and grant privileges to a family nurse practitioner to work outside that little sliver of her training, people die. And that's what this case was about. It was about taking a license and stretching it to make money."

Unfortunately, patients were not informed that Mercy had replaced physicians with nurse practitioners. In fact, at the beginning of the case, Dunn said that the Ochoa family was under the assumption that a physician treated Alexus. "We didn't even know the case was about a nurse practitioner when we took it on because this particular nurse practitioner represented herself to the family as a physician." Dunn recalled having to inform them that Alexus had not received her medical care from an emergency physician. "I remember very clearly telling Alexus's boyfriend that the person that he'd been dealing with, that he thought was a doctor, was in fact a nurse practitioner. And this was a year after she died. He had no idea."

In their defense, the corporation argued that they were forced to hire nurse practitioners because Mercy-El Reno Hospital was located in a rural area. Dunn laughed as he recalled one of the corporation's Atlanta-based defense attorneys attempting to paint the facility as being rural. "He was not familiar with Oklahoma City at all, and during jury selection, he kept saying El Paso instead of El Reno, [at one point saying], 'you know, El Paso is an hour away.' Finally, one of the prospective jurors said, 'do you mean El Reno? Because El Reno is not an hour away.'" In fact, when Alexus was finally transferred to Oklahoma University Medical Center in Oklahoma City, it was a 22-minute ambulance ride. "So, it wasn't a rural area; they have access to whatever they needed. They were just trying to save money."[143]

As Mercy was embroiled in this legal battle, the system decided to close Mercy-El Reno Hospital, announcing an end to their lease agreement with the city of El Reno in November 2018. In news reports, administrators blamed the closure on the need for 'extensive renovations' of the hospital and financial losses over the previous year, which they attributed to a decreased demand for hospital services.[144] Mercy-El Reno Hospital closed its doors on April 30, 2019, just six weeks after a jury returned a $6.19 million verdict for the wrongful death of Alexus Ochoa.

THE RISE OF FOR-PROFIT HOSPITALS AND PRIVATE EQUITY

In 2010, the Affordable Care Act prohibited physicians from owning hospitals, ostensibly to prevent doctors from abusing their positions to make money. This ban on physician-owned hospitals was supported by nonprofit and for-profit hospital lobbying groups, and the American Hospital Association and Federation of American Hospitals have opposed proposed legislation to repeal the ban.[145] While vigorously protecting patients from potentially unscrupulous physicians, the government seems to have less hesitation about allowing for-profit companies to own their own hospital systems. Today a quarter of all U.S. hospitals are owned by companies that answer to shareholders, who fully expect to profit generously from their investments.[138]

Increasingly, for-profit hospitals are owned by private equity companies, investors who buy, manage, and sell companies to maximize profit. Private equity ownership is a relatively new phenomenon in medicine, but it is growing rapidly. In addition to owning hospitals, private equity companies also buy and sell medical practices and physician groups. Robert McNamara, MD, an emergency physician who has been speaking against corporate influence in medicine from its earliest roots, explained the problem with private equity in healthcare in a *Patients at Risk* podcast episode. "You have a group of managers that look for opportunities where, in a five-to-seven-year period, the investors can get back 15 to 20% return on investment." At the same time, those running the private equity firms are making money for themselves earning healthy salaries. "The trouble is that when they come into an industry, they create practices to make money that can have negative effects, they can shut down hospitals. Their goal is to profit when the goal for healthcare is to take care of the patient."[146]

Mitch Li, MD, the founder of *Take Medicine Back*, an advocacy group that is fighting corporate ownership of medical services, joined McNamara on the podcast. He said that to understand the problems with private equity, one must understand the definitions of profit and profiteering. "Many doctors have private practices. Technically, for us to have a salary or to pay ourselves something, we have to have a profit. So, there's a reasonable amount, even if you're an employee of a government-owned system, that doctors need to make to live." Li contrasted reasonable profit with profiteering. "The corporate model is one in which somebody is disproportionately profiting off the top. That could be an individual physician that owns the group, it could be the public market, or in the extreme, it could be private equity ownership."[146]

CONTRACT MANAGEMENT GROUPS

Robert McNamara, who has been called 'an encyclopedia of corporate medicine' by his peers, traces the rise of corporate medicine and private equity in hospitals to contract management groups. "If you look at the arc of Emergency Medicine, it started with great intentions: a moral imperative to deliver care to the poor, the uninsured, anyone arriving in emergency departments, but there were two pathways," said McNamara, who began his emergency medicine residency in 1982. He explained that one pathway began with doctors at big hospitals, academicians who were focused on creating the specialty of emergency medicine to serve the needs of the patients. The other were the entrepreneurs who were realizing that they could make a lot of money from emergency medicine, in part by replacing physicians with non-physician practitioners. "The problem was started by physicians that saw the profit motive and the chance to take advantage," he said.[146]

These physician entrepreneurs compiled a network of physician colleagues for hire, creating staffing agencies now known as contract management groups (CMGs). Acting as intermediaries to sell physician services to hospitals for a percent of the share, CMGs became highly profitable. As they gained market share, many merged or were acquired by private equity corporations. The result is that today, 50% of all emergency physicians are employed by a contract management group, giving these companies control over emergency departments across the country.[147]

McNamara has been warning about the dangers of corporate influence in medicine for decades. In a 1994 letter to the Annals of Emergency Medicine, he wrote: "The specialty must take a firm stand in opposition to the principles that allow these groups to function and flourish," noting that patients were being overcharged and deceived.[148] In his article, McNamara accused emergency medicine leaders of failing to act to protect patients, pointing to a conflict of interest regarding personal ties to contract management groups. Just two years later, former American College of Emergency Physicians president Leonard Riggs would go on to earn $38 million when he sold his staffing firm EnVision, formerly EmCare.[149]

However, emergency medicine leaders mocked McNamara's concern. In fact, in a rebuttal written immediately after McNamara's letter was published, Ronald A. Hellstern, MD the founder of an emergency medicine contract management group accused McNamara of "innuendo and exaggeration as if it were scientific fact." Hellstern, an entrepreneur who also started an air ambulance service, an urgent care chain, billing and transcription companies, and a large multi-specialty group practice management firm,[150] wrote, "Although well-intentioned, [McNamara] attempts to paint a picture of group influence and greed that simply does not exist." Hellstern says that McNamara is wrong and that he "errs terribly in attempting to rewrite our history by asserting that contract management groups threaten the specialty status of emergency medicine." He added, "The exact opposite is true—were it not for contract management groups, the specialty of emergency medicine … would not exist." Hellstern mocked, "I love a good argument, but please spare us the propaganda."

McNamara notes that academic physicians and medical journals did little to oppose the profession's move towards corporate medicine. "The moral force of academics was not brought to bear on emergency medicine leaders," he said. "The academicians that should have watched the shop were too busy trying to create journals and research and censoring each other for taking pens from pharmaceutical companies. Meanwhile, there was the creation of an industry to exploit your colleagues to make money off of them." Not only did the specialty fail to stop these schemes, but McNamara says they shut off discussion on the topic. "I can show you a letter to the editor where they said, 'We are not going to discuss this stuff in the journals,' and they shut off the press to suppress debate."[146]

Nearly thirty years later, history has proved McNamara right. Although some attempted to paint McNamara as a conspiracy theorist, he correctly predicted the astronomical growth of corporate influence in medicine, which he says has led to the replacement of physicians by non-physician practitioners. McNamara points to a 2021 PowerPoint presentation by a large corporate medical group, titled 'Staffing Your Emergency Department Efficiently, and Safely: Core Concepts.' Key points from the presentation read:

> Leveraging Your Available Talent Pool:
> - Employ the least expensive resource to accomplish the mission.
> - APPs (advanced practice providers—nurse practitioners and physician assistants): In many EDs, up to 25–35% of the cases can often be effectively and successfully seen independently by APPs.[151]

Ultimately, McNamara says that the bottom line for corporations is the need to appease investors. "The most expensive piece of the equation is what they pay the doc. So, the more you can replace an expensive doctor with a cheaper provider, the better it is [for profits]. But a 'simple' sore throat could be epiglottitis [a life-threatening infection]; the kid with 'the flu' could have sepsis [an overwhelming blood infection]." McNamara says that patients are at risk when a trained emergency physician is not available during a truly life-threatening situation. "We have our fire departments standing ready to take care of fire. Fire doesn't happen every day, but when it does, you want professional firefighters to respond." In the same way, substituting board-certified emergency physicians with non-physician practitioners without proper emergency training creates a danger to patients. "Yet it's right there in the cold corporate slideshow that they want to use the cheapest provider available to get the mission done." Of greater concern to McNamara is that patients may not know that they are not seeing a physician. "A lot of times they are deceived," he said. "They think they are seeing a doctor, or that there's a doctor in charge, [but] that's not always the case."[146]

THE CORPORATE PRACTICE OF MEDICINE

In many states, laws prohibit corporations from employing physicians. "The same thing exists for lawyers; you don't want the business interest getting between the patient and the doctor or between the lawyer and the client," said Mitch Li. "The problem is that in medicine, these laws have not been enforced."[146]

Indeed, evidence shows that when corporations put profits first, physicians and patients suffer, such as when Los Angeles-based private equity firm Leonard Green & Partners bought control of hospital management company Prospect Medical Holdings for $205 million. Prospect manages many safety-net hospitals that serve mainly low-income patients, with the company estimating that most of its revenue comes from public funding through Medicare and Medicaid. According to a ProPublica investigation, since its acquisition by private equity, Prospect hospitals have struggled with staffing shortages, facility problems including broken elevators, water leaks, and damaged surgical instruments, and a lack of funding for gas for their ambulances and basic medical supplies.[152]

During the early days of the COVID-19 pandemic, one of Prospect's hospitals in New Jersey became infamous for the death of an emergency room physician after he complained of being unable to obtain adequate personal protective equipment (PPE). At another Prospect-owned hospital in Rhode Island, multiple housekeeping staff members contracted COVID-19, and the department head died after receiving limited PPE.

According to reports, Prospect's hospitals rank in the bottom 17% of U.S hospitals, and government inspectors have cited the company 14 times for serious violations to patient safety. The company closed down one hospital that it had promised to keep open and required a $15 million emergency grant from New Jersey legislators to keep a second hospital open. Unfortunately, while hospital staff and patients suffered and Prospect shuttered hospitals, private equity company Leonard Green cashed in $400 million in dividends. Prospect CEO Sam Lee took home $128 million and a second executive $94 million.[152]

WHY DON'T PHYSICIANS WALK AWAY?

If physicians face difficulties with private equity companies, why are they choosing employment? Mitch Li believes that one of the reasons that doctors initially allied with private equity is to counter increasing control of healthcare by insurance companies, but as companies have merged and gained market share, it is now hard for hospital-based physicians to find jobs that aren't under corporate control. Further, doctors who speak out for patient safety may soon find themselves unemployable.

For example, Roy Brovont was hired by physician staffing company EmCare as the emergency department medical director at Overland Park Regional Medical Center, a for-profit hospital near Kansas City, Missouri in 2012. Shortly upon his arrival, Brovont identified a potentially dangerous situation: Emergency physicians were expected to respond to "Code Blues" across the entire hospital. A code blue indicates that a patient is facing an imminent life-or-death situation and requires an immediate emergency response. Due to limited staffing, leaving the emergency room to attend to these critical patients elsewhere in the hospital would leave the emergency department without a physician for an undetermined amount of time.

Having served in the U.S. military in combat zones in Iraq, Brovont understood quick action and chain of command in solving problems. He reported his concerns to his medical director at EmCare and asked the company to hire another emergency physician to ensure patient safety. The response was 'no.' According to court documents, EmCare declined to provide additional staffing, responding in an email, "Profits are in everyone's best interest."[153]

Unsatisfied, Brovont continued to press the issue, sending a detailed memo documenting his concerns. Six weeks later, he was fired from his position. Further, he was blackballed from working at any hospital staffed by EmCare. Since EmCare contracts with an extensive network of hospitals across the area, Brovont was left virtually unemployable. The emergency physician sued EmCare, arguing that he was fired for speaking out about patient safety. A jury agreed, awarding him $29 million, including $20 million in punitive damages.[153]

Robert McNamara has heard similar stories from physicians across the country who are being threatened into practicing medicine unethically. Doctors are being forced to admit a quota, or be fired. If they complain about staffing issues, such as having too many non-physicians to safely supervise, they are told to refer to their employment contract, and advised that they can easily be replaced. "The stories that we hear are just unbelievable and would shock the public." Physicians are often required to supervise nurse practitioners and physician assistants as a term of employment, even if they have concerns over the clinicians' skill levels or billing practices. "They are being told 'you've got to supervise them, but don't interfere; let them operate independently,'" McNamara said.[146]

Some of these companies may also be holding back physician pay for the work of supervision. In March 2022, TeamHealth settled a $15 million class action lawsuit by emergency physicians who claimed that they were cheated out of pay for supervision. The suit alleged that TeamHealth manipulated data when calculating physician pay, removing credit that they should have earned for supervision.[154]

While some doctors like Ray Brovont have fought back, many physicians are too afraid to act. Mitch Li says that by participating in corporate healthcare, physicians have indirectly contributed to patient suffering. "We've lost the trust of patients for good reason because we've sold out to business interests everywhere. And so, the individual altruism of a physician is lost upon the public," he stated. Li believes that physicians must unite against private equity, which he says is exploitative to both patients and physicians, "Only then can we take on profiteering insurance companies."[146]

Physicians have had difficulty unifying, says Robert McNamara, in part because of messaging that doctors should be doctors and leave business decisions to others. "There are pretty clear reasons why we wound up as we did," he said. "The people that choose emergency medicine are doing it with a strong sense of social justice—we take care of the homeless, we take care of the uninsured. We can be taken advantage of—that's the nature of the emergency physician." McNamara says that physician leaders and administrators created a web of mystery around the business of medicine, telling doctors that the system was too complex for them to manage. "We were the perfect foils," said McNamara, "There was a lot of profit to be made, and it was easy to victimize emergency physicians."[146]

McNamara said that rather than being too complicated for doctors to manage, emergency medicine follows a relatively simple business model, which is what made it initially attractive to corporations. McNamara blames emergency physicians and their leadership for allowing themselves to be used for corporate profit. "A whole generation, we were sheep, and we had sheep herders telling us, 'We're taking care of you. This is beyond you.' A lot of docs do realize now that they had the wool pulled over their eyes."

Further, McNamara believes that allowing corporate medicine into the emergency room opened the door to the practice in other fields. "The specialty of emergency medicine needs to apologize to the rest of medicine," he said. "We led the way to corporate takeover, and then it morphed into radiology, anesthesia, dermatology, urology, and GI." McNamara says that private equity is becoming rampant in medicine because investors see an opportunity for profit.[146] Indeed, over half of all physicians are now owned by corporations, and there has been an 86% growth in corporate practice acquisitions in the last few years. Private equity now owns a sizeable chunk of practices in the field of dermatology (7.5%), gastroenterology (7.4%), urology (6.5%), and ophthalmology (5.1%).[155]

As companies invest in the medical field, they may emphasize profit over patient safety. For example, in 2021, private equity-backed company U.S. Dermatology Partners was accused of replacing physicians with non-physician practitioners with little or no formal training in dermatology.[156] At the largest private equity dermatology chain, Advanced Dermatology, doctors were reportedly asked to allow physician assistants to bill at a higher level as if the physician was directly supervising them, even though the dermatologists were not on-site. Doctors also alleged that when they complained that physician assistants were providing inappropriate care by missing skin cancers or performing unnecessary procedures, the physician assistants were simply relocated to another clinic rather than being fired or placed under stricter supervision. In response, the company's attorney noted that, "all PAs get six months of training and are supervised by experienced doctors."[157] For contrast, dermatologists complete a 3-year residency (after medical school and an intern year), which includes at least 12,000 hours of training specific to the field.

Private equity is also working to squeeze profits out of the lowest paid field of medicine, primary care.[158] In the last few years, retail giant Walmart began opening primary care clinics staffed by nurse practitioners[159] and in 2021, the creators of MinuteClinic teamed up to open a brand-new primary care chain run completely by nurse practitioners.[160] Focusing initially on states with independent nurse practice, 'The Good Clinic' is owned by Mitesco, Inc, a "growth-oriented holding company."[161]

In 2022, Operose Health, the largest owner of primary care clinics in the U.K. was accused of replacing physicians with lesser-trained physician assistants. An investigative report found that the U.S. company, owned by Centene Corporation, was potentially compromising patient care by staffing half as many full-time physicians and 6 times as many physician assistants compared to other U.K. clinics. Critics accused the company of "putting profits and money ahead of quality care."[162]

Corporations are also taking over nursing homes and hospices, cutting staff, and replacing physicians. Reports of increased death rates of up to 10% at private equity-owned nursing homes have caused enough concern that in 2022, the Government Accountability Office launched an investigation into the practice.[163] Private equity companies are buying up community hospices, consolidating them into a chain, and then selling them to a larger company, with a goal of flipping their purchases in 3–7 years for big bucks.[164] With a model focused on profit, studies show that private equity hospices employ fewer clinical staff and offer less care than their nonprofit counterparts, replacing registered nurses with licensed practical nurses, and providing hospice patients with fewer physician visits.[164]

Mitch Li says that the focus on short-term profit is the foundational problem with private equity ownership of healthcare. "You can argue that a publicly traded market is somewhat aligned with creating long-term value .... If they do a good job, then the shares will go up, and people make money and everything's good, although not even that's perfect." This is not the case with private equity in healthcare, he said. "The entire rubric of operations is to cut expenses and increase revenue. You can do that quickly, and then sell to another buyer, which could be a health insurance company. It could be the public market. They can sell it off in pieces, but as something more profitable." Li argues that when this model is applied to staffing companies, the only way that the company can increase profits is to decrease staffing costs. "You decrease how much you're paying physicians, or you change it to a lower training model of hiring non-physicians, whatever the market will tolerate, to get the lowest cost."[146]

Robert McNamara points to this pattern in emergency departments. "In many emergency departments you walk into, private equity owns it," said McNamara, "and the danger to the patient is that the corporation determines who sees them. Private equity says, 'What's the business decision here? Are we going to hire a board-certified doctor, or is it going to be a non-physician practitioner? How can I get away with the cheapest model?' Because the number one cost to delivering that kind of care is the cost of the clinician."

As private equity has become more aggressive, McNamara believes that the public is beginning to take note. "Patients are starting to ask, 'Why is that Wall Street company determining staffing levels?' It's an opportunity for the public and doctors to step back and ask why we are allowing private equity in medicine."[146]

CHAPTER 6

IS THERE A DOCTOR IN THE HOUSE?

Richard Curbelo was a 51-year-old Detroit sports reporter who cared for an elderly mother with Alzheimer's disease. He had recently become engaged to be married for the first time when he checked into Beaumont Health, one of Michigan's largest healthcare systems, for a routine colonoscopy on January 21, 2021.[165] Less than a year before, Beaumont had elected to terminate its long-time anesthesia company and replace it with NorthStar Anesthesia, a private equity company that promised lower staffing costs by using mostly nurse anesthetists (CRNA) rather than anesthesiologists. Richard Curbelo's colonoscopy was scheduled just three weeks after NorthStar's contract began, and his anesthesia was provided by a CRNA, without a supervising anesthesiologist standing by. At the end of the procedure, Curbelo stopped breathing, and the CRNA was unable to resuscitate him. By the time the anesthesiologist and an emergency response team arrived, Richard Curbelo was dead from an anesthesia-related complication during one of the most routine medical procedures: a colonoscopy.[166]

PHYSICIANS REPLACED

In 1994, when Robert McNamara tried to warn emergency medicine physicians of the dangers of corporate intrusion on patient care, he was accused of exaggeration and innuendo. Fast-forward to today, and the replacement of physicians with lesser-trained practitioners has become commonplace.

For example, Clear Lake Regional Medical Center, located outside Houston, opened as a community hospital in 1972. The hospital merged with Mainland Medical Center, and announced a corporate rebranding in 2019 to include the name of for-profit company HCA Healthcare. CEO Todd Caliva told journalists that, "Taking the HCA name signals our commitment to be held to the highest standards in the industry," and announced several planned improvements, including upgraded obstetrical services, adding operating rooms, and expanded cardiology services.[167]

Unfortunately, retaining physician staffing did not seem to be part of the HCA upgrade plan. Within two years, the hospital announced that it would be replacing emergency physicians with non-physician practitioners. A memo from Caliva read, "Consistent with most emergency departments, HCA Houston Clear Lake will have mid-level providers, nurse practitioners and physician assistants, providing care with an emergency medicine physician in the Emergency Department."[168] With decreased emergency physician staffing at HCA Clear Lake, patients presenting for emergent care may be more likely to be treated by a non-physician practitioner. Additionally, HCA's patient consent form seems to try to minimize the company's liability, requiring patients to sign the following disclaimer:

> **Legal Relationship between Hospital and Physicians and Advanced Practice Professionals.**
>
> I understand and acknowledge that the physicians and advanced practice professionals [nurse practitioners and physician assistants] providing services to me in the hospital are independent contractors and not agents or employees of the hospital ... Advanced Practice Professionals are responsible for their own actions and the hospital shall not be liable for the acts or omissions of any such independent physicians and/or Advanced Practice Professionals.[169]

A similar situation occurred in 2015 when Watertown Regional Medical Center (WRMC), a community hospital in Wisconsin, entered into a joint venture with Life Point Health, granting the private equity company 80% ownership of the hospital.[170] The hospital contracted with staffing group Envision to provide physician services, and in April 2021, announced the replacement of all its anesthesiologists with certified registered nurse anesthetists (CRNAs).[171] CRNAs are nurses that attend a two-year nurse anesthesia program, while anesthesiologists are physicians—either an MD or a DO, who have completed medical school and then gone on to undertake four years of residency training in anesthesiology (Figure 4).

In a letter to key staff members, CEO Richard Keddington wrote,

> Please be aware that WRMC is moving to a 100% CRNA model in our anesthesia department. This is a very common model in hospitals our size ... and the literature is clear that care quality and outcomes are just as good with CRNAs. This will not impact the availability of anesthesia or the support the anesthesia department provides ... You shouldn't see much of a change.[173]

While Keddington is nonchalant in his claim that CRNA care is just as good as care by an anesthesiologist, the American Society of

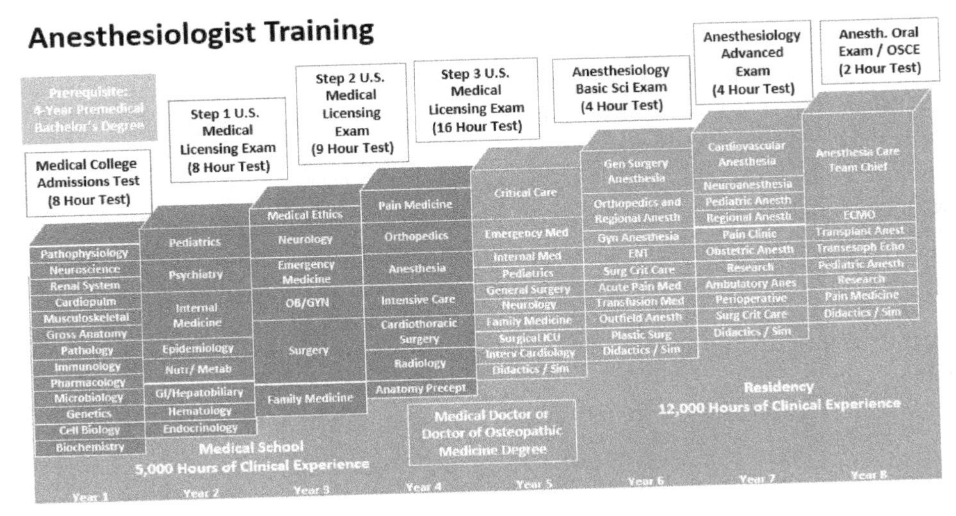

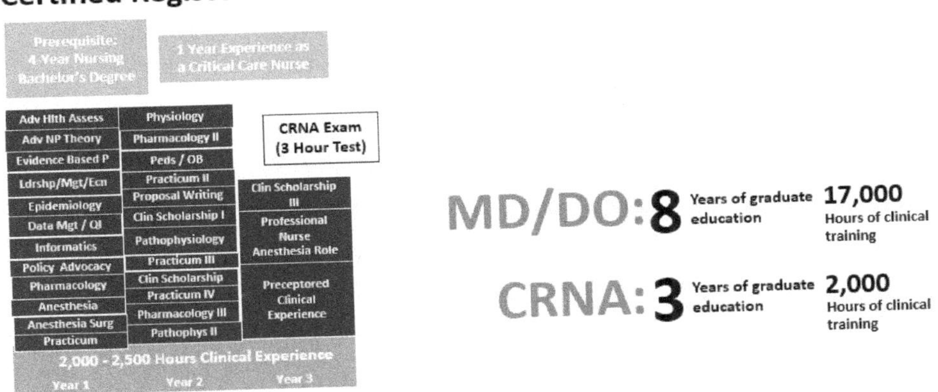

Figure 4. Anesthesiology Training—Physicians vs CRNAs[172]

Anesthesiologists disagrees, pointing out that studies of independent CRNAs have always included low-risk patients during low-risk procedures, and that it is impossible to draw conclusions about the care of higher-risk patients and surgeries.[174] In fact, in cases in which anesthesia or surgical complication occurred, as in the case of Richard Curbelo, physician-directed anesthesia was associated with lower rates of morbidity, preventing 6.9 excess deaths per 1000 cases.[175]

Keddington's memo continues:

> Kristen Burg will be the Lead CRNA. I have 100% confidence in her ability to manager [sic] anesthesia services at WRMC. Kristen will be supported by Dr. Odell the regional director of anesthesia services for Envision.

> He will be credentialed as a member of the medical staff and will also be available as needed.[173]

Physicians were outraged by the policy, which they argued represented the illegal corporate practice of medicine and fee-splitting[176] and the memo was shared extensively on social media. In response to the physician outcry, Envision released a document called, *The Facts about CRNA Care Models*. The letter, signed by Envision Physician Services President Doug Smith, MD, and Anesthesiology Chief Clinical Officer James E. Johnson, Jr, MD, claimed to clarify what they call "a lot of misinformation spreading about Watertown Regional Medical Center and Envision's approach to care."

In contrast to Keddington's memo, Envision insisted,

> **CRNAs are not 'replacing' physicians in Watertown**—Unlike what is being reported, physicians were **not** 'replaced' by CRNAs [emphasis in original]. In fact, CRNAs have been the primary providers at WRMC for years and have done an outstanding job supporting the community. An Envision anesthesiologist will still be on staff at this hospital and work closely with the CRNAs.[177]

The company further denied that the decision had anything to do with corporate profits, stating,

> After careful evaluation, the hospital—armed with an in-depth understanding of its community and following consultation with Envision—decided the CRNA model is appropriate for its patients. The fact that people who were not a part of the decision-making process are insinuating this approach is somehow driven by private equity or as a means to cut costs is simply inaccurate.

While the hospital insisted that these decisions were not influenced by private equity, just months after this staffing change, Watertown Regional announced that it had been selected by LifePoint Health to become part of a new, larger health system called ScionHealth. The merger came after LifePoint bought Kindred Healthcare, a company specializing in rehabilitative care for patients after acute illness or surgery. CEO Richard Keddington told reporters,

> The opportunity to join ScionHealth is exciting .... Very little change to day-to-day operations is anticipated ... patients will continue to receive the great care they've come to expect over the last 115 years from the providers they know and trust, and there will be no changes in any services—or in how patients or providers access care.[178]

PHYSICIANS FIRED FOR SPEAKING OUT

Administrator assurances that care will remain unchanged despite staffing changes are common, and physicians who complain are silenced or fired. For example, when Beaumont elected to replace anesthesiologists with CRNAs, senior hospital physicians wrote to the board chairman warning that the change in staffing would be dangerous to patients. Several physicians, including the head of pediatrics, were fired for complaining that cutbacks would lead to patient harm. About half of the anesthesiologists, as well as multiple surgeons and specialists resigned over the transition plan, citing deep concerns about the skill levels of staff hired by the outsourcing firm.[166]

Indeed, the CRNA in charge of colonoscopy anesthesia at the time of Richard Curbelo's death had less than five years of experience. Reports stated that rather than perform routine sedation for the procedure, the CRNA decided to intubate him. In a *Patients at Risk* podcast, Karen Sibert, MD, a clinical professor in the Department of Anesthesiology and Perioperative Medicine at UCLA and past president of the California Society of Anesthesiologists, who was not involved in the case, said that intubation during a routine colonoscopy is rarely required, and that the decision may have been made to intubate because of the patient's weight. "We are told that he was six foot one and 300 pounds. Now that's not morbidly obese, that's only a body mass index [BMI] of 39, which is getting up there, but is really a blip these days." She noted that she provides anesthesia for patients with this BMI routinely and that intubation isn't generally indicated for this reason alone. "Typically, colonoscopies are just done under sedation. I don't understand why the decision would have been made to intubate."[179]

Regardless, the CNRA chose to intubate Curbelo. At the end of the procedure when the tube was removed, Curbelo stopped breathing. According to Sibert, the patient may not have been ready to be extubated. "My whole job as an anesthesiologist is to try to make sure that people are ready when they have the breathing tube taken out. In fact, I would say that obese patients, and certainly morbidly obese patients, can be tricky to intubate. I worry far more about extubating them than I do about intubating them because that is the point where they're probably at the highest risk of getting into problematic airway obstruction. If they do encounter airway obstruction, the level of oxygen in their bloodstream will plummet far more quickly than a thin person, as well. So, it's just a riskier business all the way around, and that's one of the reasons why well-managed, relatively light sedation can be a much better choice for colonoscopy in the obese population."

Removing a breathing tube before a patient is ready can be catastrophic, said Sibert. "If a patient is given a muscle relaxer for intubation, then you have to make sure that it's worn off completely or that you've used a reversal agent to get completely rid of it, because if the patient has any residual muscle weakness, that can impair their ability to breathe on their own." An anesthesiologist would normally measure tidal volume and respiratory rate, as well as consider several other variables to assess readiness for extubation. "Whole chapters and articles have been written on extubation criteria and complications after extubation," she said.

Sibert notes that when supervising CRNAs or anesthesia residents, an anesthesiologist needs to be present during the two most dangerous aspects of anesthesia—induction, or the initiation of anesthesia, and emergence, coming out of anesthesia. "A lot of people make the analogy to airline pilots; that takeoff and landing are the riskiest parts of the procedure. Most operations, particularly long ones, will have a long, steady sort of cruising altitude when it's very unlikely that anything is going to change acutely unless something happens during the course of the surgery." Oftentimes, Sibert is required to supervise the anesthesia of multiple surgeries at once. While she may not be present throughout an entire individual surgery, she is constantly monitoring the situation, and she is always present at induction and emergence. "I follow the case; I know when to be there. Obviously, I'm there at the start, I'm there at the finish, and I'm there any time in between that's necessary," she said.

When CRNA supervision is performed this way by an anesthesiologist, Sibert says that it is a very safe model. "The difference in training [between an anesthesiologist and a CRNA] is quite considerable. Nurse anesthetists can be superb, but the issue is what kind of collaborative or supervisory model you're working under. When that model is working happily for everybody, the anesthesia care team is incredibly safe, but when nurse anesthetists are asked to substitute for anesthesiologists, or even worse, when in an effort to cut costs, anesthesiologists are asked to supervise more nurse anesthetists than is really feasible or safe, that's when problems can occur."[179]

A 2022 study of nearly 600,000 patients receiving anesthesia confirms Sibert's opinion. Anesthesia care teams involving an anesthesiologist supervising 3 to 4 CRNAs had a 14% increased risk of patient death or injury compared to teams in which an anesthesiologist supervised just 1 or 2 CRNAs.[180] Reports indicated that under Beaumont's new staffing model, anesthesiologists were not directly supervising the emergence of anesthesia. The anesthesiologist supervising the CRNA handling Curbelo's anesthesia was not present during the removal of his breathing tube and was only called in to help when the patient showed signs of distress. Unfortunately, the supervising anesthesiologist was unable to successfully reintubate the patient and an emergency team was called to assist.

Here, again, staffing company changes affected the team's ability to respond. Before NorthStar's takeover, procedures requiring intubation were performed in surgical areas where emergency teams were on-site. A change in this protocol caused a delay in receiving emergency assistance. By the time the emergency team arrived to help, the patient had been without a pulse for 30 minutes and was unable to be resuscitated.[166]

Karen Sibert argues that anesthesia has become a victim of its own success—because it has become so safe, there is now a misconception that anyone can do it. "Monitoring has improved the safety of anesthesia tremendously, with mortality decreasing from 1:1000 to one or two in hundreds of thousands." This success is a direct result of efforts by anesthesiologists, she said. "Anesthesiologists take a great deal of pride and credit because inventions like pulse oximetry and end-tidal CO2 monitoring have increased safety." She also points out that anesthesiologists have had to fight those who wanted to cut costs to get these safety measures universally implemented. Moreover, even though anesthesia has become much safer, it is not without risks. "The fact is that in anesthesia, there are minor procedures, but there are no minor anesthetics," said Sibert. "There's an element of art and judgment and experience that goes into it, and if that's not there, you can get into trouble no matter how good your monitoring equipment is." Indeed, studies show that having anesthesia directed by an anesthesiologist saves lives, especially in the event of an anesthetic or surgical complication.[175]

Sibert also notes that when procedures occur in places other than operating rooms, additional safety measures may not be available. "For example, your institution might not have end-tidal CO2 monitoring in an endoscopy suite, or they might not have every resuscitation drug you might want. Sometimes the equipment in endoscopy suites is woefully less than what you would find in an operating room, even though you may be doing the same type of anesthesia."

Although the news media reported on the death of Richard Curbelo, observers noted that staff members were under pressure from NorthStar not to speak publicly about the case and were even threatened with the loss of their jobs.[166] "All I can tell you is that patients should never die during a routine colonoscopy," said Sibert. Unfortunately, this needlessly tragic outcome is likely to happen again as companies across the U.S. increase involvement in healthcare. "I find it alarming and distressing that this is happening over and over again, that it's happened in my state, California," she said. She notes that the temptation of promised cost-savings from private equity groups may prove irresistible to hospital administrators.

Sibert says that during staffing company changes, hospitals will generally offer employed nurse anesthetists the opportunity to join the new entity. "If they don't want to join, they lose their positions." However, these corporate interests may or may not offer positions to the current anesthesiologists. "Very typically, the model is that they will want far fewer anesthesiologists than they had before and higher ratios of supervision." While Medicare payment rules require that anesthesiologists only supervise up to four cases at a time, states are allowed to opt-out of these requirements, allowing facilities to use their own discretion about supervising ratios. "They'll often have one anesthesiologist try to supervise six, eight, or even twelve—who knows how many anesthetizing locations. I'm sorry, you just cannot provide immediate backup or, frankly, any kind of reasonable oversight of that many cases at a time."[179]

DECREASED PHYSICIAN ACCESS

While hospitals promise little change to patient care after corporate takeovers, the evidence shows otherwise. In 2019, nonprofit healthcare company Mission Health, based in Asheville, NC, was purchased by for-profit HCA Healthcare, the largest hospital corporation in the U.S. Shortly before the sale of the hospital, president and CEO Ronald A. Paulus promised that the hospital would continue to have "the exact same people and exact same doctors and exact same nurses." Within three years, over 200 physicians had left the health system, including 33 family physicians, 25 surgeons, and 15 pediatricians. According to reports, physicians chose to leave Mission because of the change in leadership strategy, stating that rather than being led by clinical staff, the hospital is "being run by businessmen." Other physicians left because of a decline in staffing and quality patient care and increased focus on metrics and corporate benchmarks. HCA has declined to comment on the number of physicians currently on staff, other than to say that physician staffing is 'relatively the same.'[181]

North Carolina leaders, including State Senator Julie Mayfield, expressed strong concern for the loss of community physicians after HCA's takeover, saying that "it is truly unfortunate that HCA chose from the start to prioritize its profit over the people." Indeed, HCA has profited from the acquisition of Mission, increasing revenue by $548 million. While watchdogs note that some of these profits have come from cutting clinical staff, HCA also increased prices for patients by about 10%.[181]

An exodus of physicians also occurred at Lake Norman Medical Center in Charlotte, NC. The hospital was established in 1926 as a nonprofit and later acquired by for-profit company Health Management Associates (HMA). In 2018, HMA paid a $260 million settlement to the U.S. Department of Justice for False Claims Act allegations, some of which occurred at Lake Norman.[182] In 2019, Community Health Systems (CHS) acquired Lake

Norman Medical Center as part of its purchase of HMA for $7.6 billion. Just two years later, Lake Norman replaced the hospital's board-certified pediatricians and neonatologists with nurse practitioners.[183]

According to reports, administrators said that the hospital did not care for enough seriously ill newborns to justify keeping a neonatologist on staff, replacing the physician with a neonatal nurse practitioner at about half the salary. Two hundred local women doctors signed a letter protesting the move, calling the replacement of physicians dangerous and saying that the staffing change "purposefully jeopardizes the care and well-being of our most valuable asset—newborns."[183]

Nevertheless, a hospital staffer insisted to journalists that nurse practitioners are more than adequate, stating, "They're better than a doctor … They are more experienced than a pediatrician is with sick babies." While North Carolina requires physician supervision of nurse practitioners, this supervision does not have to be on-site. According to the hospital staffer, "if nurses have questions or concerns, they can call a neonatologist or ask one to come to the hospital." While hospital insiders said that pediatricians were no longer seeing babies by their own choice, stating, "they decided they don't want to come in on the weekends and in the middle of the night," an anonymous hospital physician told reporters that pediatricians were blocked from rounding because the hired nurse practitioners had an exclusive contract with the hospital.[183]

NON-PHYSICIAN 'HOSPITALISTS'

In addition to staffing emergency departments and anesthesia suites, hospitals are increasingly utilizing non-physician practitioners to work in the wards, with 83% of hospital groups employing nurse practitioners.[184] About 28% of all nurse practitioners work in hospital settings, with 12% working in critical care. Of physician assistants, 38.5% work in a hospital.[185] According to hospital nurse practitioner Tracy Cardin, "If you are going to have successful collaborations with nurse practitioners and physician assistants, you have to treat them like a doctor."[186] Despite these types of statements, there are few studies examining the safety and efficacy of non-physicians in hospital settings. A 2019 literature review found just 44 research studies over ten years examining care provided by non-physician practitioners in hospitals, including only two randomized, controlled trials, both of which examined follow-up care after cardiac surgery.[185]

Further, a 2020 report found just 10% of nurse practitioners working in hospitals are properly certified for the role. Instead, most hospital-based nurse practitioners are certified in primary care and receive 'on-the-job training' as their qualification. The study authors noted that "there is no current national certification that specifically confirms or validates preparation as an NP [nurse practitioner] hospitalist," and suggested that "the mismatch between the primary care educational preparation of an NP and the knowledge, skills, and competencies required for the NP hospitalist must be reconciled."[184]

Despite a lack of certification, patients are increasingly receiving care from non-physicians when hospitalized. John Chamberlain is a former hospital executive who is currently the board chairman of Citizen Health, a healthcare cooperative working to redesign healthcare. In a *Patients at Risk* podcast, he discussed his surprise to find that a nurse practitioner 'hospitalist' was in charge of his wife's hospital care when she was admitted for a hip fracture. "We were admitted through the ER, and I was surprised because two years prior, I went in for a hot gallbladder and I saw a physician hospitalist," said Chamberlain, "but this time, we only had a nurse practitioner."[187]

Although Chamberlain's wife had a straightforward hospital stay, he believes that replacing physicians with non-physician practitioners in hospitals is a dangerous step. "It's happening more and more in hospitals across the country. I think they're doing it primarily from a cost standpoint. Hospitals, both not-for-profit and for-profit have become more and more greedy. They have a lot of regulatory pressures, they're looking for ways to continue to put money to their bottom line, and that's why they're using lower cost practitioners."

In some cases, hospitals are staffing wards with nurse practitioners and skirting state laws for physician supervision requirements. Terence Alost, MD, an emergency physician in Louisiana said he was fired from his position when he refused to admit a patient to an unsupervised nurse practitioner. "Nurse practitioners require supervision in Louisiana, but the hospital had recently instituted a pilot nurse practitioner hospitalist program without a supervising physician," he said. When Alost wrote an order admitting the patient to the usual hospital physician, he was immediately confronted by a charge nurse, who insisted that he change the order to the nurse practitioner's name. Disturbed by the fact that he had been asked to commit an action that seemed not only dangerous, but fraudulent, Alost declined. "I refused because I believed that to be unsafe, foolish, and illegal."[188]

A hospital administrator contacted Alost, ordering him to change the name on the admission order. Instead, Alost called the hospital's CEO to report the situation. During that discussion, Alost said he was shocked to learn that the nurse practitioner-hospitalist program had been planned and approved by physicians at the facility, who he believes were forced to accept the change. The CEO told Alost to admit the patient to the nurse practitioner—or be fired.

Ultimately, Alost was terminated from his position. He filed a complaint with the Louisiana State Board of Medical Examiners, which acknowledged that unsupervised nurse practitioners were illegal in the state but failed to take any action. "My interpretation of their answer was that there was nothing they could do about it." Alost filed a qui tam lawsuit against the hospital but says the assistant Attorney General declined to take the case. A whistleblower suit he filed against the hospital and contract management group was dismissed by a U.S. District Court judge. Although Alost's struggle for accountability was unsuccessful in Louisiana, he is proud of the efforts that he made. "I'm glad that I tried because few doctors can. Most don't have the energy to fight or they correctly fear being blackballed for even fighting," said Alost. "I fear for the practice and the quality of medicine in this country."[188]

While hospitals profit from replacing physicians, patients may face harm. Robert Painter, a plaintiff's attorney in Texas, discussed cases he has seen involving this scenario in a *Patients at Risk* podcast. "Right now, we're looking into this situation of a nurse practitioner intensivist," said Painter, who finds the term inaccurate. "By definition, an intensivist is a critical care specialist, who has extensive training to treat the most acutely or chronically ill patients," he said. In the case he was reviewing, Painter said that the nurse practitioner providing intensive care lacked the qualifications to fill that role. "You start looking into the background of the training to ask what qualified this person to be an intensivist, the person who is seeing a really ill person. You start digging into it and [find] ... this nurse practitioner in particular had an online degree from a for-profit nursing school, and it's unclear that there was much clinical emphasis at all," said Painter. "You see that over and over."[189]

He described a similar case involving a physician assistant. "The physician assistant was tasked to see neurosurgery consults at a level one trauma center. So, you have a guy that hits a tree at 65 miles an hour. Head and spine surgery is consulted, and a PA shows up. I deposed the PA and her level of supervision by the spine surgery service was exclusively through text messaging," said Painter. "Imagine if it's you or your loved one in a hospital with a loss of sensation to the extremities that is slowly moving upward. They ask for a spine surgeon consult, and you have a PA show up texting the spine surgeon ... We see that over and over again." Painter, who worked as a hospital administrator before becoming an attorney, believes that this trend is the result of managers making healthcare decisions. "When you have administrators who aren't physicians making calls on the way medicine is practiced, there is a problem," he said.

If replacing physicians is dangerous, why do corporations continue to do it? According to Painter, it is a financially driven decision. "Rather than looking at physicians as having independent duties to the patient, they see them as a revenue center. If you aren't generating enough revenue, then that's a problem." Painter said that while non-physicians originally were meant to serve as a way to allow physicians to be able to see more patients, they are now substituting for physicians entirely. "What they're doing is really hard to rationalize," he said. "How does this make sense in terms of patient care? In my view, the solution is to put more qualified physicians on the medical staff, and then you can use mid-levels to assist under appropriate supervision. But they're looking at it as lower overhead, a lower expense to have a nurse practitioner or physician assistant. Then if they have independent practice authority, they can order all the diagnostic imaging, lab work, and other things that end up making the hospital a lot of money."[189]

As a former hospital executive, John Chamberlain agrees with this assessment. He notes that utilizing non-physicians does more than save money—it can increase revenues because these clinicians order more tests. "Obviously from a financial standpoint, if you're working for the hospital as a nurse practitioner or a PA, where are you going to refer those patients for imaging and diagnostic labs? Well, to the hospital, of course." While ordering more tests makes hospital stays more expensive for patients, it adds to the company's bottom line. "The hospital CEO thinks that it's great because it's revenue in the door. They're revenue driven, whether you're for profit, or as we're coming to find out, more and more not-for-profits are even worse. Not only do they have a tax advantage, but they can get away with these things because of [the excuse of] 'community benefit.'"[187]

SAFE MEDICAL STAFFING LEVELS

While safe nursing staffing is well-defined in the scientific literature,[190] little attention has been focused on safe medical staffing ratios, and there are few studies evaluating the number of physicians needed to optimize patient safety.[191] Although there are no standard safe medical staffing guidelines in the U.S., the Royal College of Physicians developed recommendations for U.K. hospitals in 2018, addressing the role of physicians, physicians-in-training, and non-physician practitioners.[192] The recommendations divide clinicians into three tiers:

> *Tier 1: Competent clinical decision makers—clinicians who are capable of making an initial assessment of a patient.* Tier 1 clinicians are first- or second-year resident physicians as well as nurse practitioners and physician assistants (called physician associates in the U.K.).
>
> *Tier 2: Senior clinical decision makers—clinicians who are capable of making a prompt clinical diagnosis and deciding the need for specific investigations and treatment.* These are senior residents near the end of training.

Tier 3: Expert clinical decision makers—clinicians who have overall responsibility for patient care. These are attending physicians or specialty physician consultants.

The staffing guidelines spell out how different tier doctors should be available throughout the day, at night, and on weekends or holidays, as well as the timeliness of patient evaluations. While Tier 1 clinicians may assess patients, they must report all findings to a higher-level clinician who is the clinical decision-maker, and unwell patients must be seen at least daily by a Tier 2 clinician or greater.

The guidelines are clear that medical evaluation by non-physician practitioners is considered on the same level as an intern, or first-year physician, and always requires further assessment by a senior doctor. Not so in the U.S., where there are no rules regarding safe staffing levels for physicians and non-physician practitioners. In many cases, hospitals often allow nurse practitioners to function completely independently of physician involvement, pointing to studies that purport to show that substituting nurse practitioners for physicians in hospitals improves patient care.

WHEN THE HEADLINES DON'T MATCH THE FINDINGS

In October 2021, the journal *Medical Care* published a study that claimed that having more nurse practitioners in hospitals improved patient outcomes. In the discussion section, lead author Linda H. Aiken, Ph.D., a longtime advocate for nurse practitioners and the author of *Charting Nursing's Future: Agenda for the 1990s* (1992), extrapolated the findings to argue in favor of expanding independent hospital practice for nurse practitioners. However, an analysis of the study methodology shows the article to be a prime example of propaganda rather than serious research. For example, the core data point, the number of nurse practitioners working in a given hospital, was gleaned not by any objective measure, but by simply asking staff registered nurses to *estimate* the number of nurse practitioners working at their facilities. Dylan Golomb, MD, who examined the study, believes that the use of this measuring tool invalidates the study. "I couldn't even begin to guess how many nurse practitioners work at my facility," he said in a podcast interview about the report.[193]

Despite this methodological flaw, the conclusions make logical sense, said Marsha Haley, MD, who also reviewed the article for the podcast. "Adding more nurse practitioners, more staff, to existing physician and RN professional care, improves outcomes. That I can believe," she said. "The part that I have an issue with is their discussion section, how they say that their findings are relevant to policy debates about NP scope of practice and unsupervised nurse practitioner practice."[193]

Dylan Golomb agrees, noting that the study did not address independent practice. Rather, the authors elected to examine data in four states requiring physician supervision for nurse practitioners. "They concluded that NPs have value in this role," he said. "But then the discussion was about autonomous practice and eliminating collaborative care with physicians. They could have easily sent this survey out to nurses in states with full practice autonomy, but they didn't."[193]

Headlines reporting this study were typical examples of sensational reporting without accurately reflecting demonstrated outcomes. Lauding, 'Increased number of inpatient NPs linked to improved patient outcomes,' news articles failed to note that nurse practitioners in the study were functioning in physician-led teams, and that the 'hospitals' were actually orthopedic surgery centers.[194]

Overstating or stretching the results of studies is a common technique used to justify non-physician practice. For example, in a discussion about urgent care practices, AANP past president Sophia Thomas said that owning and operating a freestanding urgent care without physician supervision is well within the scope of a nurse practitioner, saying, "The question of quality and safety around NP care has been asked and answered by more than 50 years of rigorous evaluation."[195] But where exactly is this data? In a 2013 review article on the role of nurse practitioners in an urgent care setting, just two studies are cited.[196] A 2003 British study of nurses in a minor injury unit, treating cuts, scrapes, sprains, and strains, found that nurses provided safe care in these low-risk situations. However, the nurses cost more money and had significantly greater referral rates compared to physicians.[197] Further, a 2012 study on nurse practitioners in rural urgent care centers examined patient satisfaction, but not outcomes.[198]

URGENT CARE

Despite a lack of data, nurse practitioners and physician assistants provide much of the care at urgent care clinics, with just 20% of all urgent cares hiring physicians exclusively.[199] In some instances, non-physician practitioners run their own facilities. For example, Just 4 Kids Urgent Care, the facility where 7-year-old Betty Wattenbarger was treated before her death from influenza and streptococcal pneumonia, was owned by three partners: medical director and pediatrician Michael Cowan, pediatric nurse practitioner Madeline Broemson, and the nurse practitioner's father, Frank R. Scheer, acting as a silent investor. Nurse Broemson later became the majority owner of the practice, and geriatrician Dale Swanholm took over as her supervising physician—an unusual choice of specialty to supervise a nurse treating children.[199]

No supervising physician was apparently on-site when physician assistant Melanie Choos misdiagnosed 53-year-old Joseph Dudley with the flu. The Iowan man presented to the UnityPoint Health urgent care clinic with fever and mental status changes. According to reports, the patient was confused and resisted a flu swab, and the physician assistant questioned whether he was using illegal drugs. Although the flu test was negative, Choos diagnosed Dudley with influenza and sent him home. Because Dudley could not walk due to dizziness, he was escorted out of the clinic in a wheelchair. Unfortunately, Dudley's erratic behavior wasn't caused by drugs or the flu. He had meningitis, an infection of the brain and spinal cord. By the time he was taken to an emergency department days later, he had developed multiple strokes, leading to permanent disabilities. A jury awarded the Dudley family $27 million. Nick Rowley, the family's attorney, said that "physician assistants shouldn't be running clinics on their own without any supervising physician."[200]

The state of North Dakota disagrees. They have determined that physician assistants can indeed work without physician supervision, becoming the first state to allow the practice in 2019. South Dakota may be following suit, with the introduction of a similar bill in 2022. The American Association of PAs supports such legislation, which leaders say will "eliminate outdated administrative burdens and allow PAs to practice to the full extent of their education, training, and experience."[201]

Based on his experience as a malpractice attorney, Travis Dunn says that non-physician leadership is putting patients at risk by urging their members to work up to the very limits of their training—and beyond. "All you have to do is compare the education and training that goes into becoming a physician to the education and training that goes into becoming a nurse practitioner [or physician assistant], and there's a big difference," he said. Dunn believes that NP and PA organizations are doing a disservice to members by comparing them to physicians. "If they want to truly do what's best, they should focus on scope of practice, and encouraging them to stay within their scope, not putting their members in a position to fail."[143]

Emergency physician Andrew Wilson, MD agrees, noting a recent conversation with a nurse practitioner employed at an urgent care. Wilson called the nurse practitioner to discuss a patient she referred to the emergency room for an abnormal EKG obtained during a routine work physical. "The computer readout said, 'sinus arrhythmia,' which is an innocent finding, but it sounds scary to a non-trained person," said Wilson. The patient reported no symptoms and had a normal examination, leading Wilson to worry that he was missing something. "After a fairly long hold, I was finally able to get on the phone with the nurse practitioner," he said, noting that his frustration at the situation immediately turned to empathy when the nurse practitioner explained herself. "She disarmed me instantly, because she was so much more frustrated with her own job," said Wilson. "She said she was expected to see up to 50–60 patients a day, and that she had already put in her notice." With her supervising physician out of town, the nurse practitioner decided to send the patient to the emergency department because she wasn't sure what to do with the abnormal result and was afraid that not acting could cause the patient harm. "I felt badly for her because she found herself in a situation without the skill set," said Wilson.[464]

CHAPTER 7

THE FALL OF THE IVORY TOWER

The fact that healthcare organizations have turned to non-physician replacements is rooted in money and politics, said Laura Kendall, MD in a 2020 article in the *American Journal of Medicine*. "National organizations that govern [non-physician practitioners] are on a mission to obtain unsupervised practice," she wrote. "This is advantageous for healthcare corporations who have already started cutting costs by replacing physicians with midlevel practitioners."[14] Why has there not been more of an outcry from institutions that train physicians? Kendall believes that academic centers have simply pivoted away from medical education and towards training and hiring non-physician practitioners to act as physician replacements.

RESIDENCY WORK HOUR RESTRICTIONS: THE CASE OF LIBBY ZION

Teaching hospitals and academic centers have long relied on the labor of physicians in training to care for patients. In fact, the term *resident*, also called *house staff*, was used because these physicians either literally or virtually lived on-site at the facility during their years of training. Until about 2003, when residency work hour restrictions were put into place, resident physicians routinely spent 80–100 hours per week on duty at the hospital for anywhere from three to seven years after medical school. Physician residency training is designed under a careful supervision model. Interns, first-year physician trainees, are directly supervised by more senior and experienced residents. Fully trained physicians, called *attendings*, rotate through the hospital daily, seeing patients with residents and evaluating their diagnoses and treatment plans. Resident physicians remain on-site at the hospital throughout the night, on weekends, and on holidays.

"It was like trial by fire," pediatrician Niran Al-Agba said of her residency years in a podcast episode. "I remember covering seventy children at the hospital at night on call, and there were always codes and not enough [intensive care physicians] to go around." She also recalls having her mistakes corrected by her senior physicians before they harmed patients. "It's important to get slapped in the face over and over because that's what medicine is about—learning from your mistakes and being properly afraid of making a mistake." Al-Agba noted that without this intensive supervision, her mistakes would have gone uncorrected, and patients would have suffered. Worse yet, she would have unknowingly continued making the same mistakes in the future.[202]

In the 1980s and '90s, residency positions were cut in response to predicted physician surpluses, but hospital workloads remained unchanged, creating stress on systems that relied on resident physician labor. At the same time, the Accreditation Council for Graduate Medical Education (ACGME), the overseeing body for residency training programs, began to mandate reduced residency work hours, sparked by the death of a young woman named Libby Zion.

Roy Stoller, DO explained in a *Patients at Risk* podcast. "In 1984, a teenager named Libby Zion, unfortunately, dies in New York City from a medical intervention complication called serotonin syndrome." Libby's father, an influential attorney and former *New York Times* writer, blamed her death on overworked resident physicians. "Although serotonin syndrome was virtually unknown at the time, politically it was investigated and the powers that be came down on the medical education system and said that residents were spending too many hours in the hospital," said Stoller.[202]

At the time of Libby's death, resident physicians routinely worked more than 100 hours per week. In 1989, New York restricted the hours of residents to a maximum of 80 hours per week with no more than 24 consecutive hours of duty. Other states followed suit, and in July 2003, the ACGME mandated work hour restrictions for all residents across the U.S. "They cut resident hours by about 20%," said Stoller. "Now you have resident physicians who are the backbone of the hospital system working 20 hours a week less. When you multiply that by thousands of doctors, now we have a void." With cuts to both the total number of residents and resident work hours, hospitals needed help. Rather than hiring fully fledged physicians at regular wages to make up the hours previously worked by low-paid resident physicians, hospitals looked to allied health practitioners to fill the gap.

Physician assistant Elizabeth Ennis was one such clinician. After college, she attended a two-year physician assistant program at the University of Florida. Immediately after graduating, Ennis was hired by an acclaimed academic institution to work in Pulmonary and Critical Care, one of the most rigorous fields of medicine. She says she was told that she was expected to function at the level of a physician fellow. The term *fellow* in medicine refers to a physician in their final year or two (or more) of subspecialty training, after completing medical school and at least three years of residency. Fellowship programs for physicians are intensely competitive, and physicians who enter them are already experts in the foundations of medicine and are now honing highly specialized skills. Yet Ennis says that as a new graduate from a two-year training program, she was expected to function at this level. "It just wasn't a great environment," said Ennis. "One of the attending physicians told me, 'The only reason we hired a PA is because we're not allowed to hire physicians'—it was a financial decision." Ennis realized that her physician assistant education had not prepared her to provide this level of care. "I didn't think it was fair to patients and I didn't think it was fair to our team. I decided that it just wasn't something that I wanted to stay with."[203]

Not all clinicians have the same insight as Ennis, and many have flocked to work in academic settings. Most teaching hospitals today include a large team of non-physicians assisting in the care of patients, but less than 30% of these institutions track the outcomes associated with nurse practitioner or physician assistant care.[204]

Another factor that has increased the hiring of allied health professionals is the growing administrative burden in medicine over the last few decades. The HITECH Act of 2009, introduced by the Obama administration, required the implementation of electronic medical records.[205] Physicians are now required to act as data entry clerks, spending increasingly more time on documentation and tasks like manually entering orders into a computer, which was previously done verbally or by using a checklist in a much shorter amount of time.[206] Resident physicians have taken on much of the burden of these administrative responsibilities.

To understand the amount of work handled by medical residents, consider the case of the University of New Mexico School of Medicine. When the school lost its neurosurgery residency program accreditation in 2019, the hospital had to hire 23 nurse practitioners and physician assistants to handle the workload of the departing eight residents.[207] In an analysis of the staffing change, physician blogger Bryan Carmody noted the irony: "It required 3 paid professionals to replace the clinical work that was previously accomplished by each of the residents. Since the average neurosurgery nurse practitioner earns around $115,000 a year—nearly twice as much as a resident—the loss of accreditation cost the university five times as much as they would have paid if they had kept their residents."[208]

Residency funding

Most of the funding for physician residency training comes from Medicare, which pays an average of $171,000 per resident physician. Hospitals may also receive supplemental funding from sources like state Medicaid and the U.S. Veterans Administration. While Congress froze the total number of residents funded at established residencies in 1997, Medicare will fund new programs, capping the total number of residents at year five.[209]

This funding policy has restricted residency growth at established facilities, but has been a boon to for-profit companies like HCA, which jumped into the residency market in 2015. Within the five-year Medicare funding cap time limit, HCA had become the largest sponsor of residency programs in the U.S., training more than 5,000 physicians per year.[210] Since it costs an estimated $2–8 million to open a new residency program,[206] corporations with large operating budgets are uniquely positioned to enter the market, and in some cases, may benefit from political relationships. For example, in 2013, Florida Governor Rick Scott, formerly the chief executive of HCA, provided $80 million in Medicaid funding for new residency programs.[211] Companies that open residency programs anticipate a return on investment from future Medicare payments, affordable resident labor, and the expectation that many graduating residents will stay with their organization to work.

Evidence indicates that there is money to be made in resident education. When private equity-backed Hahnemann University Hospital in Philadelphia filed for bankruptcy, the owner agreed to sell its 550 residency positions to Tower Health for $7.5 million. However, during the company's bankruptcy auction, Tower was outbid by local health systems, which spent $55 million to obtain the slots. The Centers for Medicaid and Medicare Services filed court papers to oppose the sale, arguing that residency positions are non-transferrable, but a U.S. Bankruptcy Court ruled that they could be sold as assets without the government's permission.[212]

Despite criticisms that companies are flooding the market by producing too many emergency medicine residencies and concerns over corporate influence in medical education, others see alternates to academic residency centers as a positive. Ian M. Kahane, MD is a primary care physician who trained and teaches at an HCA Internal Medicine residency program. Noting that every HCA hospital is different, Kahane said that his program has worked hard to provide high-quality training, including prohibiting nurse practitioners and physician assistants from teaching residents. He also noted that, unlike many academic centers, his hospital has virtually eliminated non-physician practitioners in departments with an adequate number of residents, as they are no longer needed, therefore increasing patient access to physician care.[213]

Training non-physicians

With caps on established residency positions, many academic teaching hospitals are not only turning to non-physicians for labor, but creating programs to train them. Ivy League schools once renowned for creating top-tier physicians, are now promoting nurse practitioner and physician assistant programs, including an online PA program at Yale University.[214] These programs provide academic centers with added income from tuition fees.

For example, in 2022, the Michigan State University College of Osteopathic Medicine (MSUCOM) announced plans to train physician assistant students 'synergistically' with Doctor of Osteopathic Medicine (DO) students. A letter from Dean Andrea Amalfitano Ph.D. DO wrote that the new program would be among the first in the nation to have "PAs sitting side-by-side with DO medical students." Amalfitano used the physician shortage as the rationale for training more physician assistants, writing, "there's a shortage of doctors across the country, and PAs can help offset those difficulties."[215]

Leah C. Davis, DO, an alumnus of MSUCOM, was concerned when she read about this program. "I've never seen a College of Medicine so proud to announce a new program without a single benefit to osteopathic medical students," she said. Davis discussed her concerns with osteopathic medicine leaders and sent a letter to Dean Amalfitano, noting a potential negative impact on the training of future physicians. Davis objected to the use of terms that conflate PA students with DO medical students, and wrote that the program will "provide direct support for the American Association of Physician Assistants (and other organizations) to expand their push for the unsupervised practice of medicine." The Dean met with Davis via Zoom and vowed to ensure that DO students would be prioritized in every discussion moving forward and promised more transparency in titles. While Davis asked the Dean to reconsider the program, MSUCOM is currently enrolling PA students.[216]

Aside from providing basic training for non-physician practitioners, medical schools and academic centers are also developing postgraduate training programs that they call 'residency' or 'fellowship' programs. Physician groups like the American Academy of Emergency Medicine oppose the use of these terms, noting that 'residency' and 'fellowship' implies the far more lengthy and rigorous process that physicians complete.[217] Most non-physician postgraduate programs last no more than a year, include 40-hour work weeks, and have salaries that are far more generous than those paid to physician residents. Further, while physician residency training is standardized and overseen by a single credentialing body, postgraduate training for non-physicians is more haphazard, without published standards or guidelines.[218]

"It's a total hot potato topic," said emergency physician Thomas Cook, describing the uproar when the medical community learned of the hushed formation of physician assistant 'residency' programs at several prominent university teaching hospitals. Cook said that medical students and program directors were outraged. "The word went out like wildfire ... there was this grassroots effort on the part of the residents, who were saying, 'what are you doing? Here I have killed myself as an undergraduate, I've paid a lot of money to go through a very tough medical school, and you're giving [physician assistants] residency training, which by the way, lasts a year and mine is three years?' This is craziness.'"[51]

The development of programs for non-physicians at teaching centers has led to increased competition for training opportunities, which some worry will negatively impact physician preparation to practice. "I think we should remember that it wasn't always this way," said psychiatrist Ana Natasha Cervantes, MD. "My medical school training started 20 years ago, and I can tell you, nurse practitioners and physician assistants were just not something that we saw or competed with. We never had to worry about a procedure being offered to an NP or PA versus a resident or medical student. We worried about the resident getting the procedure instead of the medical student. And then the residents worried about the fellow getting the procedure instead of them."[219]

In addition to studying together, medical schools and residency credentialing agencies are allowing non-physicians to train future physicians. Laura Kendall wrote that "some residents have reported on social media that they are being supervised by [non-physician practitioners]. Others have reported that attending physicians are not teaching [physician trainees] certain procedures anymore because they would rather train their NP or PA to do the same procedure. The mentality behind this appears to be that it is a bad investment to train a medical student or resident who will just rotate off the service eventually, but a much better investment to train a midlevel practitioner who will continue to work with that attending physician."[14]

Rishi Patel, DO, a family physician who teaches medical students and residents, has noticed the same phenomenon. "When I was going through residency, all of my training was by physicians. However, as the years have gone by, increasingly nurse practitioners are supervising medical students, especially in the intensive care unit overnight and on pediatric rotations."[79]

ACADEMIC INVESTMENT IN NON-PHYSICIAN PRACTICE

With an increased dependence on non-physicians, academic institutions are working to acculturate equivalency to physicians. In some cases, they have used social media to provide messaging that de-emphasizes the physician's role on the healthcare team. For example, on Doctor's Day in 2021, Johns Hopkins University chose to include nurses and physician assistants, tweeting:

> During COVID-19, we are thankful now more than ever to have not only our doctors but also nurses, PA's, environmental services and other healthcare workers by our side at Johns Hopkins Medicine. We are grateful to all of our staff who are on the frontlines during #COVID19. #NationalDoctorsDay.[220]

Responding to concerned physicians asking for recognition on a day dedicated to their role, Johns Hopkins posted an apology, saying that their original goal was to be 'inclusive' of non-physicians due to 'previously received feedback':

> We are revising this post due to feedback we've received from our community and the doctors that we so very much value and respect. Our intention in the original post was to be inclusive of other important members of our patient care teams due to previously received feedback. We recognize that this has deeply offended doctors, those that are intended to be celebrated on Doctors' Day. For that, we sincerely apologize. This was not our intention.[220]

The Twitter community pointed out that while Hopkins claimed a goal of inclusion, the organization never thanked other team members on days dedicated to healthcare professionals like nurses, lab technicians, or physical therapists. Several months after the criticized Doctor's Day post, Hopkins posted on Nurse's Day, "Every day nurses provide compassion and care, motivation and inspiration. They are at your side in moments of need and leading innovations that shape our future."[220]

Some critics point to the fact that Johns Hopkins is not led by a physician, but by a nurse. After rising through the ranks of the Duke University Health System from staff nurse to president of the hospital, Kevin W. Sowers, MSN was named president of Johns Hopkins Health System in 2018. Sowers also serves as executive vice president of Johns Hopkins Medicine and chair of Johns Hopkins Community Physicians, which includes more than 40 primary and specialty care outpatient clinics.[221]

With such leadership, academic institutions have become powerful advocates for nurse practitioners and physician assistants. Natalie Newman, MD, an emergency physician who writes about scope of practice issues, believes that because teaching centers tend to attract higher-than-average clinicians, academic institutions have a skewed view of the education and training of the average graduate. "Nurse practitioners in academic centers tend to be of a higher standard," she said in a *Patients at Risk* podcast. "Since academic physicians work with the cream of the crop, they have a bias—they think that all graduates are like that. But those of us out in regular practice are seeing the diploma mill graduates. We're seeing the majority who are not in the academic centers, and we're seeing the results of inadequate care."[222]

Newman suspects that the pendulum will swing, as even well-regarded Ivy-league institutions are creating online training programs. "What's happening is that Yale, Johns Hopkins, Mayo, Harvard—when they create online programs, they become degree mills, too," Newman said. "They are depending on their name, but they're just as bad if they don't guarantee clinical rotations. They're just as bad as Walden or the University of Phoenix. I don't view them any differently." While Newman has tried to explain this to academicians on social media, she finds them unconvinced. "It's not their experience, [so] they're not going to see the deficits at all. Many of them are still supervising somewhat closely, and nurse practitioners functioning at a higher level are probably more responsible about presenting the patient. So, they're not going to see those who try to be mavericks without the knowledge."

She thinks that academic doctors believe that improperly functioning non-physicians are the minority. "They think it's just a small few. I say, no; you have 23 states where they have unsupervised practice, so that's a lot of states. They are in denial, and when I try to educate them, I get blocked. They don't want to know, and they don't want to hear that side." Newman finds this attitude frustrating. "In my opinion, they don't want to protect the patients. They are more interested in protecting the virtue of the [non-physician practitioners] than they are the patients."[222]

Newman said that academic physicians often vigorously defend non-physician practitioners, and physician trainees are expected to pay obeisance. For example, in December 2020, physician assistant Sarah Rebey participated in an interview process for prospective incoming neurosurgery residents at the Mayo Clinic in Arizona.[223] When a medical student questioned the role of non-physicians in residency interviews, as well as Rebey's title of *Neurosurgery PA fellow*,[224] Rebey posted on Twitter: "So disheartened to see this. Applicants—if you don't respect the entire healthcare team, and especially a program so reliant on APPs [advanced practice providers], maybe reconsider your path."[225] The Twitterverse exploded, with physicians rushing to support Rebey. Guillermo Escobar, MD, program director for the Emory Vascular Surgery Fellowship program wrote, "We have our vascular PA and NP regularly interview our future trainees. 100% part of the team! Their experiences on interviews have directly led to the removal of people from being ranked! My trainees will always respect, support and learn from everyone they work with."[226] University of Pennsylvania hospitalist Emmanuel King, MD, agreed, noting that he requires even prospective attending physician faculty members to be interviewed by his non-physician practitioners, who he considers their 'colleagues:' "For our faculty positions, we often have APPs interview candidates because we value our APPs opinions on their future colleagues. Anyone who doesn't respect APPs doesn't get through the door with us."[227]

Some physicians supported the medical student, noting that physicians should interview prospective physicians. Christian Lamb, MD, an internal medicine resident at the time, said that while he had no problem with multiple team members talking with prospective candidates, he was concerned about increased dependence on non-physician involvement in the residency hiring process. "I have friends applying for residency interviewed by a lone PA," he wrote. "I have nothing against PAs whatsoever, or collaborative care—in fact I'm a proponent of that—but how can you expect someone who didn't do residency to have insight into that experience for a resident-to-be?"[228]

Natalie Newman says that academicians are failing to act to protect physicians-in-training and patients. "I just say we must keep educating people on the differences between the disciplines of nurse practitioner and physician assistant and physician. They are distinct, and there is a hierarchy." Newman believes that having a hierarchy and a team is not contradictory. "You can have both and be cohesive, but someone must be the leader and that is going to be the one with the most expertise in medicine—the one who is licensed and trained." She also points to a double standard in medicine, noting that while academics will defend non-physicians, "they will criticize another doctor—a colleague—with no problem. And I find that offensive." She refers to posts in which academic physicians bestow the virtues of nurse practitioners and physician assistants, claiming to have learned medicine under their tutelage. "When physicians attribute their skills to NPs and PAs, yet never say anything about the physicians who taught them, this is virtue signaling," said Newman.[222]

An example of this occurred at Stanford University when Richard Besser, MD, President and CEO of the Robert Wood Johnson Foundation was asked about the Foundation's support for independent practice by nurse practitioners. Besser responded, "At the clinic I work at in Trenton, I work there under the direction of a nurse practitioner. I have to say over the course of my career as a general pediatrician, I've learned more from nurse practitioners than I think they've learned from me."[229]

Natalie Newman finds this type of talk demeaning. "During my era, we acknowledged physicians. I think that I'm a pretty good physician, and it was physicians who taught me to become a physician. Now, there were PAs that assisted or taught me procedures when I was a medical student rotating, and I appreciated that; however, they did not teach me how to be a physician. A physician taught me that." Newman is further disturbed by physicians who insist that 'their' nurse practitioner or physician assistant is better than some physicians. "Honestly, I think it is ego-driven. The specialist will work with an NP or PA for a certain amount of time and teach them a portion of what they know. Then they decide subjectively that in their opinion, the NP or PA is qualified." She says that the specialist may then allow their practitioner to see patients independently, including consults referred by another physician. "I think that's inappropriate because you're assuming that the NP or PA understands everything that you as a physician understand—which they don't."[222]

Newman notes that some physicians falsely believe that they are teaching non-physicians medicine, as they would for a medical resident who has the foundation. "But what they are actually doing is teaching them how to mimic medicine." She points out that the Flexner report of 1910 established that a variable apprenticeship model of learning was unacceptable for physicians, instead requiring a standardized, structured model of medical education under an accredited body. "What these doctors are doing is, in essence, an apprenticeship," she said. "The physician is not an accredited body; they are just a man or a woman with a medical degree, teaching someone what they know, to an extent. So, that person is never going to be an expert. They're just going to be somebody who worked under your watch." Newman says that some non-physician practitioners will then utilize the training that they received while working with a specialist to open their own practice. "They may now go to a state that allows independent practice and claim to be a 'cardiology NP' or a 'dermatology PA,' when they are not."[222]

Newman also believes that many physicians don't understand the basic background and education of non-physician practitioners. This was the case for Brent Wilson, who was the supervising physician for nurse practitioners hired by Mercy Health Systems to work alone in the emergency department. Attorney Travis Dunn said that Wilson believed that nurse practitioners were capable of staffing an emergency room alone, in part because the hospital system credentialed them to function in this capacity. "I took his deposition; very nice guy," said Dunn, "but he really had no concept of the educational limitations, the license limitations of nurse practitioners. He was operating under the belief that they had a broad scope of practice, as opposed to being a very narrow scope of practice in a very small area of medicine. He pretty much admitted that he thought that a nurse practitioner could do anything."[139]

To try to educate physicians, Newman posts graphs of non-physician practitioner education and the courses that they take. "I used to supervise NPs. I didn't know they had zero medical training. I thought when they were listed as advanced nurses, it meant that they had some formal medical training. I had no idea that their only medical training is whatever they get at the bedside with the physicians they work under. Well, to me, that doesn't count, because if that counted, we wouldn't have needed a Flexner report. Apprenticeship is not reliable for physicians, so how the heck is it reliable for nurse practitioners?"[222]

ACADEMIC PUBLICATIONS

To justify the use of non-physician practitioners in the role of physicians, many academic centers are publishing papers intended to prove comparable care. For example, faculty at the University of Pennsylvania, considered an Ivy League institution, have published editorials and research supporting the use of non-physicians in the field of radiology. In the article, 'Navigating the Paradox of Scarcity—the Case for Physician Extenders,' Saurabh Jha, MBBS, argues for an increased role for radiology assistants, and recommends that they be trained to perform lower-complexity radiology interpretations like chest-x-rays to save time and money.[230] But radiology assistants are not trained to read x-rays, and the profession, which was established in 1994, was only recognized by the American College of Radiology under certain stipulations, including an absolute ban on image interpretation.

Radiologists Phil Shaffer, MD and Sharon D'Souza, MD, MPH say that this is because using non-physicians to read x-rays is dangerous for patients, a topic they discussed in a *Patients at Risk* podcast. "There is no such thing as a 'simple' x-ray," said Shaffer. "In a lot of cases, the findings can be very subtle, but potentially life-threatening," as in the case of pneumothorax, or punctured lung. "When a patient is lying flat on their back as they are in the ICU, all the air goes to the front of the chest. So, all you may see is a finding that's very subtle, such as the heart border is a little too sharp. You think, 'Whoa, that's a little weird,' [but] that can hide a very significant pneumothorax." D'Souza agreed. "There is this huge misconception that a chest X-ray is so easy, and I think it's because after this decade of training, and after seeing thousands and thousands of chest X-rays, we tend to make it look easy because we have this vast experience, this depth of knowledge to fall back on."[231]

To support the argument that non-physicians can be used to read x-rays, the University of Pennsylvania performed a study in 2020 that claimed to show that radiology technicians could interpret chest x-rays as well as radiology residents.[232] Phil Shaffer said that he was appalled by the study. "This is such a violation of ethics that it is hard to overstate," said Shaffer. "Radiology technicians have zero medical training—their training is all about taking x-rays, not reading them." Further, he said that radiology technician licensure specifically prohibits them from interpreting x-rays, but researchers attempted to sidestep this regulation through the use of semantics. "They said, 'they're not interpreting them, they are just writing down their impression and the attending physician interprets,'" said Shaffer. Shaffer notes that physician residents were also ethically compromised by this study, as they may have felt obligated to participate as a term of their employment. The authors failed to protect the confidentiality of the resident physicians, revealing their names in the acknowledgments section. "I would have been furious if this had been me," said Shaffer, especially since the study seemed to conclude that there was no difference between the performance of residents and technicians, which Shaffer said did not accurately reflect the reality of the study. "On final analysis by attending radiologists, 6 out of 186 chest x-rays read by radiology technicians were found to have significant errors, three of which were judged to be dangerous." Shaffer said that while this number may not have reached statistical significance for differences between the groups, "if three patients out of 186 die because of a dangerously misread x-ray, that's a big deal."[231]

Research studies that utilize human subjects are required to undergo review by an Institutional Research Board to ensure proper procedures, such as informed consent. Since the University of Pennsylvania labeled this study as a quality improvement project and not a research study, those processes were not followed. Concerned about the impact of the study on resident physicians, Shaffer and a colleague wrote to the Vice Provost for Research as well as the research integrity officer at the University of Pennsylvania. While denying any wrongdoing, the authors elected to formally withdraw the article from publication.[233]

Advocates for non-physician practice in radiology insist that they are needed because of a shortage of qualified radiologists. Shaffer believes that this excuse isn't good enough. "The argument boils down to, 'We have so much volume, and we can't keep up—we really need help. I don't have a whole lot of sympathy with that,'" said Shaffer. "They get too busy, so they try to farm out some of it to relatively unqualified people to manage the volume. But the patients are charged the same as if they had had an expert physician actually reading the study. The ethical way to do this is, if you don't want to read the studies, if you're too busy, don't do it, and don't charge people for it."[233]

NURSE COLONOSCOPIES

Another esteemed academic institution, Johns Hopkins, has published research claiming that nurse practitioners can perform colonoscopies as well as gastroenterologists.[234] In a *Patients at Risk* podcast, colorectal surgeon Amer Alame, MD said that this research is severely flawed and can have dangerous repercussions on patient care. Nurse practitioners in the Johns Hopkins study practiced 140 colonoscopies under supervision, and then completed 1,400 colonoscopies on about 1,000 patients. Four hundred exams were excluded from the study due to inadequate bowel prep or abnormalities found during examination—requiring physician intervention. Alame said that excluding patients with abnormal findings skews the results. "That's the worst thing you can do when you want to evaluate safety," he said. "I mean, are you doing it yourself, or do you need someone always on backup? Let's say the conclusion from the study is that it's safe for nurse practitioners to do colonoscopies—as long as a gastroenterologist is on backup standing next to them."[235]

While the study concluded that nurse practitioner colonoscopies were safe, Alame believes that the evidence presented is inadequate to make that claim. "If your mission is only to get a scope from the anus to the cecum and back out, and no damage was done during that journey, and you want to define that as safe, then you have defined safety in medicine in your own world," he said. Further, he states that without adequate preparation to act immediately on abnormal findings, patients will be forced to undergo another procedure. "So, the scope exits, and then they're going to tell Grandma, 'We did the scope and we found something. But now you're going to need a gastroenterologist to come back and address it.'" Failing to act immediately on abnormalities harms patients, Alame said. "If you ask me, 'Did we harm Grandma?' Yes, we did. We sure did. Because we see many elderly patients every year who have taken a bowel prep and get dehydrated, and end up in the emergency room. And now we're going to ask her to take the bowel prep again?"

As an advocate for colon cancer screening, Alame said that he was most disappointed by the institution's choice to focus on training shortcuts rather than working to develop simpler techniques to improve patient access to colonoscopies. "The barriers that have been identified by the American Cancer Society are no usual source of care, inadequate insurance coverage, and not having the test recommended by their primary care clinician." Alame notes that other barriers include logistical factors like transportation, language barriers, fear of the procedure, and lack of knowledge about colon cancer. "Notice, none of them include, 'no provider to do the procedure.' This is per the American Cancer Society."[235]

Two-tier healthcare

Another criticism of the study involved the high proportion of Black patients. Seventy-five percent of the patients in the trial were African American, far exceeding the typical demographic composition of the Johns Hopkins patient population. While advocates for non-physician practice have insisted that expanding scope will increase access to care for disenfranchised patients, critics express concern about social justice. For example, a consensus statement from a group of colorectal surgeons for health equity and justice questioned whether Johns Hopkins researchers acted with complete transparency and provided full informed consent to study patients. The authors also cautioned researchers to plan studies more carefully to avoid the creation of a two-tiered system in which some patients receive care from physicians, and others are limited to non-physician practitioners.[236]

A colonoscopy by anyone less than a fully trained clinician creates a substandard tier of care, says Amer Alame. "Why are we trying to create another tier of care and then trying to prove that that tier is in some way acceptable?" he asked. "If you have these non-physician practitioners advise patients to get their colonoscopies done, you've probably achieved more benefit than any of this." Alame says that he is passionate about colonoscopies because of his work with colon cancer. "I deal with colon cancer day in and day out; that's my life. Because I deal with it so often, I see how easily the problem can be fixed, but also, what kind of ramifications it can have when it's not dealt with properly."[232]

PHYSICIAN ASSISTANT COLONOSCOPIES

In 2020, another academic institution, Washington University in St. Louis, published a study claiming that physician assistants could perform colonoscopies as well as gastroenterologists. The study, which examined screening colonoscopies over one year, excluded patients that had an advanced risk of colorectal cancer, those who exhibited symptoms or had a family history of intestinal cancer, and those who had inadequate bowel prep. Physician assistants were completely supervised by physicians, who assisted in the interpretation of endoscopic findings. In some cases, PAs required hands-on assistance from the supervising physician, and these colonoscopies were excluded from the final data analysis.[237]

"What this is saying is that PAs are good enough at colonoscopies except when they are not," said Amer Alame, noting that eliminating higher-risk patients and cases in which the PA required help from a physician invalidates the study conclusions.[232] Despite the flaws in this study, headlines proclaimed that 'PAs and Gastroenterologists Prove Equally Capable of Performing Colonoscopies.'[238] Alame says that this reporting does not accurately reflect the study results. "What the study is saying is, 'if we have a feeling that things may be okay, we will try and give you a non-physician provider. But if we have any hint that something could arise, something weird could be going on, better give it to somebody who knows what they're doing.' If I'm the patient, I'll be like, 'You know what, just give me that person who can take care of me no matter what!'"[232]

Interestingly, because so many patients undergoing colonoscopies by non-physicians require additional testing and follow-up, a 2015 review of the practice concluded that allowing non-physicians to perform colonoscopies did not save patients or the healthcare system money.[239] Alame says that the physician assistant study shows the same thing. "PAs can perform colonoscopies as long as there's a gastroenterologist within earshot that can be dragged into the room to help. We did not solve any problem[s] with this one. You still have somebody else whose time is being consumed. You did not save anything." Further, Alame says that this type of practice subjects patients to unnecessary procedures.

Instead of training non-physicians to perform colonoscopies, Alame sees a greater role that could be played by encouraging patients to get colonoscopies. "The American Cancer Society says if you want to help these patients, tell them to get a colonoscopy. Promote them, encourage them to do it, and educate them. If there's a language barrier, translate; break that barrier. Get them to get a colonoscopy by a gastroenterologist or surgeon like myself, or anybody who already does it as a standard of care."[232]

NON-PHYSICIAN SPECIALISTS

Although academic centers and hospitals are increasingly training and hiring nurse practitioners and physician assistants to function as 'specialists,' there is little evidence that this practice is safe or effective. For example, a 2021 literature review published in the *Journal of the American Association of Nurse Practitioners* found just 11 studies on care provided by nurse practitioner specialists.[240] Three of the studies focused on positive subjective findings of patient satisfaction:

- Patient trust among African Americans with hypertension (Benkert et al 2008)
- Patient satisfaction and appointment access in pediatric cardiology clinics (Evangelista et al 2012)
- Patient satisfaction with out-patient HIV care (Langner and Hutelmyer 1995)

Outcome studies included in the review showed that nurse practitioners with additional training could provide quality care among previously diagnosed, stable patients:

- Stable HIV-positive patients down-referred from physicians in the U.K. (Brennan et al 2011)
- Stable patients with bronchiectasis, a lung condition; although the nurse practitioner patients did have more hospital admissions, increased resource use, higher cost, and more antibiotic prescriptions than the physician group (Caine 2002)[241]

- Patients with diabetes in a quasi-experimental study with limited data without statistical analysis (Conlon 2010)
- Children with previously diagnosed, stable attention deficit disorder—although the study found that nurse practitioners underestimated emotional disorders (Foreman and Morton 2011)
- Stable patients with rheumatoid arthritis in a rheumatology clinic in which the physician comparison group consisted of junior doctors (residents-in-training), not rheumatologists in the U.K. (Hill et al 2003)
- Previously diagnosed children with eczema, a medical condition heavily dependent on patient education for proper skin care (Schuttelaar et al 2010).

The final two studies included in the analysis were procedural. Gonzalez et al (2011) evaluated colonoscopy skills among nurse practitioners at an academic center, with similar limitations as colonoscopy studies previously described in this chapter.

The second procedure study involved nurse practitioners performing the cardiac procedure of cardioversion (Norton et al 2016). The study, titled, 'Effectiveness and safety of an independently run nurse practitioner outpatient cardioversion program,' was a nonrandomized study of short-term outcomes performed at Stanford University. It concluded that nurse practitioners had similar success rates to physicians in bringing patients with an abnormal heart rhythm back into a normal rhythm by applying a cardiac shock.[242]

Cardiologist and Associate Professor of Medicine Mehrdad Saririan, MD reviewed the study details. While the headline sounds impressive, Saririan said that the study did not evaluate independent medical judgment by nurse practitioners, but rather, the ability to follow a standard cardioversion protocol, which includes pad positioning and energy selection. "The nurse practitioners in this study were not making decisions as to appropriateness or need for cardioversion," he said. Saririan further points out that "a cardiac anesthesiologist was involved in every case, standing at the head of the table to provide sedation and medical support. While these specialist physicians have more than enough training to perform electrical cardioversion themselves, the nurse practitioners were nonetheless used for billing purposes: to obtain the history and physical exam and for procedure documentation." Although this study was included in a meta-analysis to justify specialty practice by nurse practitioners, Saririan said that "the study merely showed that nurse practitioners were as capable as physicians in pressing the shock button."[243]

While the literature review showed data supporting the safety and efficacy of specially trained nurse practitioners managing stable, chronic patients with physician supervision, no data has been published showing the independent care of undifferentiated (not previously diagnosed), complex, or unstable patients. However, the study authors generalized their review to all patients, concluding that "research demonstrates that specialty NPs are just as capable of caring for patients as their physician counterparts and are more likely to exceed physicians in patient education and satisfaction."[240]

Academic centers have bought into this rhetoric, and often use non-physicians to care for patients. Internal medicine physician Elizabeth C. Berigan said that this is one of the reasons she left her job in an academic setting. "Every time I referred a patient to a specialist and specifically asked that they be seen by a physician rather than an NP or PA, I was ignored," she said, noting that this even happened to her physician patients. Berigan found this unacceptable, and ultimately resigned from her position.[244]

Specialists at academic centers are encouraging more entry of non-physicians into specialty fields. For example, in 2021, *JAMA Neurology* published a viewpoint urging an increased use of non-physician practitioners in the cognitively demanding field of neurology. The article, 'Advanced practice clinicians: Neurology's underused resource,' was co-authored by Heidi Schwarz, a neurologist with the University of Rochester, and argued that that non-physician practitioners should be used more widely to provide neurology care to patients, due to a shortage of neurologists across the country.[245]

To become a neurologist, physicians must complete a four-year residency program (one year of internal medicine and three years of neurology) after medical school, with some physicians completing additional years of fellowship training in sub-specialty fields like pediatric neurology or clinical neurophysiology. There is no formal neurology training program for non-physician practitioners, says Carol Nelson, MD, a neurologist with firsthand knowledge of the topic (Figure 5). Nelson has worked with and trained many nurse practitioners in her practice, and discussed her experience in a *Patients at Risk* podcast. "I'm fortunate because, for the last eight years, I've worked with a very bright and very hardworking nurse practitioner who also enjoys her role as a physician extender and doesn't want more than that." Nelson notes that her current nurse practitioner "comes from the old school when nurse practitioners graduated from nursing school and practiced nursing for a set amount of time before they could go back to school." Although her nurse practitioner was an experienced nurse before joining Nelson's practice, she had very little clinical experience in neurology before they began to work together. "All of the neurology she learned was through me and our office," said Nelson. The model works well for the neurologist, who says that having a non-physician practitioner can help to make her more efficient. "I will train somebody to be my extender, who can do the prior authorizations, write the letters to the insurance companies, pull up the charts and get them ready for me, make calls to people, check my messages, things like that. Things that are helping me get to the patients that I need to be seeing," she said.[246]

However, the *JAMA* article demanded that non-physicians be permitted to do far more than assist a physician, urging an increased clinical role in providing direct patient care. This is dangerous, said Alyson Maloy, MD, a double-boarded neurologist and psychiatrist who participated in the podcast with Nelson. "The problem is that they don't know enough. Three months of shadowing and being taught to be on a physician-led team gives one a false sense of mastery," she said, "and it is very, very dangerous unless you have someone who is an expert in these fields at the bedside with you, guiding you and picking up things that a physician extender might miss. These poor patients don't even know what has hit them."[246]

Neurologist Training

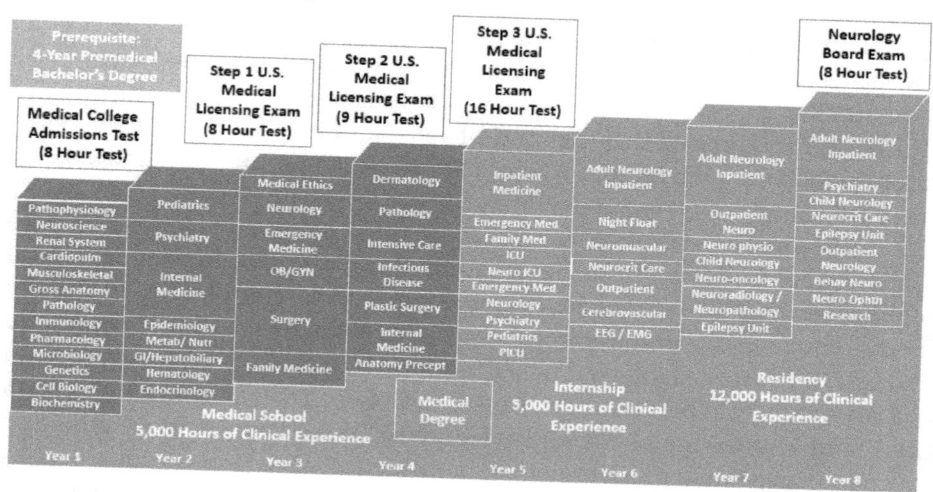

Family Nurse Practitioner Training

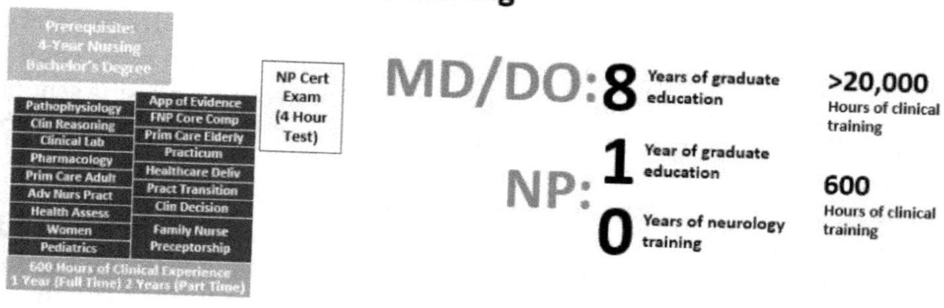

Figure 5. Neurology Training—Physicians vs NPs[247]

Maloy described a case of a patient she recently treated who was under the care of a neurology nurse practitioner. "The patient reported episodes of stumbling and memory loss, and since she was also having depression, the nurse practitioner diagnosed her with 'pseudo-dementia,' which is when depression is so severe, it causes cognitive impairment. What the patient actually had was uncontrolled temporal lobe epilepsy." Maloy noted that the patient was also misdiagnosed with bipolar disorder and treated with antipsychotics, a potentially dangerous class of medications. "If she'd seen an actual neurologist, they would have known that her temporal lobe epilepsy was not controlled, and she wouldn't have spent a year before she came to me to diagnose this."[246]

Carol Nelson notes that having inadequately trained practitioners treat neurology patients is not only dangerous to individual patients but can spread to a societal issue. "Number one, this person is potentially disabled from this, and her quality of life is poor. [Further] if ... people with epilepsy aren't controlled, they can seize and crash and kill somebody," she said. "This is a human life, but that could also impact another human life and family. I mean, epilepsy .... It's a huge responsibility." Nelson recalls her feelings of imposter syndrome despite having many years of training. "When I was in my second and third year of residency, well into it, I remember sitting back and thinking, 'Oh, my gosh, I've only got a year left, how am I ever going to be ready?' I think the more you know, the more you realize what you don't know, and what you need to study more. You realize how complex the human system is, and you just can't get that in a year. You can't get that in 2,000 hours. It's impossible."[246]

Medical malpractice expert witness and author Bob Pegritz has also seen examples of this danger in neurology. Pegritz, a former physician assistant, discussed a malpractice case he reviewed involving a neurology nurse practitioner. "The nurse practitioner was experienced in pediatrics, but decided to work in a neurologist's office, although she had no training in neurology," he said. Despite her lack of training, Pegritz said that the nurse practitioner treated a patient with progressive vision changes over seven months. "You can see from reviewing the medical record that instead of examining the patient or doing a neurological evaluation, she just cut-and-pasted the medical record," Pegritz said. "The patient came into the office about once a month, so there were seven cut-and-pastes in the medical record. During this entire time, the man was going blind, and he ultimately lost his sight." Pegritz notes that if a physician decided to practice in another specialty, they would be required to complete another residency training. "Why wouldn't that be the same for mid-levels? If they decide that they want to work in cardiology one day and rheumatology the next, that's a pretty steep learning curve."[248]

This logic seemed to go unrecognized in the *JAMA Neurology* article, which argued that nurse practitioners and physician assistants should be used as more than physician extenders and that they should be allowed to operate to the fullest extent of their license as clinicians. "One of the main points that bothered me in this article is that they say these physician extenders are upset because they're not practicing to the full extent of their licensure," Carol Nelson said, "but in that same article, they say non-physicians have little or no exposure to neurology. That means that working simply as a physician extender *is* practicing to the extent of their knowledge, because that's all [the knowledge] they have."[246]

In addition to patient safety, Nelson said that having non-physicians function as neurologists can be more expensive. "It's actually been proven that the amount of testing that is ordered by a physician extender compared to a [physician] is astronomical. It's not saving the system, or certainly the patient, money." Nelson said that using a non-physician delays care and increases profits for health systems. "It's not necessarily getting you closer to an answer—it is sort of just like buying some time and having the patient float through the system."

While the *JAMA* article argued that "the distribution of neurologists in the U.S. highlights inequitable access to care," it neglected to consider that replacing neurologists with lesser-trained substitutes may contribute to worsening health inequity. Nelson questioned who will determine which patients receive care from fully trained neurologists and who will be forced to see non-physician practitioners. "I think it's going to be unfair for the poor and for people that can't advocate for themselves," Nelson said. "There are a lot of people that are going to fall through the cracks." She also worries about the patients' understanding of who is caring for them. "A lot of these people think they're seeing a neurologist. There's not a lot of transparency in who they're seeing. So, the patient might think they're walking down the right path, and they're not." Rather than emphasizing patient safety, the *JAMA Neurology* article instead focused on the feelings of non-physician practitioners who want more privileges in patient care, writing, "neurologists also have to be mindful of our own insecurities and implicit biases stemming from the fear that we can be replaced or are no longer in charge, because such reactions are often unconscious. Comments or actions that demean or marginalize APC [advanced practice clinician] colleagues can create an unwelcome culture."

Alyson Maloy points to this as an example of gaslighting, an attempt to manipulate the feelings of physicians to make them question their reality. "They are trying to convince doctors that anyone who opposes this practice is only focused on their ego, and that speaking out is morally wrong, rather than this being a patient safety issue," she said. Maloy believes that replacing neurologists is degrading to the entire concept of team-based care. "This article was so disturbing because it made it seem like there's something wrong with a team, that there is an expert on the team, and that the other people on the team play a very important role. When I think about myself as a resident, I was a phlebotomist, I was an EKG tech, I was social work, I was transport. I was whatever the patient needed at that moment. There was no job too silly or beneath me, and that's what medical training is." However, she points out that on any team, there can only be one true leader. "They talk in this article about a culture of inclusiveness and shared leadership, but there is one leader on a medical team, and it's the physician. That's not because physicians are arrogant; it's just because of the expertise."[246]

The *JAMA* paper suggested that neurologists assist non-physicians in learning how to care for neurology patients by creating templates and onboarding materials. Carol Nelson says that the time and financial investment required to reach educational milestones appropriate for patient care should not be portrayed as a failure of practicing neurologists. "We've had a lot of nurse practitioners and PAs go through our clinic where we fully train them, and it takes months. We train them to be our extender; we teach them some neurology that is within their scope, and then they quit. [Then] they go to the VA where they practice completely independently."

Alyson Maloy points out the irony in allowing non-physician practitioners a privilege that is not granted to graduating medical students. "Although fourth-year medical students have significantly more clinical hours of training than the average new nurse practitioner or physician assistant, the authors are not suggesting that neurologists hire unmatched medical school graduates to independently evaluate new and returning neurology patients," Maloy said. "This opportunity for 'on-the-job training' is not an option to the thousands of unmatched physician graduates who are expected to continue formal training to obtain adequate expertise before they are licensed to practice."

In fact, despite a lack of neurologists, the reality is that there is currently a shortage of neurology residency positions. According to the National Residency Match data, there were 1,400 applicants for just 700 first-year neurology positions. Besides a shortage of neurologists, there has also been an increased demand on physician time to perform documentation in burdensome electronic health systems and to complete uncompensated tasks like prior authorizations. Nelson and Maloy say that helping neurologists care for patients by refilling medications, coordinating care management, and performing routine follow-up visits under a physician's supervision is an appropriate role for the training of non-physician practitioners, and this contribution may help expand access to neurology care while still ensuring that patients receive an accurate diagnosis and treatment plan from a fully trained neurologist.

Shortly after the *JAMA Neurology* article was published, Alyson Maloy submitted a letter expressing her concern which the editors declined to publish stating, "Unfortunately, because of the many submissions we receive and our space limitations in the letter section, we are unable to publish your letter in *JAMA Neurology*. After considering the opinions of our editorial staff, we determined your letter did not receive a high enough priority rating for publication."[246]

PSYCHIATRY AND MENTAL HEALTH

Psychiatry is a medical specialty that is every bit as cognitively demanding as neurology, but adds the element of patient vulnerability and the potential for decreased self-advocacy. Despite the rigors of this field, the number of nurse practitioners is growing relative to that of psychiatrists. In 2016, 1,500 students graduated from psychiatric mental health nurse practitioner programs, a 56% increase from 2014. Factoring demand and the addition of 29 new programs over three years, analysts predicted 2,000 psychiatric nurse practitioner graduates in 2020,[74] exceeding the number of psychiatry residency positions.[249]

With this growth, nurse practitioners are increasingly providing mental health care for some of the most medically fragile Americans. An analysis found that between 2011 and 2019, the number of psychiatric mental health nurse practitioners caring for Medicare patients (which includes disabled patients under 65 as well as seniors), increased by 162%, providing one in three prescriber visits, while psychiatrist rates decreased by 6%. Nurse practitioners were also found to provide over 50% of psychiatric care in rural areas in states allowing independent practice.[250] Non-physicians are providing more care to mentally ill children, with calls to expand that role.[86] However, there is very little literature examining the competency, safety, and cost-effectiveness of non-physicians replacing psychiatrists, as we will see in the next chapter.

CHAPTER 8

A STAR IS GONE: MENTAL ILLNESS AND THE RISE OF THE PSYCHIATRIC NURSE PRACTITIONER

Stevie Ryan was a rising Hollywood comedian and YouTube sensation. Described by friends as gorgeous and magnetic, Ryan moved to Los Angeles at the age of nineteen to pursue a career in show business. While auditioning for various roles, Ryan began creating and uploading videos to a brand-new entertainment medium: YouTube. In 2010, she got her big break when her sketch comedy show, *Stevie TV*, was bought by VH1. The program was a heralded success, with executives at VH1 calling Ryan, who created, co-wrote, executive-produced, and starred in the series "a rare example of successful female humor on television."[251]

In 2014, after two seasons and fourteen episodes, VH1 canceled *Stevie TV*. According to her friend, Yuni Kim, Ryan struggled with depression, and the cancellation of the series took a toll on Ryan's mental health. "Stevie was one of the first people I knew who talked about mental health openly," Kim said in a *Patients at Risk* podcast. "If she was feeling depressed and crying, she would show everybody. Honestly, I remember thinking back then, I would never cry publicly, just because that's how I was raised. But in retrospect, I see how courageous it was to share."[252]

To cope with her depression, Stevie Ryan sought treatment at Insight Choices, a mental health clinic in Los Angeles. She was evaluated in September 2015 by Gerald 'Jay' Baltz, a psychiatric mental health nurse practitioner (PMHNP) with seven years of experience after graduating from an almost entirely online nursing program.

PRESCRIPTION FOR DISASTER

Jay Baltz initially diagnosed Stevie Ryan with attention deficit disorder and started her on the stimulant medication Adderall (amphetamine salts).

Over the next year, he would continue to prescribe amphetamines as well as a cocktail of psychotropic medications—sedatives, antidepressants, mood stabilizers, and even antipsychotics.[253] Medical records kept by Baltz to justify these prescriptions were sparse, with few details about Ryan's symptoms. His initial intake note did not include any medical history, nor did he document a comprehensive mental status exam.[253]

To gain insight into Ryan's clinical picture, Ana Natasha Cervantes, a forensic psychiatrist who did not treat Ryan personally, reviewed the list of medications prescribed by Baltz, which she discussed in a *Patients at Risk* podcast. She noted that Baltz prescribed multiple anxiety medications, including seventeen prescriptions for benzodiazepines, sedative drugs that are controlled substances due to the potential risk of addiction. He also prescribed at least three different antidepressants and two drugs usually used for patients with bipolar disorder—a mood stabilizer and an anti-psychotic drug. "This tells me that it wasn't clear exactly what the diagnosis was," Cervantes said. "Or maybe there were multiple diagnoses, which makes it a more complicated situation." Cervantes said that clinicians must be aware of the risks of psychiatric medications. "For example, you'd want to be particularly careful in treating a patient with bipolar disorder with antidepressants, because there's the risk of inducing mania or what we call a mixed state, which is a combination of depressive and manic symptoms which can be uncomfortable and difficult to manage." Prescribing stimulants like amphetamine can also induce mania or lead to instability in a patient with bipolar disorder.

Cervantes also pointed out that Baltz prescribed numerous controlled substances to Ryan at the same time, including medications with opposing effects, such as Adderall (amphetamine salt), which is a stimulant, and Xanax (alprazolam), which is a sedative. While there was no evidence that Stevie Ryan had any substance abuse issues, Jay Baltz did not document that he asked her about risk factors for addiction. "There is some due diligence that should be done by the prescriber, [but] it's not clear that that was done here," Cervantes said.[219]

Crossing ethical boundaries

While Jay Baltz's diagnoses and treatment modalities were questionable, his behavior became far more egregious when he began a romantic relationship with his patient, Stevie Ryan. "She didn't start talking about him until April of 2017, which is when they started dating," said Ryan's friend, Yuni Kim. "She was like, 'I think my doctor is hot.'" Ryan told Kim that she had given Baltz her cell phone number, and the two were texting each other.[252] The American Medical Association calls romantic or sexual relationships between physicians and patients unethical, noting that "such interactions detract from the goals of the patient-physician relationship and may exploit the vulnerability of the patient, compromise the physician's ability to make objective judgments about the patient's health care, and ultimately be detrimental to the patient's well-being." The organization insists that a physician withdraw from professional care before initiating a personal relationship with a patient, and also cautions against dating former patients, which they warn may be unethical, "if the physician uses or exploits trust, knowledge, emotions, or influence derived from the previous professional relationship, or if a romantic relationship would otherwise foreseeably harm the individual."[254]

Yuni Kim acknowledges that she was concerned about her friend entering a relationship with Baltz, especially because of Ryan's fragile state. She worried that in Ryan's psychological despair, attention from a clinician she found attractive may have served as a momentary bright spot and impacted her judgment. "Did I know that it was wrong for a doctor to date his patient? Yes. Stevie was really depressed, but as a friend, I just wanted her to be happy," Kim said. "You hope for the best. You don't think the absolute worst might happen."[252]

When Ryan asked Baltz if texting was unethical, Baltz acknowledged that it was, texting, "I'm a healer, it would be unethical for me, not you. I took an oath!" Baltz seemed more concerned about his professional repercussions, adding, "If I did anything to harm you, it would not only be a dick move, but cause 10 years of school and work to disappear for me and injure you in some way." Baltz then instructed Ryan to delete all their texts.[253]

Although Baltz initially indicated to Ryan that she would need to find a new clinician for them to date, she was still under his care when they began to see each other socially. Within just a few days, text messages detailed a sexual relationship, including graphic descriptions of rough behavior. Photographs showed both of their necks with bruising that they describe as hickeys. Baltz texted Ryan, "we tore it up woman," and that he had "scratches on my chest which I don't recall getting."

"More like you tore me up!" Ryan responded, saying that her breasts hurt, and her neck was 'tweaked.'

"Oh, I'm sorry," Baltz replied, "I shouldn't have bitten. I thought you liked it at the time for some reason."

Baltz and Ryan met again, this time at the nurse practitioner's home. Subsequent text messages describe the meeting, with Ryan referring to breast and genital discomfort after the interlude. Baltz responded, "I was gentle this time; I'm sorry they hurt," and later, "PS I love your vagina." Baltz instructed Ryan to delete the entire text chain. Throughout their conversations, he expressed concern over the relationship, saying, "I do feel a strong connection and feel guilty at the same time." He repeatedly urged her to, "never say anything."[250] But rather than delete the texts, Ryan shared them with her friend, Yuni Kim. Kim recalls becoming concerned, not only because of the relationship, but because Baltz had discouraged her friend from going to the hospital, despite her reports of increased depression and suicidal thinking. Indeed, texts from Ryan to her friend indicate that the crush may have impaired her judgment: "Saw my doc. He said DO NOT go to the hospital. He's putting me on new meds AGAIN ... But he is so hot Yuni ... like FINE ... I think I'm dating my doctor now."[252]

Kim believes that Baltz kept Ryan out of the hospital for his own gain. "Either he didn't want her to check in because he wanted to continue sleeping with her, or because he didn't want to get in trouble," she said. "He knew it was unethical. I have screenshots of their texts where he says, 'this is unethical for me; not for you, but for me. I could lose my license and everything.' He seemed to care more about himself than her wellbeing."[252]

The flames of the affair seemed to fade as quickly as they began. "At the end of April, she broke it off with him. She didn't want to date him anymore," said Yuni Kim. Ryan ended it with Baltz, telling him, "I don't feel like texting anymore." He responded, "So you don't want to date anymore? It's okay. I figured you might not be thinking clearly. That sucks. I like you, but if that's what you're saying, I'll leave you alone." Baltz acknowledged that the relationship had been a bad idea, "I made a horrible error in judgment. You needed help and I worsened the situation."

A falling star

Already depressed, the breakup was difficult for Stevie Ryan, who told Kim, "Even though I don't like him, I feel super bad." Baltz had referred Ryan to another clinician at Insight Choices, but they continued to encounter each other at her appointments. "The problem is, even though he said that he would refer her to another doctor, she had to run into Baltz every time she went in," said Kim. "I remember she was telling me, 'It's so awkward to run into someone you've broken up with.' And he was still involved in her treatment, like trying to be involved, even when he had referred her to someone else." Baltz had referred Ryan for transcranial magnetic stimulation (TMS), telling her in texts that she needed to 'magnetize' her brain to improve her depression.[255]

According to psychiatrist Ana Natasha Cervantes, TMS is a course of treatment for depression that involves the application of a large electromagnetic current to a patient's brain. "The idea is that this stimulates certain parts of the brain to release neurotransmitters that might be deficient," she said. While it may be effective for some patients, TMS is expensive and requires a significant time commitment. "The course of treatment is usually five days a week for six weeks, a total of 30 treatment sessions at about an hour each time."[219]

After the breakup, Baltz texted Ryan to ask if she would be coming to her treatment. When she responded that she had been busy, he wrote, "That's fine but [the TMS clinician] wants you to follow [up] with me as the person who referred you; so that will be fun."

Ryan wrote back, saying, "Fuck it I'm not doing it. It's too much drama."

Baltz replied, "Listen I feel terrible about this whole thing. Most important thing is your mental health. This is exactly why I'm an idiot."

Stevie Ryan's mental state continued to decline over the next month. "She was really depressed," said Yuni Kim. "I mean, really, really. Like I would call her and sometimes she would be crying, but she was still trying to pull through."

Ryan was making efforts to rebuild her career. She had started co-hosting a podcast called "Mentally Ch(ill)," which discussed her journey with depression. Ryan told audiences that she had stopped the antidepressant Prozac cold turkey, and talked about her TMS experiences. However, the death of her grandfather seemed to be the final straw. Ryan shared her loss on her final podcast and said, "I am just worried that this is going to send me into a deeper depression." A few days later, on July 1, 2017, Stevie Ryan ended her own life at just 33 years of age.[255]

THE INVESTIGATION

Psychiatric mental health nurse practitioner Gerald J. "Jay" Baltz left Insight Choices a month after Stevie Ryan's death by suicide. In 2018, Ryan's parents sued Baltz and the clinic for wrongful death, and Baltz's malpractice insurance paid a $200,000 settlement. That same year, on August 30, Ryan's former boyfriend filed a complaint with the California Board of Nursing after discovering a large number of prescription medications prescribed by Baltz while cleaning out Ryan's apartment.[255]

The Board of Nursing began an investigation, including an interview with Baltz. Initially, the nurse practitioner said that he didn't remember Ryan "all that clearly," nor why he had treated her. Regarding a personal relationship with Ryan, Baltz denied any wrongdoing.

Investigators showed Baltz his cell phone number saved to Ryan's phone. He responded that he often provided patients with his personal number, but did not recall sending her text messages. Investigators then showed Baltz screenshots of texts between him and Ryan, which he denied sending. At that point, the investigator showed Baltz a photograph of a man's neck with bruising near a tattoo above the collarbone. When asked if he had a tattoo like the one in the photo, Baltz moved his shirt collar, revealing the same tattoo. Asked about Stevie Ryan's mental state, Baltz acknowledged that he was aware that she had suicidal thoughts. However, he did not thoroughly evaluate her risk of suicide, nor did he refer her for a higher level of care.[253]

According to Ana Natasha Cervantes, an in-depth risk assessment must be performed on any patient who expresses thoughts of suicide. "It's not just asking the person, 'are you going to kill yourself?'" she said. "It goes deeper than that. You want to look at what risk factors they have: whether there's substance abuse, whether there are acute stressors that are happening, any significant losses, and you also want to look at what protective factors the person has as well." Based on this evaluation, patients may need to be admitted to a hospital for more careful observation. "As uncomfortable as it is, if a person is crossing that threshold where they need a higher level of observation, it can't be done on an outpatient basis," she said. "It requires either an emergency room or inpatient level of care, or maybe a partial hospitalization program for a person to be seen every day but go home at night. There are certainly several higher levels of care that could have been considered, but it doesn't sound like that was done." On the contrary, Baltz actively discouraged Ryan from seeking emergency evaluation.[219]

The nursing board investigation report noted that Baltz failed to consult with his supervising physician regarding Ryan's care. At the time of Stevie Ryan's treatment, California law required nurse practitioners to have a supervising physician and standardized procedures to follow when treating patients. These supervisory agreements are in place to ensure that patients have access to input from a physician, especially if a patient is declining or failing to clinically improve. According to the investigation, Baltz's medical records did not show any physician consultation. Further, Baltz's supervising psychiatrist admitted that his supervision was deficient and that he had failed to review charts with Baltz or perform annual evaluations. Baltz also acknowledged that he never sought out chart reviews from his supervising physician as required by law.**

According to Ana Natasha Cervantes, who has served as a supervising psychiatrist for nurse practitioners, anytime a physician agrees to supervise or collaborate with a nurse practitioner, they are obligated to perform a minimum amount of due diligence, which is often regulated by state law. "Usually, there's a certain number of required charts or percentage of charts that should be reviewed," she said, adding that there must be a procedure

---

**Failing to follow the terms of a supervisory agreement put patients like Stevie Ryan at risk, but beginning in 2023, physician supervision is no longer required for California nurse practitioners with more than three years of experience (*AB-890 Nurse practitioners: Scope of practice: practice without standardized procedures*).

in place for how this is done. "Are you relying on the nurse practitioner to bring charts to the physician's attention? Or are you randomly selecting charts to review?" Cervantes' preference is a combination of both. "He or she should come to me as needed, but I also will pull random charts to make sure that there's due diligence that is done. Ultimately, it might be the physician's responsibility."[219]

Delayed discipline

On June 15, 2020, nearly two years after Jay Baltz was initially reported, the California Board of Nursing filed a formal complaint against the nurse practitioner. The legal document listed four causes for discipline, including gross negligence, incompetence, unprofessional conduct, and sexual misconduct. The board accused Baltz of inadequately assessing and treating Stevie Ryan's psychiatric conditions and failing to consult with his supervising physician, especially in light of her suicidal thoughts, as well as unprofessional conduct by engaging in a sexual relationship with a patient under his treatment.

Despite these serious charges, Baltz continued to work as a nurse practitioner in California for nearly two more years. Baltz was also granted new licenses to work as a nurse practitioner in Colorado and Washington state while under investigation by the California Board of Nursing.[256] Questioning the delayed discipline, Yuni Kim expressed concern. "I just don't understand how he is still practicing with a license. In this field, where he gets to prey on the most vulnerable?"[252]

Some physicians note that Boards of Nursing are often slow to act, especially compared to state Boards of Medicine. "It's hard to get bad nurse practitioners removed without the public's help—without people standing up and saying, 'Hey, this is a problem' and putting pressure on the Board of Nursing," said Niran Al-Agba in a podcast episode on the subject. "The Board of Medicine in most states is pretty quick. Anytime that I've known of a physician sleeping with a patient in the state of Washington, they've lost their license. What's fascinating to me is the Board of Nursing doesn't seem to be as upset about sex with patients."[219]

Ana Natasha Cervantes agrees that state Boards of Medicine tend to come down hard on psychiatrists who cross the line with patients—and for good reason. "In the mental health field, we're dealing with people who are potentially very vulnerable and very fragile," she said, noting that inappropriate relationships with psychiatric patients are considered particularly egregious because, during psychotherapy, patients often disclose intimate and vulnerable details. Cervantes also points out that the power differential between physician and patient may compromise a patient's judgment.

"That's why it's always considered unethical to start any kind of romantic relationship with a psychiatric patient," she said. "Baltz seemed to know this, but it didn't matter. It happened anyway."[219]

Why did it take so long for the California Board of Nursing to act? Further, why did Washington and Colorado grant a nursing license to a nurse practitioner under investigation in another state for sexual misconduct? Cervantes says it's not unusual for disciplinary cases against physicians to take several years because due process must be followed before licensure is removed. "There's usually the opportunity to have counsel and to have an administrative hearing before a decision is rendered," she said. Some critics have expressed concern that state Boards of Nursing are not adequately funded or staffed to oversee the volume of nurses under their supervision. For example, audits of the California Board of Nursing in 2016 found a significant backlog of complaints, including allowing a nurse accused of causing the death of a child to practice for over three years.[257] In 2020, the Board was further accused of falsifying documents to make it appear as if complaints against nurses were being investigated in a timely fashion when they were not.[258]

Of additional concern is why two separate states, Washington and Colorado, approved nursing licenses after an investigation against Baltz had been opened in California, leading to questions about how state nursing boards communicate. "What concerns me is that he was completely unrestricted in a state that does not require nurse practitioners to work under physician supervision," said Niran Al-Agba.[219]

In December 2021, an administrative court rendered a verdict against Baltz, calling him "grossly negligent" in the care of Stevie Ryan, and noting that he failed to demonstrate evidence that he had taken steps to prevent another such incident. Baltz filed a petition challenging the court's decision on February 16, 2022, arguing that the nursing board "misinterpreted and misapplied relevant statutes" in its disciplinary order. On February 28, 2022, nearly five years after Stevie Ryan died, the California Board of Nursing finally revoked Gerald Baltz's license to practice in the state.[259]

At the time of the California order, Baltz had active licenses in Colorado and Washington, although he agreed to a non-disciplinary cessation of practice agreement in Colorado pending his California investigation. In April 2022, Baltz faced a summary suspension of his license in Washington State. His Seattle, WA practice, Old Ballard Psych, is listed as temporarily closed on Google.[260]

While Jay Baltz is no longer allowed to care for psychiatric patients, many other nurse practitioners are filling the role of a psychiatrist, caring for vulnerable patients. How did this practice begin?

THE HISTORY OF THE PSYCHIATRIC MENTAL HEALTH NURSE PRACTITIONER (PMHNP)

While the nurse practitioner profession was designed to work alongside physicians to provide preventive care and health promotion,[261] legislative efforts over decades have expanded the role into primary and specialty medical care, including the treatment of patients with mental illness.

Nurses have received advanced degrees in psychiatry since the 1950s, and the Community Mental Health Centers Act of 1963 provided a surge in funding for master's level training. The legislation aimed to transition people with mental illness from institutions into the community, and psychiatric nurses were needed to provide psychotherapy, patient education, and to act as consultants and patient liaisons. As pharmaceutical treatments for mental health conditions were developed, nurse educators added training on the medical management of patients, and in 1973, the American Nursing Association established core competencies and began to grant certification as a clinical nursing specialist (CNS) in psychiatric-mental health nursing.[262]

In the 1990s, funding for CNS training programs dried up, and with a growing acceptance of nurse practitioners in primary care, psychiatry nurse educators shifted curricula to emphasize the diagnosis and treatment of psychiatric patients, with a goal of prescriptive authority for advanced psychiatry nurses. In 2003, the standards for the psychiatric-mental health nurse practitioner role were officially outlined.[262]

Although it requires eight years of post-college education for a physician to practice psychiatry, the nursing community has conferred the same responsibilities on registered nurses with an additional two years of training and just 500 clinical hours (Figure 6).[263] These mental health nurse practitioners are authorized to treat patients across the lifespan, including children and geriatric patients. In about half the states of the country, they are permitted to diagnose and treat mental illness independently, without physician involvement.

Psychiatric mental health nursing education

In the last twenty years, there has been an explosion in the number of training programs for psychiatric mental health nurse practitioners, with an estimated 327 programs in 2017.[86] While each nursing program has specific requirements, students must complete at least 500 clinical hours and take a certifying examination to be licensed. These clinical hours are spent with a psychiatrist or another psychiatric nurse practitioner, and telehealth sessions may be counted. As an example, Midwestern State University in

Psychiatrist Training

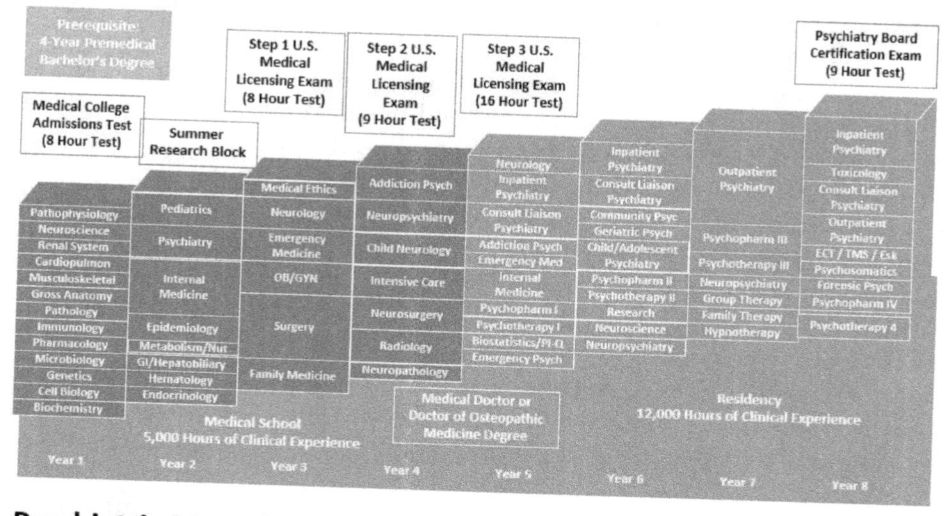

Psychiatric Mental Health Nurse Practitioner Training

Figure 6. Psychiatry Training—Physicians vs NPs[264]

Texas requires 512 clinical hours to graduate, including 256 hours caring for adults with mental illness, 100 hours with children and adolescents, 100 hours with geriatric patients, and 16 hours in the field of addiction. Students must participate in 40 hours of therapy sessions to be certified to provide psychotherapy (Table 6).[265] In contrast, psychiatrists are required to spend a minimum of one year providing longitudinal psychotherapy under supervision during residency training.[266]

Psychiatrists are required to complete training in multiple settings, including in-patient hospital units, emergency rooms, and outpatient centers, treating acutely and chronically ill patients of all ages. Psychiatric nurse practitioner students may only be assigned to one or two settings, and given the relatively small number of hours required, they are unlikely to gain experience in the full range of clinical settings. For example, a nurse practitioner student assigned to an emergency room may not get exposure

Table 6. Midwestern State University PMHNP Required Clinical Training

	Clinical Hours	Equivalent weeks (40 hours/week)
Adult	256	6 weeks
Pediatric	100	2–1/2 weeks
Geriatric	100	2–1/2 weeks
Addiction	16	< 1 week
Psychotherapy	40	1 week
Total	512	13 weeks

to more common presentations of anxiety and depression, or have the opportunity to engage in psychotherapy. Likewise, a student assigned to an outpatient setting for most of their hours may not learn how to recognize acute mania, psychosis, or substance withdrawal.

Considering that the standard reference textbook for psychiatry, the *Diagnostic and Statistical Manual of Mental Disorders* includes 450 different definitions of mental disorders, nurse practitioner graduates will likely have been exposed to only a fraction of the psychopathology in a typical psychiatric practice during their 500 hours of clinical experience.

The making of 'Dr.' Baltz-DNP

Yuni Kim is convinced that her friend Stevie Ryan believed that Gerald Baltz was a physician—specifically, a psychiatrist. "I am 100% sure that Stevie thought that he was a doctor," said Kim, who herself was unaware of the differences between psychiatrists and mental health nurse practitioners until after her friend's death. "Why are they allowed to be called doctors if they are nurses?" The answer, in the words of American Association of Nurse Practitioners President Sophia Thomas? Because "physicians don't own the term doctor."[1]

Nurse practitioners with a doctorate are indeed allowed to call themselves a doctor, as long as they follow the title with the identification of *nurse practitioner*. Patient advocates like psychiatrist Ana Natasha Cervantes believe that the use of the term 'doctor' by non-physicians in a clinical setting is misleading. "When people hear doctor, I think there's an expectation of a minimum amount of training that goes into it, but their training as a nurse practitioner is absolutely nothing like the training of a physician."[267]

Indeed, Jay Baltz followed an alternate route to becoming a 'doctor.' Before turning to nursing, Baltz received an undergraduate degree in creative writing. He briefly taught high school English Literature and then pursued a career in information technology, creating websites and providing computer support for several large companies. Baltz decided to go back to school to get a bachelor's degree in nursing. In his online profile, he says that he specifically chose nursing and not medicine because he "preferred a holistic and education-based approach to care" and "admired the fortitude and compassion of nurses."[268]

After working as a registered nurse for one year, Baltz attended an online psychiatric mental health nurse practitioner master's degree program at St. Louis University. He completed the required 500 hours of clinical experience, and became certified in 2008. Following his master's degree, Baltz practiced for two years under the supervision of three psychiatrists and an experienced psychiatric nurse practitioner. His profile lists his specializations as treating depression, anxiety, and ADHD, and notes that he "embraces alternative and complementary therapies … and provides psychoeducation as part of every session."[263]

In 2018, Baltz received a Doctor of Nursing Practice (DNP) degree from St. Louis University and began to refer to himself as "Dr. Jay Baltz DNP, PMHNP-BC," even signing his Facebook page messages, "Warmly, Dr. Jay."[269] At the time that Baltz was treating Stevie Ryan, he did not yet have the right to use the title Doctor of Nursing Practice, let alone doctor. Yet in texts, Ryan often referred to him as her doctor. "When you look up St. Louis University—which he calls medical school, by the way, in his bio—it's fascinating, because you can apply credit from your master's degree for some of your doctoral hours," Niran Al-Agba said in a podcast about the program. "What's interesting is they sort of brag on the website that there's a two- or three-day orientation at the beginning of the program, and a second 1–2-day visit at the end of the program and then you never have to show up at school again, you can completely do everything online."[267]

While the doctorate is billed as a three-year program, Ana Natasha Cervantes says that this is not as impressive as it sounds. "First, it's really two and a half years because there's no spring in the third year. If you really look at the breakdown of 28–29 credit hours, some of which can be transferred in, you're only talking about one to two three-credit courses per semester, which would hardly be considered full-time. If a medical student were doing this curriculum, I feel like this could be condensed into one and a half years of medical education just based on the number of credit hours and what's expected." Cervantes suspects that the curriculum is spread out so that a student can work full-time as a nurse or nurse practitioner while attending the program. "That's certainly not something that any medical student or resident can do while in school," she said. "If anything, we're working way more hours than in a typical job during our training."[267]

More importantly, Cervantes points out that the DNP curriculum includes no specific classes on psychiatry, psychology, the practice of interviewing patients, or learning how to generate a differential diagnosis. "It's all about nursing leadership, nursing theory, medical informatics, healthcare delivery systems. The only thing I could find that seemed clinically related was 'evidence-based practice,' of which there are two 3-credit hour courses that are expected (Table 7)." DNP students at St. Louis University are also required to complete a capstone project, worth about a fifth of their total grade. For his project, Baltz produced a paper about the use of electronic cigarettes by mental health patients.[270]

Table 7. St. Louis University Doctor of Nursing Practice Curriculum[271]

Course	Credit Hours
Epidemiology	3
Health Care Policy and the APN	3
Health Care Delivery Systems	3
Interpersonal Collaboration	3
Leadership in Health Care	3
Clinical Informatics	3
Evidence Based Practice	3
Evidence Based Practice II	3
Capstone Project Management	1–2
DNP Clinical and Capstone Project	4
TOTAL	**30**

The emphasis on non-clinical education is consistent with concerns from nurse education leaders that only 15% of all DNP programs are clinically focused.[272] Indeed, Cervantes compares the University of St. Louis nurse practitioner curriculum to her medical school and psychiatry residency training. "Most of these DNP subjects would be considered electives. Toward the end of your fourth year, both in med school and residency, usually, there are a few months where you can choose to do some electives, but it's not most of the time, like in this program."[267]

Instead, medical students and residents are expected to study medicine and develop expertise in diagnosing and treating psychiatric conditions. "To learn what mental illness looks like, you do have to see a certain threshold volume of patients, and that's why our residencies are so long," Cervantes said. She believes this is why there has not been a push to shorten psychiatry residency, despite a shortage of psychiatrists. "You can go one or two years and not see some of these rare things that we deal with, but if you are there for three or four years, you might get exposure to rarer conditions. Then you know what they look like, what to look for, what questions to ask, and how these illnesses progress over time. There's really no shortcut."[267]

PSYCHIATRISTS REPLACED BY PSYCH NPS

Psychiatrists complete a minimum of 17,000 hours of training before being permitted to treat patients because medical education experts have determined that without this level of mastery, patient care is compromised. Yet these physicians are being replaced by nurse practitioners with a fraction of the training. Ana Natasha Cervantes says that the reason is simple: to increase company profits. "There's definitely a trend toward corporations hiring nurse practitioners instead of psychiatrists," Cervantes said. "We've had this surge of nurse practitioners over the last few years because they can graduate so quickly, combined with states allowing them to prescribe and essentially do a lot of what physicians have been doing, despite less training and experience."[267]

For example, in December 2022, Providence Sacred Heart Medical Center in Spokane, WA announced that it would lay off eight psychiatrists, replacing the physicians with three nurse practitioners to save between $2–4 million. In an article about the move, chief medical officer Daniel Getz blamed the decision on financial losses but reassured the public that, "what's important to remember is that we're adding back positions," noting that the company was "restructuring our current model of delivering behavioral health care."[465]

The hospital is owned by Providence Health and Services, a non-profit, tax-exempt healthcare company with $5 billion in total revenue in 2019. While the company reported financial losses from COVID19, the Catholic organization paid nearly $11 million to outgoing President and CEO Rod Hochman and over $4 million to current President Mike Butler, with thirty other top executives earning seven-figure salaries in 2019. IRS reports also showed that the company paid for first class travel and funded discretionary spending accounts for executives.[466]

Self-employment

After being hired by companies and gaining some experience, many psychiatric nurse practitioners then go on to hang their own shingle, as Baltz did. In fact, there is an increasing trend towards self-employment with social media influencers like *The Psych NP* encouraging nurse practitioners to quit salaried jobs to open private practices or offer telemedicine as a way of gaining greater independence.[273] Patients who visit these nurse practitioners are often unaware of the differences in training between psychiatric mental health nurse practitioners and psychiatrists, and do not even think to question the qualifications of their clinician.

In some cases, nurse practitioners deliberately obscure the differences in training. For example, in a since edited post, Partners in Psychiatry, a medical practice serving patients aged 4–60 and staffed by two psychiatric nurse practitioners in Johnston, RI, a state where nurse practitioners have independent practice rights, defined the professions on their website as:

> **Psychiatric nurse practitioner** is an advanced nursing professional who may diagnose and prescribe medications to treat psychiatric problems … Depending on the time spent working in a psychiatric setting as a registered nurse, *a new psychiatric nurse practitioner is considerably more prepared than a new psychiatrist, due to the wealth of experience with patients and treatment as a registered nurse* [emphasis added].
>
> **Psychiatrist:** A doctor who specializes in the field of psychiatry who may diagnose and prescribe medications. It generally costs the system or private payers much more to acquire the services of a psychiatrist. The healthcare system at large is moving towards employing physician assistants and nurse practitioners due to comparable patient outcomes, yet lower costs to operate.[274]

Despite this very public insistence that nurse practitioners are 'considerably more prepared' than psychiatrists, academic nurse practitioners disagree, with one textbook writing, "in our current clinical reality, the [psychiatric mental health nurse practitioner] is expected to function like the physician despite the significant difference in academic and supervised clinical practice exposure. Quantitatively speaking, the newly trained NP likely does not possess equivalent knowledge, skills, and abilities compared to a newly trained physician. Any attempt to argue otherwise avoids an inconvenient and quantitative truth."[275]

Regarding claims of similar outcomes for psychiatric mental health nurse practitioners, there is little data on the subject. A 2004 review found no specific outcome studies for nurse practitioners in the mental health field, but noted favorable previous research in different specialties. The article called for more research, saying that, "outcome studies comparing the efficacy of different mental health professions are important, [because data] can be used to influence health policy and legislation" for the profession.[276]

More recent publications on the topic have also failed to find outcome data. While a 2022 commentary urging an increase in the use of psychiatric nurse practitioners extensively documented workforce data and research on access to care, it cited just two studies analyzing clinical outcomes.[277] The first, a 2018 study of psychotropic prescriptions for Medicaid-insured children, found that nurse practitioners were far more likely to prescribe psychotropic medication to children, noting a 51% increase in psychotropics prescribed by psychiatric nurse practitioners and a 29% increase by non-psychiatric nurse practitioners, while prescribing by psychiatrists and non-psychiatry physicians both decreased.[278] The commentary also cited a 2022 analysis of prescribing patterns for nursing home residents with dementia, which found that nurse practitioners and physician assistants prescribed more pain medications, including opioids, as well as a larger proportion of benzodiazepines than physicians.[279]

A 2016 review of mental health nurse practitioners in public health gave high marks to the profession for its "whole-person perspective, collaborative approach, and interpersonal communication," but noted "significant knowledge gaps" as a barrier to the field.[280] These knowledge gaps can be the difference between life and death.

The danger of replacing psychiatrists

Clinical training and experience matter, especially when evaluating and treating patients with psychiatric illnesses. Psychiatrists must develop a strong foundation in developing a differential diagnosis, a rigorous process in medical training detailed in the book *Patients at Risk*. Correct diagnosis is essential; otherwise, treatments will be ineffective and potentially dangerous. For example, prescribing an antidepressant to a person with bipolar disorder can trigger a manic episode, which can be dangerous and even life-threatening. Giving a stimulant drug can cause a cardiac event in a patient with underlying heart disease, and can induce psychosis in patients with schizophrenia. Prescription medications, especially in psychiatry, must be carefully monitored. Overprescribing or mixing medications can lead to serious physical and mental side effects, and even death. There can be a risk of suicide or psychosis when medications are started, if the proper treatment is not instituted and if careful follow-up is not in place.

Medical standards exist not to withhold care from those who need it, but to ensure that clinicians do not unintentionally harm patients. All patients with psychiatric symptoms deserve a thorough evaluation by a fully trained physician, including a full biopsychosocial assessment, comprehensive physical examination, and diagnostic testing when appropriate to exclude medical causes for symptoms. In other words, the medical standard is to create an individualized plan of care. In some cases, patients may be best served by treatments other than medications, such as psychosocial support, lifestyle changes, and cognitive therapy. Most of the time, patients need more than just a quick check-in with a non-physician practitioner and a handful of prescriptions. Unfortunately, in the name of access, this is exactly what some of our nation's most vulnerable patients are getting.

Yuni Kim said that she only learned about the role of nurse practitioners in mental health after her friend Stevie Ryan died, and can't help but wonder if Stevie might have had a different outcome if she had received care from a qualified psychiatrist. "I feel that it's just really easy to be exploited in the mental health industry, and I want people to know that sometimes they might not be talking to a psychiatrist. You've got to make sure what their qualifications are: are they really a doctor? That's a really good first step," she said.[252]

Are policymakers and legislators listening? It seems not, based on policies that emphasize training for more nurse practitioners, rather than for more psychiatrists. For example, in 2020, UCLA announced that it would use a $1.5 million grant to offer a new online certification for mental health nurse practitioners to 'increase access.' At the same time, zero residency slots were added to UCLA's psychiatry programs due to a "lack of funding."[281]

Ana Natasha Cervantes believes that this shortcut to education is diluting the quality of care. "One of the problems is that they don't know what they don't know. They may believe that they have the experience that's needed, but if you've never seen it and you don't know what to look for, you're missing things. It is very problematic." For example, Cervantes says that she sees many patients diagnosed with psychiatric conditions by nurse practitioners and physician assistants based on questionable criteria. "Then medications are being started and continued with the risk of significant side effects, expense, follow-up—and this also takes resources that might no longer be available for somebody who really does need mental health care." She speculates that as psychiatrists are increasingly replaced by nurse practitioners, "in the next few years, we will see an increase in certain diagnoses all of a sudden, probably due in part to misidentifying symptoms as mental illnesses."[267] Indeed, there is evidence of this already occurring in psychiatry, with a recent surge in attention deficit disorder being diagnosed by nurse practitioners working at for-profit mental telehealth companies. The explosion of this online mental health care industry has also put patients at risk for other serious consequences, including drug addiction and suicide.

CHAPTER 9

PHONING IT IN: VIRTUAL MENTAL HEALTH CARE

Anthony Kroll was just 17 years old when he enrolled in Cerebral, an online mental health service. During a 24-minute video appointment, Anthony reported depression and suicidal thinking to a nurse practitioner, who prescribed the antidepressant drug fluoxetine (Prozac). Fourteen days later, Anthony took his own life.[282]

Anthony's parents only discovered that he had sought treatment for depression on the day that their son died. They questioned why Cerebral failed to inform them about his diagnosis. Had they been aware, they said, they would have taken precautions, including removing firearms from the home. While Cerebral said that Anthony had misrepresented his age, an investigation found that the company's identification checking system had not functioned properly.

While the risk of suicide is inherent in the treatment of depression in any setting, Anthony's death brings special attention to concerns over the virtual treatment of mental health conditions. Over the last few years, telehealth startups have exploded, including companies offering psychiatric care and staffed predominantly by nurse practitioners.

Case examples: Cerebral and Done

The COVID-19 pandemic created financial opportunities in the healthcare sector. One major winner: telehealth startup companies offering virtual medical care. As patients faced stressors related to worries about illness, working from home, and economic uncertainty, the timing was ripe for private equity investors to cash in on mental health. The model was simple. Patients would fill out a short self-assessment form online, arrange a quick phone call or video chat, and voila! A prescription for their preferred medication was transferred electronically, or even better, the medication was shipped directly to their door.

Cerebral was one of the first players in this burgeoning telehealth market, launching in January 2020. The company offered online mental healthcare at a low fee—for just $85 per month, patients could consult with a 'prescriber' by phone or video. Instead of psychiatrists, Cerebral's model relied heavily on nurse practitioners who were hired to evaluate and treat patients with psychiatric disorders.[283] Cerebral also offered 'care counseling' by social workers or mental health counselors, and patients could upgrade to receive weekly sessions with a higher-level psychotherapist for $325 per month.[284]

The startup was a huge success. With an initial private equity investment of $300 million, the company was valued at $4.8 billion just a year later.[285] An even bigger game-changer came when the U.S. Drug Enforcement Agency relaxed requirements for prescribing controlled substances due to the COVID-19 pandemic. Cerebral and other online mental health companies quickly shifted gears to prescribing medications previously available only through a face-to-face clinical visit, including stimulant medications for attention deficit hyperactivity disorder (ADHD). Not only did the number of controlled substances prescribed skyrocket, but patients with contraindicating medical conditions and medications were put at risk for dangerous drug interactions, addiction, and death.[283]

While patients with true ADHD may benefit from increased access to stimulant drugs, others face serious harm. Many ADHD medications are controlled for a reason: They carry the risk of misuse and addiction, may cause adverse effects in patients with cardiovascular disease, and can induce panic attacks and psychosis in vulnerable patients. The real winners in these 'pay for prescription' schemes are not patients, but private equity investors, who have been raking in the cash. For example, mental telehealth company Done reported earnings of more than $3 million per month from prescriptions for Adderall and other psychiatric medications.[286]

Done's model offers quick ADHD assessments and 24/7 online support for an initial fee of $199 and then $79 per month. According to its website, it's as easy as 1-2-3:

1. *1-minute assessment—take an online clinical assessment to see if Done can help*
2. *30-minute appointment—available the same day, or as soon as the next day, with one of our licensed ADHD clinicians*
3. *Get ongoing care at ease—enjoy online visits, worry-free refills, 24/7 care with clinicians and care team.*[287]

Despite concerns that abbreviated visits could lead to improper diagnoses and prescribing, other for-profit companies jumped on the mental telehealth bandwagon, including Minded, Lemonaid, and For Hers, which offers the simplest prescription option: text messaging. For $85 per month, patients log onto the website and answer a questionnaire that 'matches' them with a prescriber for 'messaging-only consults.' The service promises that patients will be connected with a provider in 24–48 hours, with unlimited online check-ins and dosage adjustments. Once prescribed, medications are shipped directly to the patient.[288]

Virtual mental health companies aggressively market the ease and convenience of online mental health treatment. They promote a message of care and concern by their clinicians, as compared to physicians, who they say are rushed, don't listen, and don't care. One Facebook advertisement for Cerebral reads:

> At Cerebral you will NOT talk to:
> - Doctors who don't have time to listen.
> - Doctors who write a prescription and say goodbye.
> - Doctors who aren't interested in you and your story.
> - Doctors who talk at you instead of to you.
>
> Get care from people who care. Cerebral offers prescription anxiety meds, ongoing care and someone to talk to. To do our part during quarantine, we are offering your first month for just $45.[289]

In the comments, prospective patients asked questions about the model. Responding to the question of whether patients would be paired with a physician, Cerebral was adamant that a psychiatrist would directly oversee all care:

> Our providers are all board-certified psychiatrist physicians, physician assistants and nurse practitioners. They have all done extensive training to be able to prescribe medication and all of our non-psychiatrist providers are directly overseen by our psychiatrists.

However, the staff listing of 'prescribers' on Cerebral's website includes nearly 1,400 nurse practitioners and just five physicians (four psychiatrists and an internal medicine physician).[290]

Other commenters on the Facebook post inquired about specific medical concerns. Valarie asked, "I'm currently on Cymbalta, Klonopin, propranolol, Xanax as needed, and Ambien. Would you be able to help someone like me?"

Cerebral's response: "Messaged!"

Veronica wrote, "I am currently on Xanax for my high social anxiety and Ambien for insomnia. Would your doctors be able to help me?"

Cerebral: "Messaged!"

Steven wrote, "Can I please get Xanax 2 milligram so I can dose with 0.5–1 mg as needed? I don't appreciate the other doctors saying that they don't want it out there for abuse. Or I'm going to start using it a lot recklessly. I just want relief and not to have to purchase fake Xanax."

Cerebral responded,

> Hi Steven. We can prescribe Xanax and we leave that to the discretion of our providers. If you are already prescribed controlled substances, you must show proof during your provider visit of a past prescription within the last six months for your prescriber to consider immediately including it in your medication plan.[289]

PILL MILLS

Benzodiazepine medications like Xanax (alprazolam) may be used for the short-term relief of anxiety, but are generally not recommended for long-term use, due to the risk of addiction. For this reason, the drug class is categorized as a controlled substance, and clinicians are cautioned to follow strict medical standards when prescribing. While some patients may like the way they feel when they take medications like Xanax, there are often better and safer choices to treat anxiety.

While the need for expanded mental health services is without question, substituting lesser-trained clinicians and failing to follow medical standards puts patients at risk. Private equity corporations, accountable first and foremost to shareholders, face an inherent conflict of interest between profit and patient care. In a worst-case scenario, the corporation may incentivize or even require clinicians to provide unnecessary medications to increase profits.

How does this play out concretely? If a startup retains more customers by prescribing feel-good pills, even if they are dangerous to the patient, then they are financially incentivized to do whatever they can to prescribe more of those pills and keep more patients/customers. That incentivization can manifest as pressure on doctors or non-physician practitioners to prescribe up to quotas, or may lead to the firing of those who don't prescribe in ways that maximize profit.

This seems to have happened at companies like Cerebral and Done, with reports of serious deficits in patient care. An investigation into the company Cerebral revealed over 2,000 incident reports from employees citing misdiagnoses and dangerous prescribing practices. Nurse practitioners complained that 30 minutes for new patients and 15 minutes for follow-ups were inadequate. Care coordinators reported feeling improperly trained to manage suicidal patients. Multiple reports documented a failure of prescribers to check state-controlled substance databases, resulting in patients being prescribed multiple overlapping addictive medications. A Cerebral psychiatrist reported that nurse practitioners were inappropriately treating patients with severe mental illness, including schizophrenia and bipolar disorder.[291]

For example, 30-year-old Jeneesa Barnes was treated by several nurse practitioners through Cerebral. At her initial eighteen-minute video consult, Barnes was diagnosed with bipolar disorder and prescribed a five-month supply of antipsychotic medication. She followed up four times with various nurse practitioners over the next three months, and received five additional medication prescriptions: three antidepressants, an anticonvulsant mood stabilizer, and an antipsychotic. As her mental state acutely declined and she began to develop suicidal thinking, Barnes checked herself into an inpatient facility, where she was stabilized and referred to an in-person psychiatrist.[292]

The company was also accused of pressuring nurse practitioners to prescribe medications quickly, including controlled substances. Nurses were paid to refill medications like Adderall between appointments. At one point, more than 13,000 controlled medications were being prescribed per week. Employees of Cerebral say they were pressured to prescribe exactly what patients asked for as quickly as possible. Nurse practitioner Angela Rasheed, who worked at Cerebral for nearly a year, compared the model to a fast-food restaurant, saying that she was assigned thirty patients a day and pressured to prescribe medications despite short patient visits that she felt were inadequate to make a correct diagnosis.[293]

According to a lawsuit by former Cerebral executive Matthew Truebe, who claimed that he was fired for complaining about the high volume of ADHD medications being prescribed, the company "egregiously put profits and growth before patient safety." He also cited concerns about data security and failure to address safety issues such as drug overdose or suicidal thinking.[294] While the company uses a messaging app to communicate patient concerns to a clinician, insiders reported that messages were often assigned to staff members with minimal training in addressing psychiatric symptoms. Melissa Butorac, a former client-coach with Cerebral, described the system as chaotic and dangerous, and expressed serious concerns about patients with suicidal ideations.[293]

The company Done also churned out medication prescriptions, especially after November 2020, when the company stopped requiring patients to have a monthly phone or video appointment with a clinician. Instead, patients were allowed to simply fill out an online form for a medication refill or to request a dose adjustment. Nurse practitioners were expected to write prescriptions on demand, a policy that Done clinical president David Brody called the company's 'patient-first philosophy.' Paid $10 per prescription, nurse practitioners reported earning as much as $20,000 per month simply renewing medications.[295]

Some physicians believe that companies like Cerebral and Done were primarily motivated by the opportunity for profit with limited regulatory oversight in the emerging telehealth marketplace. Natalie Newman wrote, "In my opinion, Cerebral was never about the care; it was about the potential to profit. When profits were threatened because of decreasing subscriptions to Cerebral, a decision was made to target patients with ADHD to prescribe more stimulants such as Adderall. Medical standards were tossed to the wayside."[296]

Focusing on mental health services "made it easier to take advantage of a population that is inherently vulnerable to begin with," said Newman, who pointed out that "the discipline and practice of medicine are tightly regulated for good reason because the health and safety of the public are paramount." She noted that the COVID-19 pandemic opened the door for a decline in medical standards, and private equity companies were eager to take advantage. "Regulations designed to keep the public safe were lifted by the government so that patients could have access to medications previously unattainable online."

According to Newman, this practice led to a dangerous increase in the use of controlled medications. "It does not take a rocket scientist to understand that in a country rife with substance abuse, the now easy access to these drugs would inevitably lead to a snowballing of prescriptions, and revenue for Cerebral would explode. That is exactly what occurred, with Cerebral's worth reaching 4.8 billion dollars."

Supervision in-name-only

To cope with the growing demand for medication prescriptions, Cerebral hired recruiters to find and onboard new nurse practitioners quickly. Since some state laws prohibit the independent practice of medicine by a nurse practitioner, the company recruited physicians to oversee up to 75 to 100 nurse practitioners at a time, depending on state law. (While some states restrict the number of nurse practitioners that can be supervised by a physician, others have no specific ratio).[293] Physicians have reported numerous solicitations from Cerebral, with one physician receiving seven email messages from various Cerebral recruiters in six months. One email read:

> SUBJECT: Dr., Join Cerebral!
>
> Hello, Dr.,
>
> I came across your profile online and wanted to invite you to apply for a remote position with Cerebral. We are looking for remote Physicians who

will support our Nurse Practitioners as part of a Collaborative Agreement. Our physicians must be board certified.

A bit about us, Cerebral is a telemedicine platform offering mental health care to all that need it. We are breaking down barriers to access, reducing wait times and eliminating stigma. Most important is our client outcomes are well above industry standards! Join our mission to transform access to high quality long term mental health care.[296]

An advertisement for the role of Cerebral physician supervisor on the job search site *Indeed* read in part:

The Ideal Candidate Should Be:

- Flexible
- Patient Centric
- Self-motivated
- Energetic
- Vigilant
- Professional
- Technologically Savvy
- Comfortable working remotely in a virtual team setting
- Please ensure that you can supervise 4 Nurse Practitioners

Minimum Qualifications: Current/active MD/DO license (multiple state licensure strongly preferred) PSYCHIATRY PREFERRED/not required.

- Active licenses must be in good standing
- Strong clinical background (Family medicine, Integrative medicine, and Mental health experience preferred; 2+ years minimum experience)
- Active DEA License
- National Board Certification Two-years as a Physician
- Ability to understand and navigate Google Apps, Slack, and EMR[296]

With physicians supervising nurse practitioners in various states, the lines of responsibility have become blurred. For example, psychiatrist Michael Boggs, the director of clinical safety for Cerebral, insisted that he was not the supervising physician for the nurse practitioner who treated Anthony Kroll, the 17-year-old who died by suicide. While Boggs's name was listed on Anthony's bottle of fluoxetine, the psychiatrist said that he was not involved with Anthony's care, writing in an email, "If my name was on a prescription bottle for a patient in Missouri, it should not have been." According to reports, Boggs was the supervising physician for nurse practitioners in Illinois and Oklahoma, but not in Missouri, and that a different Missouri-licensed physician was supervising the nurse practitioner in that state. Cerebral acknowledged this and stated that software issues caused the misidentification of the patient's medication bottle.[282]

Natalie Newman warns her colleagues to avoid this type of work. "Take note—psychiatry is 'preferred but not required,'" she says. "One physician to 4 nurse practitioners who are not directly supervised. This is not a job opportunity. It is a disaster waiting to happen." Newman urges physicians to reject participating in the corporate practice of medicine. "Physicians have got to stop allowing companies like this to use and abuse our medical licenses."[296]

PROFITING FROM THE ONLINE TREATMENT OF ADDICTION

Certain medications are controlled substances because they have the potential to cause addiction, and patients need to be informed about both risks and benefits. For example, people with a history of addiction issues may be at risk for relapse. Patients need to be monitored carefully for side effects, and clinicians must do their best to avoid prescribing to patients who are using the drugs for non-therapeutic reasons.

While the liberal prescribing of amphetamines like Adderall is a brewing problem, America continues to suffer the consequences of years of overprescribed opioids, a crisis caused in part by the same 'patient-first' philosophy espoused by Done president David Brody regarding ADHD treatment with stimulants. In the early 2000s, physicians were encouraged to treat pain as the '5th vital sign,' and the risks and danger to patients were downplayed. Following this liberal prescribing of opioids, many patients became addicted, with some turning to illegal sources, including heroin and fentanyl.

Opioids can be very difficult to stop using because of the physical and psychological effects, including tolerance and dependence, as well as the discomfort associated with stopping them. Medication-assisted addiction treatment, most commonly buprenorphine/naloxone (Suboxone), can be prescribed to decrease the symptoms of withdrawal and block the urge to continue to abuse these drugs. However, since buprenorphine is a partial opiate itself, prescribers must exercise caution. The medication should not be mixed with other opioid drugs or sedating medications like benzodiazepines, as the combination can cause a person to stop breathing and die. Certain other medications taken with Suboxone can increase or decrease the amount in a person's system, and clinicians must be aware of these factors. For this reason, drug testing is routinely ordered to monitor compliance with treatment and to ensure the absence of other drugs that the patient may be taking illicitly.

The Drug Addiction Treatment Act of 2000 allows physicians to prescribe buprenorphine to up to 30 patients (or as many as 100 with additional requirements) outside of substance treatment centers. Doctors who treat 100 patients may apply to increase the limit to 275 after a year of practice. Due to the need for more access to medication-assisted therapy for opioid use disorder, the Drug Enforcement Agency (DEA) expanded prescribing rights to nurse practitioners and physician assistants in 2016.[297] On March 31, 2020, in response to the public health emergency caused by COVID-19, the DEA eased prescribing restrictions for Suboxone, temporarily removing the face-to-face visit requirement and allowing clinicians to prescribe medication by telephone.

Enter private equity once again. In 2021, addiction telemedicine startups offering online prescribing of buprenorphine began to flourish. Bicycle Health, Boulder Care, Groups Recover Together, Ophelia, and Wayspring raised large amounts of capital from investors, with Quit Genius raising $64 million[298] and Workit Health $140 million. By the following year, Workit Health had provided treatment to more than 20,000 patients and was valued at $500 million.[291] The model works similarly to that of companies like Cerebral and Done. For example, Ophelia, which is staffed by 18 nurse practitioners and physician assistants, but just two physicians, offers memberships for $195 per month. The program includes video visits with "a prescribing clinician, a nurse, and a care coordinator" and promises "you'll be able to pick up your first Suboxone prescription the same day as your initial visit."[299]

Important questions include whether these shortcuts to medical standards are safe and whether monitoring of virtual addiction treatment services is being adequately performed to ensure patient safety. For example, telehealth programs arrange for drug testing by mailing out drug tests, which patients self-administer. Workit Health notes that the tests are proctored by video or photographic evidence:

> If you use video drug testing, you'll use the Workit app to ... show your counselor the sealed, new test on camera, and then go off-camera to a private space to collect your sample. Then you'll get back on camera to review your results with your counselor.
>
> If you use automated drug testing, you'll use the Workit app ... You'll be prompted to prepare your testing materials, label them properly, take the test, and clearly photograph the results. Because there will not be a counselor on the line with you, there is a time limit for photographing the results, and you will also need to take a photo of yourself with the completed test afterward.[300]

Nurse practitioners and physician assistants are increasingly providing addiction services, with the number of buprenorphine waivers steadily increasing, especially in rural areas.[301] Yet, there is little data to show whether this practice is safe, especially when performed via telehealth. Information regarding the preparation of nurse practitioners to manage addiction problems is limited, but a 2020 review on buprenorphine found that nurse practitioner programs rarely provide training on opioid use disorder within their core curriculum.[302]

Nurse practitioners interested in learning more about treating patients with addiction are encouraged to take online courses, such as one offered by the *Elite Nurse Practitioner*. Course creator Justin Allan promises that in only 3 hours, "this course will teach the nurse practitioner who has ZERO experience with opioid addiction treatment on how to practice this niche service." Further, he notes that any nurse practitioner can offer addiction care, stating, "You do not have to be psych certified to practice this niche service line. Anyone from a [family nurse practitioner], [acute care nurse practitioner], to a [psychiatric mental health nurse practitioner] can do this!" Allan points out that starting an addiction clinic is "very simple and cheap to start. All it takes from you is the courage, focus, and dedication to take action and get started."[303]

Academic nurse practitioners disagree with this message, writing in an article that "care for the patient with [opioid use disorder] is complex and carries significant risk to patient safety. The patient in withdrawal is visibly ill, which could be intimidating for a novice provider, and many times, the patient has biopsychosocial factors that can complicate the treatment process."[302]

Unfortunately, the divergence between academic recommendations and real-life treatment of addiction may result in patient harm. For example, emergency physician Seth Aron described a patient he recently treated. "The patient had just discontinued long-term alcohol use, and was developing withdrawal symptoms, including a rapid heart rate." Rather than appropriately using a well-established standard therapy protocol for alcohol withdrawal using a benzodiazepine drug, a nurse practitioner treated the patient's rapid heart rate with propranolol, a beta-blocker. While this medication does indeed slow the heart rate, it does not treat the underlying cause of the symptom: alcohol withdrawal. Still experiencing withdrawal symptoms, including severe anxiety, the patient went to an urgent care center, where a physician assistant started him on buspirone, an anti-anxiety medicine that is also ineffective in treating withdrawal. Without correct treatment, the patient progressed into a more dangerous stage of alcohol withdrawal called delirium tremens. He began to hallucinate that he was being chased, and when police found him running wildly, they took him to jail.

Finally, the patient was brought to the emergency department, where Aron properly diagnosed him and started the correct treatment. Identifying and treating withdrawal correctly is essential, Aron said, because patients can die without proper treatment.[304] Before the development of standard therapy to treat alcohol withdrawal, delirium tremens carried a 37 percent mortality rate, which is lowered to 5 percent with correct treatment.[305] Aron worries that with an increase in untrained practitioners treating these patients, the death rate for alcohol withdrawal will return to early 20th century levels.

THE OPIOID CRISIS

One undeniable fact is that the U.S. desperately needs more treatment options for opioid addiction. One reason is the liberal prescribing of pain medications by unethical practitioners, which includes physicians, nurse practitioners, and physician assistants. While some physicians are guilty of overprescribing, studies show that nurse practitioners and physician assistants are more likely to prescribe opioids, and have more outliers that prescribe at higher doses and frequency.

For example, a database review in Oregon found that patients of nurse practitioners and naturopaths received more high-risk opioid prescriptions and had more hospitalizations related to opioids than patients of physicians.[306] (Oregon is one of several states that allows naturopaths to prescribe medications.) A 2019 study showed more opioid prescribing by nurse practitioners and physician assistants than by physicians, especially at higher dosing levels.[133] This was again demonstrated in a 2020 study that showed that 8% of nurse practitioners and 9.8% of physician assistants overprescribed opioids, compared to 3.8% of physicians. Nurse practitioners and physician assistants were more likely to prescribe an opioid to 50% or more of their patients (6.3% of NPs and 8.8% of PAs, compared with 1.3% of physicians). Nurse practitioners and physician assistants in states allowing more prescribing autonomy were greater than twenty times more likely to overprescribe than those in states with more restrictions.[307]

Several factors have contributed to increased prescribing by non-physicians, including targeting by opioid makers. In 2019, the state of Tennessee accused opioid manufacturers Endo, the maker of Opana, and Purdue Pharma, the maker of OxyContin, of targeting high-volume prescribers, including nurse practitioners and physician assistants, "who generally had less expertise in pain management and were more receptive to marketing from sales consultants."[308]

Another factor involved in the increase in prescribing by nurse practitioners involves slow action by state Boards of Nursing. For example, the Tennessee Board of Nursing allowed nurse practitioner Christina Collins to continue to practice even after state attorneys recommended that her license be revoked.[309] Collins, one of Tennessee's top opioid prescribers, was accused of prescribing massive amounts of controlled substances in 2012. According to news reports, Collins defended herself to the board by pleading ignorance, arguing that she was simply refilling prescriptions and that she later learned that the doses were too high. In 2018, state attorneys accused the nursing board of making an error in allowing Collins to keep her license and asked the court to order the nursing board to reconsider the case.[310]

In 2019, Pittsburgh nurse practitioner Larry Goisse, the owner of Prime Psychiatric Care, was charged with illegally prescribing narcotics despite having a suspended nursing license. Former employees of Goisse expressed frustration with delays in action by the Board of Nursing, including nurse practitioner Jacob Corbin, who initially reported Goisse. Corbin said that he received an email that it would take 9–12 months for the state to investigate his concerns.[311]

In 2020, Alaska nurse practitioner Kris Kile was indicted on 18 felony counts after one of her patients overdosed on opioids. News reports stated that the victim's mother had to push for an investigation into Kile's practices and that it took years before she was arrested. The family is now advocating for legislative changes to increase action against unscrupulous nurse practitioners.[312]

One of the differences between physicians and nurse practitioners is that state Boards of Medicine regulate physicians, while in most states nurse practitioners are regulated by a state Board of Nursing. This distinction is important because while nurse practitioners are being permitted to practice in the same capacity as physicians—ordering and interpreting tests, making medical diagnoses, and writing prescriptions for medications, they are being overseen by a regulatory body that includes nurses without experience in that role.

The "Rock Doc" NP

Consider the case of nurse practitioner and self-proclaimed 'Rock Doc,' Jeffrey Young, who was under investigation by the Tennessee Board of Nursing for 5 years, during which time he prescribed over 1.4 million opioid pills. Young was finally stopped not by the Board of Nursing, but through the efforts of the Department of Justice, which urged the court to strip his prescribing privileges. The DOJ argued, "the Court should do what the Board did not: stop Young from further harming the community by prescribing dangerous substances and exploiting his patients in the process." The prosecutor further told the court, "By the end of this hearing, you will be asking what on earth took the Board so long?"[313]

'Rock Doc' Jeffrey Young became known nationally from a pilot reality television show in which he was portrayed as "a medical bad boy who's willing to break free from the establishment to deliver real talk." The show featured after-hours drinking, a rock-and-roll soundtrack, and the occasional obscenity.[314] Young's work-hard, play-hard persona and tattooed, leather-clad aesthetic gained him a strong patient following in the Jackson, Tennessee area, where many patients liked his relatable, down-to-earth approach. When Young started his own practice called PreventaGenix in 2014, he was perceived as providing affordable, quality medical care. Patients appreciated that he "took pain seriously," and wasn't afraid to prescribe opioid medications.[314]

It wasn't long before Young's liberal opioid prescribing and hard-living lifestyle began to affect his medical practice. As word spread about his prescribing habits, patients wanting pain medication increasingly sought his care, and Young was eventually treating 50–85 patients per day. Some of these patients entered through the back door, where Young would trade opioid prescriptions for sex. Young's behavior became increasingly erratic, and he began to show up late to work, sometimes arriving intoxicated.

Complaints about Young began to pile up at Tennessee's health department as far back as 2012, including accusations that Young had been supplying high school boys with testosterone to 'bulk up.' In 2013, Young was accused of overprescribing the stimulant Adderall to a patient with undiagnosed and untreated hypertension who subsequently died of a stroke. In 2015, reports claimed that a patient died of a drug overdose when Young prescribed the pain medications oxycodone and hydrocodone, as well as the sedative Valium—without performing an examination.

In November 2016, the health department threatened to file charges and asked Young to surrender his license, which he declined to do. By then, the Tennessee Board of Nursing had opened an investigation that would continue for four years, stymied by slow-moving bureaucracy. At the same time, the Tennessee Bureau of Investigation began to evaluate complaints that Young was overprescribing opioids. In 2017, the DEA raided Young's clinic, seizing about 10,000 individual doses of hydrocodone. Despite these actions, Young's nursing license remained active and unrestricted.

PreventaGenix closed soon after the DEA raid, but Young quickly opened a new clinic called GeneXis Health where he continued to prescribe drugs for two years. According to reports, Young would sometimes treat over 50 patients per day. Complaints of inappropriate sexual behavior with patients continued, and the health department sent him a letter of warning about this activity without any specific disciplinary action in March 2019. Meanwhile, the Board of Nursing continued its inquiry, assigning investigator Shirley Pickering. During her investigation, Pickering reported feeling afraid of Young after experiencing harassing phone calls with strange whispers, her car doors being opened overnight, and a person running across her yard into the woods.

It wasn't until 2018 that the Board completed its evaluation, concluding that from August 2013 to November 2016, Young prescribed controlled substances in amounts and for durations that "were not medically necessary, advisable, or justified for a diagnosed condition." In a settlement with the board, Young received a 2-year nursing license probation, during which time he could not prescribe certain Schedule II or Schedule III controlled substances, including drugs such as oxycodone and Adderall. He would still be allowed to prescribe certain weaker controlled medications and would be eligible to have full prescribing privileges reinstated in 2020, as long as he agreed to extra monitoring.

But in April 2019, Young was caught up in a sting operation in which undercover officers posed as patients asking for drugs. He was arrested and indicted for prescribing controlled substances to patients "to obtain money, notoriety, and sexual favors."[315] When Young was released on bond, he continued to prescribe benzodiazepines Xanax and Valium, addictive sedatives, as was allowed by his nursing license settlement. Due to this ongoing prescribing of controlled substances, prosecuting attorneys with the Department of Justice urged the Court to revoke Young's bond and detain him pending trial, which the judge granted. Young remained detained to face trial on 15 counts including drug conspiracy, maintaining drug-involved premises, and unlawfully dispensing controlled substances, with his case delayed to 2023.

Differences between medical and nursing boards

Teresa Camp-Rogers, MD, MS is an emergency physician and hospital Chief Quality Officer who has studied the differences between disciplinary hearings for nurse practitioners and physicians. In a *Patients at Risk* podcast, she explained that while press coverage of the Young case has been extensive, one critical point has been missed: "This story could not have happened with a physician, because if this had been a physician, they would be investigated by the Board of Medicine and held to medical standards."[316]

During her review of disciplinary hearings from nursing and medical boards, Camp-Rogers found it easy to see a distinct difference in process and accountability. "Things like this will, unfortunately, happen with physicians. That's the first thing to come to terms with when we see this happen with a nurse practitioner. We're not saying, this would never happen with [a physician]. We're saying that if it happens to a physician, when the physician comes before the medical board, the processes are robust, they are swift, and they are non-negotiable."

Finding the gaps in regulatory compliance is critical, says Camp-Rogers, who believes that nursing boards need to upgrade their processes to prevent bad actors from continuing to practice. She notes that in the early 1990s, the Department of Health and Human Services and the Office of the Inspector General critically examined state medical boards to determine the total number of alleged violations, how long it took for a case to be closed, and types of disciplinary action given. The agencies issued guidelines that medical boards must follow to ensure that physicians are properly disciplined.[317]

Camp-Rogers says that nursing boards should be held to these same standards. "Go to your state's Board of Medicine website and look through the disciplinary summaries—they are so detailed and so patient-centered," she said. "When there's a medical practice concern, the Board takes their time and goes line by line." Further, Camp-Rogers noted that conclusions about medical acts are determined by a board of people who are trained in medicine, not nursing. While most medical boards may include several public members, most board members are licensed physicians. Nursing boards, by contrast, include licensed practical nurse and registered nurse members, who are not trained to assess quality standards for nurse practitioners acting in a provider role.

In most states, the disciplinary hearings of physicians are public. "The intensity of questioning is objective evidence that the medical boards take their job very seriously," Camp-Rogers said, noting that nursing board reports don't show the same degree of careful oversight. "I have looked, and I cannot find the same objective evidence that nurse practitioners are interrogated to the same degree." Camp-Rogers encourages skeptics to review Board of Nursing reports. "You can judge by the type of consequences, like the disciplinary actions. I just don't see the same thing when I compare the two." Camp-Rogers believes that improving quality processes for nursing boards will serve to promote the nurse practitioner profession, not bring it down. "Shying away from these discussions or vilifying those that promote them only creates a culture of silence," she said.[316]

It is also critical that patients know how to access nursing boards to register complaints. After Betty Wattenbarger died, her father Jeremy sought answers regarding care provided by a nurse practitioner working alone at an urgent care, but was given a runaround. In a podcast episode, Jeremy explained his efforts, noting that when he attempted to contact the Texas Health and Human Services Department, he had no response. "I had to call Washington DC because I couldn't get anyone in the state of Texas to answer." Once an ombudsman was assigned to investigate, Jeremy's complaint was rejected. "They said, 'no, we can't do anything with it,' and advised me to file a consumer complaint." But when he filed a consumer complaint, he was told, "This is a medical issue, not a consumer issue."[12]

Jeremy said that his complaints to the Texas Board of Nursing were repeatedly rejected. "You see, you constantly run into this back and forth with the nursing board when you file a complaint." For example, when he reported that staff was not wearing identification badges, he says the nursing board told him he had to prove it. "Well, I'm sorry, but I don't have a picture of her not wearing her name badge. They never believe the person at the other end; they always believe the nurse, and that's where you get stuck."

The family sought help from their state Senator. "A staff member told me how to submit it in a certain manner and way, and it was like mojo magic; all of a sudden, the nursing board began doing their first investigation," said Jeremy. The Texas Board of Nursing concluded that nurse practitioner Madeline Broemson's care did not meet nursing standards, and disciplined her with three years of probation and mandatory remedial coursework. According to Jeremy, the nurse practitioner's sanction related to her documentation of vital signs, rather than medical mismanagement.

Amy Townsend shared her own hurdles to report concerns about a nurse practitioner. "Even as a physician, it was very difficult to find the right avenues of exactly where to send the complaint. If the complaint happened to end up in the wrong person's hands, there was no assistance in redirecting [to the right person]. It was really just trial and error and trying over and over and over again."[12]

Regarding holding nurses accountable for medical mismanagement, Townsend noted the challenges with overseeing the practice of nursing as opposed to the practice of medicine. "The big issue here is, what is the standard of care for the profession? Essentially nurse practitioners are practicing medicine, yet they are responsible to the nursing board, not the medical board, so they're not held to a medical standard of care." Townsend said that nursing boards evaluate nursing tasks, not medical judgment. "That's what makes it very difficult to hold people accountable. In these situations, you have nurses that are practicing medicine, but only held accountable to nursing standards."

In addition, many nursing boards are chronically underfunded and understaffed, making it difficult to regulate nurse practitioners promptly.[318] In 2019, Carol Moreland, RN, the executive administrator for the Kansas State Board of Nursing opposed a bill allowing the independent practice of nurse practitioners in the state, in part for this very reason. "Revising and implementing significant APRN regulations will, quite frankly, overwhelm an already stretched agency," she testified, noting that the Board would struggle to absorb the financial implications of the change. "Cutting either services or personnel impacts negatively on our mission of public safety.[319] Nonetheless, on April 22, 2022, Kansas Governor Laura Kelly signed independent nurse practice into law.

Similarly, the state of California legalized independent practice for nurse practitioners despite concerns from an already strained Board of Nursing, which faced allegations of delayed investigations and falsified documents. In a discussion on the legislative battle in the state, Natalie Newman points out that ironically, the nursing board was the only nursing association that opposed the law change. "They didn't want to supervise nurse practitioners because they could not manage the volume." Newman says their concerns were dismissed. "They were forced to do it anyway."[320]

BEING NICE IS NOT ENOUGH

Jeffrey Young's patients said they loved the nurse practitioner because he made them "feel comfortable" and "took their pain seriously." In fact, many advocates for non-physician practitioners allude to what they describe as 'more holistic' care, noting that nurses are good listeners and care about their patients. While these qualities are essential, good intentions are not enough. Without thorough medical training and standards for proper care, patients are placed at risk. Bob Pegritz, a former physician assistant and malpractice expert witness says that it's important for patients to distinguish between 'nice' and competent. "When I'm talking about the importance of physician-led care, a lot of times what I hear is, well, patients prefer nurse practitioners and physician assistants because they listen, and because they're nice. It's really good and helpful to be nice and to listen, but first and foremost, there must be a certain level of skill and knowledge."[298]

For example, nurse practitioner Jessica Spayd, owner of Eagle River Wellness in Alaska, advertised that her clinic was founded "to increase access to quality pain management for the chronic pain patient using the holistic approach" and emphasized a "working partnership between patient and provider ... to meet the individual's needs." Her holistic approach to care without proper training was not enough to keep patients safe. In 2019, Spayd was charged with the deaths of three patients due to opioid overdose, with an additional 20 deaths under investigation. According to reports, Spayd prescribed potentially lethal doses of opioids to over 450 patients over 18 years.[321]

Patients decried the loss of access to Michigan nurse practitioner Sue Drust when she was suspended for six months in 2019 after the deaths of two patients due to drug overdose. Patient Bonnie Drier told reporters, "I don't understand it because she was forthright, and she was always there when I needed her."[322] Although Drust was one of the highest prescribers of controlled substances in Michigan in 2017 and 2018, she did not have the education to do so, and indeed responded to complaints by pleading ignorance about these medications. She claimed that she was, "not familiar with what controlled substances are abused and diverted," and that she "only recently understood" that one dose of pain medication is not equivalent to the same dose as a different one, acknowledging that she "was not as educated as she could have been."[323] It is for this reason that the public needs to understand that the conflation of niceness with expertise is dangerous.

Lack of knowledge is compounded when clinicians are focused on maximizing personal profit over patient care. Nurse practitioner Julie Anne DeMille worked at a county health department in Portland, OR. To supplement her income, she also worked at Fusion Wellness Clinic, where she prescribed opioids to patients who were known drug addicts. The clinic was located across the street from the county parole and probation office, and DeMille's business partner recruited patients from Narcotics Anonymous meetings. The pair charged patients $200 per visit, earning about $400,000 in 2015 from the illicit practice. DeMille was ultimately sentenced to four years in jail, becoming the first medical professional in Oregon to face federal charges for illegal opioid prescribing. According to prosecutors, Oregon was an attractive place for the nurse practitioner to work due to a lack of required physician supervision.[324]

While most non-physician practitioners are not ill-intentioned, there has been a surge in those seeking profit-based practices. Nurse practitioners and physician assistants are increasingly turning away from conventional medical practice and towards alternates, especially the cash-based practice.

CHAPTER 10

NON-PHYSICIANS AND THE CASH-BASED PRACTICE

Despite promises from independent practice advocates that nurse practitioners and physician assistants would fill the gap for primary care and underserved patients, most non-physicians are not choosing to work in these fields. The number of nurse practitioners entering primary care has declined by 40% since 2004,[325] and while the American Association of Nurse Practitioners reports that 78 percent of nurse practitioners are primary care-prepared,[326] only 48 percent of nurse practitioners practiced in primary care in 2012.[327] The situation is worse in underserved states like Oregon, where just 25% of nurse practitioners work in primary care, despite being legally allowed to work in the field independently.[328] Few physician assistants choose primary care, with just 34 percent working in family medicine, general internal medicine, or general pediatrics in 2012.[329]

Instead of choosing primary care or underserved work, some non-physicians are choosing to open practices offering exclusively cash-based services like botox injections and vitamin infusions. Registered nurse Rayne Thoman has studied this phenomenon. "There are all sorts of groups devoted to side hustles, nurse business[es] and 'elite nurse practitioner' groups," she said. "They're encouraging one another to do this. To me, that's more alarming than anything because they're teaching each other. This is not what health care is."[151] So many non-physicians are seeking this kind of work that websites are popping up to teach them how to start their own cash-based practice. One of the most interesting examples is "The Elite Nur$e Practitioner"—and no, the dollar sign is not a typo.

THE ELITE NURSE PRACTITIONER (ELITE NP)

Family nurse practitioner Justin Allan created the 'Elite NP' model in 2019. On his website, Allan explains that after spending eight years as a nurse practitioner in multiple settings, including urgent care, emergency medicine, addiction medicine, and family practice, he decided to 'break free' from the system and open his own practice. Having increased his income to over $450K a year over a three year span, Allan promises to teach other nurse practitioners how to follow in his footsteps, offering dozens of courses on various aspects of medical practice. "I spent hundreds of hours and thousands of dollars becoming an expert in the clinical and business aspects of starting my own practice," he writes. "I've taken all that experience and knowledge and put it into these courses. My mission is to help create a group of nurse practitioners that are wealthy, powerful, and professionally fulfilled."[330]

The principles of the Elite Nurse Practitioner model include having multiple streams of income so that you can leave a job at any time. A major advantage, according to Allan's website: "You don't have to put up with 'collaborating' physician bullshit. They don't control your life; you can give them the finger because you have 3–4 other income streams!" Thanks to this increased revenue, he claims nurse practitioners can retire earlier than physicians. "Let the physicians work until they are 70 years old," writes Allan. "I plan on being done around 50 and enjoying a simple stress-free life."

Allan says that nurse practitioners must own their own businesses, due to market saturation as "nurse practitioner programs continue to pump out" graduates, which he says will lead to decreased income. "I know COUNTLESS nurse practitioner graduates who cannot find a job or can make just as much, if not more, working as a registered nurse," he writes. "Our market is saturated, and it will only continue to get worse ... You must mitigate this future risk by starting your own business."[331]

Allan makes no secret of his goal to help nurse practitioners earn money, using symbols like images of Benjamin Franklin on the $100 bill throughout the website. The key, according to Allan, is to offer services that are not covered by insurance: "If the service you provide is not covered by Medicare, then you can charge the patient cash." He provides the link to Medicare coverage rules and recommends sticking with services that Medicare never pays for, like medical marijuana, aesthetics, and stem cell injections. "When you are a cash practice, you do not have to follow insurance protocols and guidelines. You do as you wish within reason." Allan also dissuades nurse practitioners from entering primary care. "If you want headaches, high expenses, long hours, and little return, look into general primary care," he says. "On the other hand, if your goal is professional and financial independence, seriously consider this niche service line" of providing cash-based treatments.[330]

Allan emphasizes the practicality of his approach, writing, "This is not a care bear blog filled with a bunch of non-sense [sic] nursing theory, non-practical BS advice from educators and administrators, and how to get in touch with your inner being. This is a blog for those nurse practitioners out there that want to take control of their lives and have professional FREEDOM through practical real world actionable advice and content." This includes freedom from physician supervision: "No more physicians dictating your life: telling you how to practice, offloading all the work they don't want to do onto you, being an asshole to you for no reason and treating you like you are an inferior medical provider."

Allan calls physicians sharks who take advantage of nurse practitioners. "They lobby and lobby and lobby, preventing nurse practitioner independent practice from passing because they LOVE the easy money that comes off our backs," he writes, describing a previous physician who charged him $3,000 per month for supervision. "Oh bologna … There was no supervision going on. I called her ONE time in 2 years; that is it. She made $60,000 for practically doing nothing over the span of 2 years. Do you think this physician wants to give up that gravy train? Absolutely not, I wouldn't either. Hell, you could supervise 3–4 nurse practitioners and pay off your mortgage in 2 years."[332]

While some physicians charge more, a 2019 survey found that the median monthly physician supervision fee was $500.[333] *Collaborating Docs*, a company created by family physician Annie DePasquale, MD in 2020 estimates the average physician supervision fee at $750 per month, which includes physician availability during business hours for questions, a 10% chart review, a monthly check-in video call, as well as fulfilling "any other state-specific requirements."[334]

Justin Allan recommends that nurse practitioners requiring supervision by state law search for just the right physician to meet their needs. In a since-edited post, Allan advises:

> If you cannot find one, keep looking. There are plenty of physicians out there that have restrictions on their license, or who have been in trouble, that are always down for making some side money. These are the best ones to hire as a 'collaborator.' They will take their money and let you do whatever you want within reason. Look on the state medical boards monthly quarterly disciplinary action list. This is public knowledge.
>
> Best of luck! I feel for my colleagues in restrictive states …[335]

Cash-based courses

Courses offered by Justin Allan range the gamut from hormone therapy, medical weight loss, and botox injections, to opioid addiction and medical marijuana, costing anywhere from $249 to $699 for streaming content ranging from two to seven hours per course. His website boasts that "The

Elite Nurse Practitioner is accredited as a provider of nursing continuing professional development by the American Nurses Credentialing Center's Commission on Accreditation."[336]

A common thread, other than financial remuneration, is the urging of nurse practitioners to have the courage to get started providing patient care in various areas with the barest minimum training. Allan constantly promises that nurses with no starting knowledge will develop the necessary patient care skills after completing his courses, which generally consist of a few hours of streaming video or audio, which he says you can listen to while driving or exercising. Allan often emphasizes the 'low liability' of cash-based practices, and rarely mentions patient risks, other than his guarantee of teaching "bulletproof documentation to CYA [cover your ass]" with every course.

Every patient intervention carries some risk. Outside of the ethical issues of offering non-evidence-based services for financial gain to desperate and potentially vulnerable patients, there is a real risk of physical harm. This harm may occur both from treatments that are provided improperly or from delays in receiving appropriate medical care. Taking a deeper dive into the course offerings demonstrates the risks that patients being treated by a practitioner with a minimal level of training may face.

Telemedicine

Providing high-quality medical care during a face-to-face visit requires thorough training, and even the most skilled physicians find it challenging to provide care through a virtual medium, which precludes a comprehensive physical exam. While some specialties function better than others via telemedicine, developing patient rapport and making an accurate diagnosis requires skill and nuance that are unlikely to be acquired in a short one or two years of school. In addition, very few nurse practitioner schools incorporate telemedicine into their curriculum, with most training occurring on the job.[337] Further, studies show that there is a lack of best practices or standards of care for nurse practitioners using telehealth platforms.[338]

Despite these limitations, Justin Allan promises that after watching his two-hour video course, nurse practitioners with no experience practicing via telemedicine will be ready to create their own practice. The course includes "how to document telemedicine visits to CYA" and teaches nurse practitioners how to properly code to be paid by insurance companies for their medical advice.

While half the states in the Union require physician supervision, Allan says that telemedicine offers a workaround. "Did you know you can live in a restricted state and practice INDEPENDENTLY in a full practice authority state via telemedicine?" he writes. "All you need is a state license in another state! That's it!"[339]

Intravenous (IV) infusions

The average American can now take part in the celebrity craze for intravenous infusions on demand. Got a hangover or feeling a bit rundown? Just stop by your local infusion center for a liter of saline or a vitamin concoction—or have them bring their mobile unit right to your doorstep!

While there is no evidence to support the use of IV hydration over oral hydration when drinking fluids is possible, and very little evidence to support intravenous vitamin infusions among healthy individuals, clinicians like Theresa Abdul-Massih, a nurse practitioner and self-proclaimed 'aesthetics and wellness guru' offers a variety of treatments that are promised to "virtually eliminate dehydration, promote adrenal function, [and] release those unwanted toxins." For an additional fee on top of the $200 per dose base price, Abdul-Massih will add supplements that she claims will improve your immune system, brain functioning, and libido. Abdul-Massih, also known as 'The Glam NP,' is trained as a family nurse practitioner. While she initially "dedicated herself to the field of primary care," she says that her "tremendous gain in skills, experience, and knowledge throughout her career has enabled her to pursue her true passion in wellness and aesthetics."[340]

Thanks to the Elite NP, any nurse practitioner can follow in Abdul-Massih's footsteps and open an IV bar after completing a four-hour course. Allan raves that "IV-Infusion Clinics and Injection Bars are very hot right now and the demand continues to increase. This sector of the alternative medicine industry is BLOWING UP, and for good reason. Patients are demanding this service and it results in healthy profits for the practice owner!" Little mention is made of the well-known risks to such non-medically indicated procedures, including vein inflammation or infection, extravasation of IV fluids into surrounding tissues, compartment syndrome, fluid overload causing stress on the heart and lungs, or air embolism in which air bubbles enter the vein—which can be fatal. Instead, Allan focuses on the best part about opening an IV clinic: "You can make money and not even be present in the practice itself! Depending on your state's regulation, an RN or LPN can be there doing the work while you make all the money sitting at home. All they need is your standing order! And the standing orders you need to develop a powerful PASSIVE INCOME stream are included in this course!"[341]

While Allan insists that the nurse practitioner can be 'sitting at home,' the Texas Board of Nursing begs to differ. Jonathan Mendoza, a nurse practitioner and chiropractor, was called before the Board for failing to personally assess patients before IV infusion administration by a registered nurse. In response to the complaint, Mendoza disagreed with the Board of Nursing, stating that "intravenous and injectable vitamins are an emerging industry, and [he] believes no prescription is required [for them], which consumers may order over the counter and self-administer." Ultimately, Mendoza agreed to the Board of Nursing that he would 'revise' his protocols.[151] The Elite NP may need to do the same.

Stem cell treatments

Stem cell therapy is an emerging treatment that the FDA says has the potential to treat many medical conditions and diseases. However, the agency also warns that these treatments are still considered experimental, and that "for almost all of these products, it is not yet known whether the product has any benefit."[342] Justin Allan advertises on his stem cell course that "chronic pain and degenerative conditions can improve significantly after just one injection," and that patients "love" the results of stem cell injections, which will bring them back to the clinic "time and time again."[343]

Indeed, desperate patients seeking an improvement in their health are willing to pay big bucks for these unproven remedies, so much so that Allan teamed up with Oliver Brown, a nurse practitioner entrepreneur to co-create the course. The ad notes that Brown's stem cell clinic "consistently generates $100,000 a month being open just 2–4 days a week for a few hours." The Elite NP promises that after watching its two-hour online course, nurse practitioners with ZERO experience with stem cells and regenerative medicine" will be able to start "one of the least complicated side practices" and earn a "SEVEN figure income … part-time!"[343]

Is this practice safe? The FDA has warned that there is not enough evidence on the risks of stem cell injections, which include infection, tumor growth, and even blindness—a consequence that patient Patsy Bade experienced. In June 2015, the 79-year-old paid $5,000 to have stem cell injections that she hoped would save her eyesight from gradual loss due to macular degeneration. Nurse practitioner Alejandro Perez, who Bade said identified himself as a physician, injected fat cells into both of her eyes. Within a few weeks, Bade was completely blind.[344] Elite NP says that "millionaires are being made by people who are running stem cell and regenerative medicine clinics. It is time for some nurse practitioners to get a piece of the pie now!" With the cost of the injections averaging around $5,000 each, Allan writes, "You literally only need to see 3 patients a month to generate a six-figure income … This is not an exaggeration."[341]

Is it any wonder that nurse practitioners are attempting procedures that they should never perform? For example, a family nurse practitioner working at Allied Wellness Centers, a chiropractic clinic in Waco, TX was sanctioned by the Board of Nursing for performing experimental amniotic fluid injections into a patient's spine. In her defense, the nurse practitioner told the Board that "she has had a number of years of experience in intra-articular joint and trigger point injections," (not quite the same thing), and added that "stem cell therapy treatments were wholly voluntary and performed with patient consent." Another family nurse practitioner working at Medical Pain Solutions in Garland, TX also faced the Board of Nursing for injecting non-FDA-approved human umbilical stem cells into patients' joints.[151]

Peptides

Peptides are chemical compounds comprised of short chains of amino acids. There are 60–70 FDA-approved drug therapies that include peptides, with many others under investigation for the treatment of various diseases.

One of the best-known peptides is growth hormone, which is approved for children with short stature due to chromosomal issues or natural deficiency of the hormone. While some promote the anti-aging effects of growth hormone, there is no scientific evidence that the peptide benefits aging or wellness. Further, the FDA warns that growth hormone is associated with an increased risk of cancer and shorter life spans.[345]

Since the FDA restricts the use of growth hormone, wellness clinics have substituted peptides that are growth hormone precursors. There is no clear evidence of benefit for these peptides, and they may have similar side effects to growth hormone. Nonetheless, the Elite NP endorses the use of peptides for "an assortment of conditions/diseases where mainstream medicine fails to provide results." The website states that "they also decrease healing times from surgery/injuries, increase lean muscle mass, accelerate weight loss, improve skin quality, improve cognition and have been used by anti-aging clinics for years." Of course, peptide clinics are a high revenue source, with Allan's clinic generating "$3000–5000 in revenue monthly from peptides alone." According to Allan, the best part is that it's a "cash service, so you can skip the pre-authorization headaches from insurance companies."[346]

Foot and ankle clinic

As of the time of this writing, the Elite NP's course on foot and ankle treatments is listed as 'coming soon.' While it is not known exactly what the course will entail, the treatment of neuropathy will likely be included. Neuropathy is a painful chronic condition involving burning, tingling, and numbness of various parts of the body, often the feet. It may be caused by diabetes, poor circulation, vitamin deficiencies, or genetic causes, but in many cases, there is no clear diagnosis.

The symptoms can be distressing, so patients like Nancy Murphy are often desperate for help. "I had been having numbness in my toes—they feel like they are frostbitten—for probably two and a half years," Murphy said in a *Patient at Risk* podcast. The condition made it difficult to walk and drive. While watching television, the 65-year-old saw an advertisement that promised a cure from what turned out to be a chiropractic office. "There was nothing that said chiropractic," Murphy said. "The sign out front said, 'Neuropathy Center,' and there was nothing on their folder with the information they gave me."[347]

Murphy had a consultation, and when she returned for her results, "I was told if I didn't take care of the matter, I would be putting myself in jeopardy of losing my feet." She was quoted $8,000 for the treatment; money Murphy did not have. "They said, 'we can take $1,950 to start the program.' So, they got me loans through a medical care credit card." Murphy refers to short-term financing credit cards meant for healthcare expenses. While these credit cards often offer a short promotional interest-free period, if not quickly paid off, they can have interest rates of up to 26.99%.[348] "I just signed on the dotted line because you're just in so much pain, so distraught, willing to do whatever you can do to get yourself back to your real personality." Murphy ended up borrowing the rest of the money from her boyfriend. "In 31 years, I never took one penny from him, but that's how much pain [I was] in. It affects your mental state a lot. I had no choice, you know, I have to do something, or I'm just going to commit suicide or just cut my feet off."

After paying the $8,000, Murphy said she never saw the consultant again. She received ten electrical treatments on her feet from various staff members with no improvement in her symptoms. She was given a "boot with lights on it," and told to eat a special diet. "They said I pretty much needed to live on a paleo-Mediterranean diet, and they gave me a cookbook." When she returned at the end of her treatment course without improvement, Murphy said she was told it was her fault. "At the very end when I had no results from them, they said, 'Well, if you don't live on the cookbook, it won't work.' And that was their final solution with me. So, I got no results for my $8,000."[347]

With continued pain and numbness, Murphy sought care from Dhruv Joshi, MD, a neurologist who is very familiar with these cash-based neuropathy clinics. "I'm an academic neurologist, and I see a lot of neuropathy patients who have gone to these centers for non-FDA-approved treatments," he said on the podcast episode. Joshi explained that the clinics discourage patients from seeking medical care from a physician. "They advertise in a way that [sends the message that] you don't want to take medication [because] it has side effects, [or] it's not going to make you better,' versus the non-medication treatment that they claim will reverse your neuropathy."[347]

As with Nancy Murphy, patients are told that if they don't get treated with the clinic, they will lose their balance, end up in a wheelchair, or even lose their feet, said Joshi. "That's the way they try to convince people who are already in a lot of pain and suffering to sign up for these non-approved treatments." Joshi points out that these treatments are not approved for good reason—because they are not effective. "A lot of time it has a great placebo effect. When the patient gets the treatment, they temporarily feel better, maybe for a few hours, or perhaps a day. But once they stop, they will return to how they were before or maybe even worse."

Neuropathy clinics like the one Murphy visited rarely involve a licensed physician, much less a neurologist. "Most of them are run by chiropractors. Since they have a doctorate, they just introduce themselves as a doctor," said Joshi, who visited several of these clinics to perform his own investigation. "If you ask them about their degree and their experience with neuropathy, they just avoid those kinds of questions." Joshi said that it is difficult for patients to know who will be providing their treatment at these centers. "They do everything in their power to not let the patient know that they're not a real physician. On their website, they don't have any information about the doctors; they have generic pictures of people in their white coats."

Joshi said that most patients will see the clinician for a quick visit, and then another staff member will take over for the sales pitch. "The medical evaluation literally spans less than five minutes. Then you will be dealing with another person who is most like a salesman, and they want to sell you their treatments and products." He said that when he presented to a neuropathy clinic pretending to be a patient, there was no investigation into his symptoms. "They don't dig deeper into whether I even have neuropathy or not. They just took my word for it." As a neurologist, Joshi notes that the medical evaluation of this condition includes not only an adequate history and physical, but also a laboratory evaluation to rule out reversible factors.

"There are standard neuropathy labs I do as a neurologist, and more detailed tests may be indicated depending on the patient's age, risk factors, and other comorbidities," Joshi said. "There is always some initial workup that we have to do to find the reason for the patient's symptoms. At the same time, we have to find some reasonable treatment for it that is effective and FDA approved; we don't just throw treatments at the patient."

Once inside these clinics, patients are bombarded with propaganda about the benefits of their treatments. "They have televisions in the waiting room and the exam rooms playing constant video testimonials," Joshi said. In both Murphy and Joshi's cases, the clinic recommended electrical and light-based therapies, which Joshi says are not effective other than a placebo effect. "If you have neuropathy acting up in your legs and you do some kind of electric stimulation, the nerves will calm down momentarily, but that doesn't mean that you're getting better." Joshi theorizes that electric shock therapy hyperpolarizes nerves, causing a temporary pause in the signal. "But it doesn't cure anything. It just might momentarily make you feel better. Then the next day, you will get the same problem."

To provide informed consent for medical treatment, physicians must ensure that patients have a thorough understanding of all factors. At these centers however, Joshi says that patients are advised on the benefits of treatments offered by the clinic, with no discussion of risks or alternatives. "The only discussion that I know of is all about benefits and that's it. They don't even [ask], 'What if this doesn't work? What's the cause of it?'"

Since these centers are cash-based and do not accept any insurance, patients have little recourse when treatments fail. "If there is a patient who is willing to pay cash for a treatment, even though it's not approved, no laws are stopping them from giving the treatment as long as they say the patient understood the risks and benefits," said Joshi, who believes that these centers are no more than money-making scams. "They are popping up everywhere, even in small communities and rural areas." Joshi says he tries to educate patients to avoid these centers. "They are not run by real doctors, and these treatments don't work."

Instead, he encourages patients with neuropathy to seek an evaluation with a physician. That's what Nancy Murphy finally did. Joshi prescribed an FDA-approved treatment, which worked. "To be honest, I have to say it's never been better. I called Dr. Joshi the other day because I'm so happy," said Murphy. "Of six days, only one day I had some partial pain in my feet."[347]

Men's health

Excessive levels of testosterone can cause heart problems, including atrial fibrillation and heart attacks. In 2017, 47-year-old Brad Guilbeaux died from excessive testosterone dosing prescribed by Texas nurse practitioner Kevin Morgan. According to reports, the level of testosterone in Guilbeaux's body was so excessively high that the coroner's office was unable to measure it.[349]

The FDA has cautioned against the use of testosterone for its supposed anti-aging effect, stating that "the FDA has become aware that testosterone is being used extensively in attempts to relieve symptoms in men who have low testosterone for no apparent reason other than aging. The benefits and safety of this use have not been established." The FDA mandated an update to the labeling of testosterone, informing prescribers of a possible increased risk of heart attacks, and stating that it should only be prescribed for low testosterone levels caused by certain medical conditions—disorders of the testicles, pituitary gland, or brain—confirmed by laboratory tests.[350]

The Elite NP insists that men's health and testosterone supplementation is "a hot service line and practice area for the aspiring nurse practitioner entrepreneur for one main reason: high revenue potential and low expenses!" Justin Allan promises that this field of medicine is "a very straightforward and low liability service to learn and implement." In just four hours, the "nurse practitioner who has ZERO experience with men's health" will learn how to open and operate this type of practice.[351]

On the Elite Nurse Practitioner Facebook discussion site, Justin Allan discussed his best practices when it comes to testosterone therapy. "I require labs before the appointment, it is my policy. If they don't like it, they can go somewhere else." He explained that he charges patients for testosterone based on the duration of their treatment. "If they come in for injections or want to do home supply but are on monthly recurring payments, then it is $129 a month. If they want to buy 3–12 months in bulk, I discount it by 5–10%. The high rollers buy the bulk deal, everyone else is mostly on the recurring payment."[352]

Selling twelve months of testosterone at a time is a questionable practice, as the drug is a class 3 controlled substance, which means that it may not be refilled more than six months past the prescription date. Further, men on testosterone generally require blood monitoring more frequently than once a year, not only for the hormone level, but for prostate cancer screening and other tests. But be careful not to question Allan. Like he says on his advice page, "You don't want patients who question you. Trust me … They are a pain in the ass and will make your life hell … If they don't like it, let them go somewhere else."[352]

Women's health and hormone therapy

Allan teamed up with another nurse practitioner to create a 'comprehensive' women's health and hormone replacement therapy (HRT) course. Why should nurses take this course? According to the Elite NP, it's because "Women's health, and especially HRT, have [sic] been a very HOT service line for years, and for good reason: WOMEN WANT TO FEEL BETTER! What does that mean? High PROFIT potential for the astute nurse practitioner entrepreneur and making an impact on the health of the female population!" The website points out that this type of clinic can earn a nurse practitioner high profit on a part-time basis, because "the aging female demographic are willing to drop CASH on these niche service lines, which results in a high revenue practice that can be done only 1–2 days a week."[353]

Joyce Varughese, MD, is a gynecologist oncologist who discussed serious harm caused to women from inappropriate dosing of hormones on the *Patients at Risk* podcast. "I take care of women with cancers of the gynecologic organs—the uterus, cervix, ovaries, vagina, and vulva," she said. The specialty requires four years of medical school, four years of OB/GYN residency, followed by 3–4 years of gynecologic oncology fellowship. Varughese says that the implication that nurse practitioners can learn how to prescribe hormones after a few-hours-long course is insulting.[354]

"Even after four years of an OB/GYN residency, in your first couple of years in practice, you're still looking to your more senior partners for advice on hormone treatment," Varughese said. "It is very nuanced. I'm insulted because, despite all my training, there are still newer products coming out that I'm learning about. Instead, NPs are being told they can learn this in just a four-hour course with zero experience. It's just scary that somebody who goes through this course is then being unleashed on the public."

Varughese points out that while she prescribes hormone replacement to her patients, it is very important to be aware of the potential risks of these treatments, which are not harmless and can include increased cardiovascular risk, blood clots, and cancer. "The reason I see these patients is because they are prescribed inappropriate doses of hormones, and then develop hyperplasia or pre-cancer of the uterus, and in some cases, actual cancer of the uterus." Varughese notes that sometimes patients are unaware that the hormones they are given can lead to these cancers. "A lot of women will say, 'Well, I didn't get any estrogen, I just got testosterone.' No one ever told them that testosterone gets converted to estrogen in the fatty tissue."

Hormonal treatment can be especially problematic when given in the form of pellets, a delivery method in which hormones are injected into a muscle or subcutaneous tissue so that they are released over time. Varuguese notes that she has seen a rise in pellets in the last four or five years. "What's scary about these pellets, is, some of them advertise just having estrogen. Some have estrogen and progesterone; some have testosterone and estrogen. It's sort of like Russian roulette as to what's being advertised and what you're getting."

During her research into pellets, Varuguese found that many of these products are compounded by pharmacies or the medical practitioner. "They say they check your hormone levels with a whole bunch of tests and then specifically compound them to personalize the therapy—whether you need a touch of testosterone, a little more estrogen, and maybe a medium dose of progesterone." But Varuguese said there is no scientific basis to this process. "I am a big fan of personalized medicine and it's the future of cancer treatment, but this isn't something that anyone can accurately determine."

Once the pellet is introduced, it cannot be removed. "They are almost like a grain of rice, and they dissolve over time," said Varughese, a process that can take anywhere from 3–6 months. If the pellet has inadequate progesterone to stabilize the uterine lining, patients may develop cancer. "That's how they then come to me. In the past several years, I've unfortunately treated women who would never have needed a hysterectomy, but now they need surgery, which has its risks, then potentially close follow up if they have cancer."

Another concern is a lack of accountability, with hormone treatments being promoted as wellness products that will make patients feel younger, stronger, thinner, and just all around better. There is no clear evidence for any of these benefits, and when used improperly, hormone therapy can cause serious risks to patients, including death. Varughese said that she has found that her patients were not made aware of the risks. "Just recently I had a patient with uterine cancer and no other risk factors for developing it other than taking these pellets. She had not been made aware of the risks." Varughese believes that some practitioners are failing to disclose or underestimating the risks. "The folks who are selling these things are often very charismatic. Patients like that they are sitting with them maybe for an hour, and they feel listened to, but they are being sold a product."

While the Elite NP course states that it includes a discussion of the risks of these hormones among its "nifty treatment protocols that you can use as a quick reference," it also includes a section on "how to create bulletproof documentation to CYA." Varughese believes that this is the reason that it is difficult to gain accountability for improper prescribing of medications. "I haven't heard of anybody losing their license for doing this, and part of it is probably that they document: 'patient counseled on potential risks.'"

Joyce Varughese said that patients who are harmed by these practices may not receive justice in a malpractice case. "It's not enough to show that you've deviated from the standard of care in most states for a lawsuit to go to fruition; you must also show evidence of harm and quantify that harm. The issue is that some women develop uterine cancer, but we never find a reason—it can just be completely sporadic. So, it's really hard to prove causation in a court of law."

The Elite NP course promises to teach nurse practitioners about the differences between bioidentical and synthetic hormones, which Varughese says preys on the desire of the public for more natural treatments. "There is a perception that these bioidentical hormones are more natural, but no data suggest that they have any fewer side effects or any greater benefits than using the ones that are FDA approved."

Ketamine

In another collaboration, this time with CRNA Heather Pearce-Shew, "who owns a very successful ketamine infusion clinic and is now finishing her [nurse practitioner] degree," the Elite NP offers a course on ketamine therapy for the treatment of depression and chronic pain. After a seven-hour video, NPs with "ZERO experience with ketamine infusion" will supposedly be prepared to offer treatments to patients with mental health disorders and chronic pain for high profits.[355]

Ketamine is generally used as an anesthetic or pain medication given by an anesthesiologist or pain specialist, and as a treatment for depression by psychiatrists. Not surprisingly, the Elite NP says that any nurse practitioner can offer this service, from family NPs to psych NPs, writing, "Many of you are wondering 'Can nurse practitioners even administer ketamine infusions?' And the answer is, **ABSOLUTELY**! You are a nurse practitioner and it is within your scope to treat mental health disorders and chronic pain." Nurse practitioners are encouraged not only to prescribe ketamine, but to administer the dosing themselves: "You are also a registered nurse; therefore, you can manage intravenous infusion therapies."

Jason A. Duprat, CRNA, also offers training for nurse practitioners wishing to open a ketamine clinic. "I was supposed to be living the dream lifestyle after sacrificing over 8 grueling years of my life to become a nurse anesthetist," he wrote in a Facebook advertisement for his program. "I almost gave up on the idea in the nursing profession and then something LIFE CHANGING happened." Duprat said he realized that he could open "a new type of clinic that offered a novel treatment ... One that is HIGHLY effective AND in high demand." Duprat promises to teach other nurse practitioners how to open their independent ketamine clinic, including a "100% compliant workaround" for nurse practitioners in physician supervision states.[356]

Duprat and the Elite NP downplay the risks associated with ketamine. "The other great news is that it is very safe and has few contraindications outside of pregnancy or active schizophrenia," says the Elite NP. Is ketamine safe? The American Society of Anesthesiologists warns that one in three pain patients may develop serious side effects after ketamine infusions, including dizziness, detachment from reality, and elevated blood pressure.[357] Critics have noted a lack of long-term safety past 60 weeks, and three suicides during clinical trials of ketamine for depression. Though the drug costs nearly $5,000 for the first month of treatment, it "did not work for the majority who took it."[358] Nonetheless, the Elite NP refers to ketamine as highly efficacious, and urges nurse practitioners to consider this "great instant revenue generator."

Patient Ariane Resnick expressed regret about trying ketamine offered through an online program and prescribed by a non-physician. In an article, she wrote that she decided to try the drug because social media ads made it seem harmless and promised an immediate improvement in mood and energy, "akin to a shot of wheatgrass or a sound bath." Resnick said that she answered a short online medical questionnaire and had a phone consult with a physician assistant, who approved her for ketamine therapy within minutes. The ketamine was shipped to her door a few days later. Rather than experiencing the wellness and relaxation effect that Resnick expected, she developed heart palpitations, anxiety, and insomnia, bordering on what she described as mania. Researching the drug on her own, Resnick learned that the medication should be used with caution in patients with thyroid disorders, a condition she had disclosed during her online medical evaluation, but was apparently ignored by the physician assistant prescriber. Resnick reported her experience to the company, but said that they took no responsibility, stating that "the risk was worth the reward," and that she had made her own decision to take the medication. Resnick warned other patients to beware the use of powerful drugs for 'wellness,' and urged more oversight to protect patients from unscrupulous companies marketing online medical therapy.[466]

Other than the potential dangers of ketamine, there is also serious concern over a delay in the appropriate psychiatric treatment of patients with mental illness. Untreated depression can lead to self-harm, including suicide. Will a nurse practitioner without an extensive psychiatric background know how to assess for suicide risk and refer appropriately? While a non-physician practitioner may be able to prescribe ketamine, are they trained to correctly diagnose the patient and provide other interventions like psychotherapy? Many patients seeking ketamine have failed other therapies, making them especially high risk and in need of quality psychiatric care.

Dermatology

Physicians know that dermatology is one of the most competitive specialties, as only the top medical students are accepted into the four-year residency programs. But who needs all that schooling, when you can simply watch the Elite NP's six-hour video dermatology course, which promises to provide the training to "empower [NPs] to evaluate, diagnose, and treat 90% of the dermatological complaints you would ever see in clinical practice." Oh, and by the way, Justin Allan also includes "a plethora of actionable cosmetic skin care topics to sweeten the course."[359]

This is a great opportunity for a nurse practitioner to "step up to the plate," says the Elite NP, since "thousands of patients are in need of quality and affordable dermatological care **RIGHT NOW.**" In addition to acting as a virtual dermatology residency program, the course will teach nurse practitioners how to provide compounded skin products through telemedicine visits to "build a passive income stream from your practice's website." As always, "This course is designed to provide the nurse practitioner who has ZERO experience in dermatology and cosmetic skin care the necessary knowledge to get started with this growing field!" Don't worry, says the EliteNP, dermatology is "low liability, high margin, and relatively straightforward." Unless a poorly trained nurse practitioner misses a melanoma diagnosis, of course.

Aesthetics and cosmetic surgery

In response to "hundreds of requests," Justin Allan now offers a course on the "super-HOT" field of aesthetics. Botox is a "BOOMING field over the past 10–15 years, and for good reason: the population is aging, and they want to look younger! The good news? This population has the disposable income to spend on cosmetic and aesthetic services!" The Elite NP advises nurse practitioners to "get a piece of the pie … You would be a fool not to!" In fact, Allan opines, "I think it would be very unwise for any nurse practitioner out there not to be integrating aesthetic services into their practice … the demand is there, so why not fill it?!"

The course promises to teach a nurse practitioner with "ZERO experience" to perform aesthetics and botox injections in just seven hours of streaming content. "If you are looking for a high revenue, low liability, and relatively simple practice to get started, then you need to take this course!"[360]

While poorly administered botox can cause an unsightly cosmetic appearance, it also carries serious medical risks, including difficulty swallowing and muscle weakness, with a rare risk of anaphylactic shock. Other cosmetic procedures like vampire facials have been associated with the transmission of HIV and other infections.

While the Elite NP does not advocate for more advanced plastic surgery techniques yet, other nurse practitioners are entering into the arena of tumescent liposuction. Although this procedure may be safe when performed by experienced physicians, documented risks include bleeding, infection, swelling, and asymmetry or irregularity of the treated areas.[361] Despite these risks, in 2021, Indianapolis family nurse practitioners Shelley Clayton and Abbie Bledsoe, the owners of Ageless Aesthetics, posted a video of themselves performing liposuction on a patient on social media. The video showed Clayton manipulating a metal wand that had been placed through a skin incision back and forth to remove 'stubborn pockets' of fat while Bledsoe narrated. Bledsoe shared with the audience that the procedure had taken about three and a half hours, and that after the liposuction, the two would be performing fat transfer into the patient's buttocks.[362]

Reviewers familiar with proper liposuction procedure were taken aback by details shown in the video, including the nurse practitioners wearing T-shirts with bare arms exposed, no surgical draping, no surgical masks, and a background that appeared disorderly and unsterile.[363] In their defense, representatives from Ageless Aesthetics stated, "This is an aseptic dermatological procedure, not a surgery. The opening is skin deep, not opening the actual fascia of the abdomen."[364]

While most physicians who perform this type of procedure have completed years of formal residency training, the nurse practitioners seemed to have learned how to do these procedures by attending short workshop courses. On her LinkedIn page, nurse practitioner Shelley Clayton purported to have 'specialized expertise in Aesthetics and Anti-Aging Medicine.'[365] She listed her master's degree as a family nurse practitioner received in 2019 from for-profit Chamberlain University, which advertises "FNP in As Few As 8 Semesters. Coursework is 100% Online with No Group Work and No Mandatory Login Times."[366] Under licenses and certifications, Clayton included a 2-day course on office liposuction and fat transfer offered by the International Society of Cosmetogynecology, a private teaching organization.[367] She also listed an in-office liposuction masterclass from Elite Medical Workshops, taught by Jennessa Iannitelli, DO, a family medicine-trained physician and self-proclaimed expert in "Cosmetic Regerative [sic] Medicine."[368]

Clayton's partner at Ageless Aesthetics is listed as "Dr. Abbie Bledsoe, DNP, RN, FNP-C." Bledsoe received her master's in nursing in 2015 and then earned a Doctor of Nursing Practice at Indiana State University in 2020 with a 4.0 GPA.[369] Indiana State University's DNP program is a 37-credit hour online program that requires 350 hours of supervised clinical preceptorship. An asterisk by this requirement notes that doctorate students must obtain 1,000 clinical hours per the American Association of Colleges of Nursing, and that up to 650 of those hours may be granted from the student's previous master's degree program.[370] Bledsoe listed her certification in 'Aesthetics and Anti-Aging' from Empire Medical Training, a private seminar educational training company.[371]

Since nurse practitioners require a collaborative agreement in the state of Indiana, the two teamed up with physician Martial Kneiser, but Kneiser was not specialized in this type of practice—he was a pathologist, a physician that specializes in examining body tissue and managing laboratory testing. It is unclear how a pathologist would be qualified to supervise family nurse practitioners providing any type of clinical care, much less surgery.

Following a social media uproar directed at their posted video, Ageless Aesthetics no longer lists liposuction on its website, but does offer the facial plastic surgery technique of thread lifts.[372] Thread lifts involve the insertion of sutures into the face to create a lifting effect. According to the International Society of Aesthetic Plastic Surgery, thread lifts carry a complication rate of 15–20% even among trained plastic surgeons, which can include bleeding, infection, suture reactions, and painful extrusion of threads.[373]

Thyroid optimization

One of the most recent additions to the Elite NP curriculum is a course on so called 'thyroid optimization.' In six accredited hours (two of which can be used for formal pharmacology credits), the nurse practitioner with 'zero' experience is promised to learn much more than the management of 'standard hypothyroidism.' Rather, Justin Allan says that the course involves "looking at the patient from a holistic point of view" to treat sub-optimal thyroid levels. He states, "just because the TSH/T3/T4 are below the threshold for diagnosis of standard hypothyroidism, that doesn't mean that the patient couldn't benefit from thyroid optimization as it often times can resolve their non-specific symptoms," including "depression, insomnia, low libido, erectile dysfunction, cold intolerance, poor skin/hair/nail quality, and foggy thinking."[374]

This advice flies in the face of guidelines from the American Thyroid Association, which warns against prescribing thyroid hormone to patients without clearly abnormal thyroid levels, because excess thyroid medication can have serious risks, including atrial fibrillation and osteoporosis. In addition, the guidelines specifically advise *against* the use of thyroid hormone to treat depression, obesity, or nonspecific symptoms without conclusive biologic evidence of low thyroid function.[375]

Prescribing unnecessary thyroid hormone in a misguided attempt to treat symptoms like weight gain, low energy, or fatigue puts patients at risk. For example, multiple patients were harmed when nurse practitioners at Optimum Medical Weight Control and Family Wellness prescribed high doses of thyroid hormone to patients with normal thyroid lab tests, including an 11-year-old girl. The girl's mother said that her daughter was misdiagnosed as having a slow thyroid after having 15 vials of blood drawn—even though thyroid testing guidelines recommend just one starting test for hypothyroidism. Nurse practitioner Randall Locke started the child on thyroid hormone, causing her symptoms to significantly worsen. A state review later found that the child was overdosed on thyroid hormone, leading to a toxic hyperthyroid state.[376] Despite these risks, the Elite NP encourages nurse practitioners to consider adding thyroid optimization as "a great additional revenue stream," promising to "easily add an additional $1–5K a month in revenue."

Because it can be tempting to prescribe thyroid medication inappropriately, either for financial gain or in the hope that it may alleviate patient symptoms, the American Thyroid Association cautions clinicians to follow the ethical principles of beneficence (focusing on the patient's best interest and avoiding harm) and non-maleficence (not harming patients, including by starting treatments that have no clear benefit). The organization says that "offering patients formulations of thyroid hormone or other preparations that are known to be inferior to the standard of care, potentially futile, or even harmful contravenes the Principles of Beneficence and Non-Maleficence."[375]

The guidelines also point out that patient autonomy does not obligate clinicians to cater to patient demands for treatments that may cause them harm, and that doing so violates ethical principles. "Beneficent care recognizes there are limits to patient autonomy when patients request substandard, unsound, or untested medical procedures or therapies that could be either futile or harmful." It cites recent judgments against clinicians who gave in to patient demands for inappropriate care. Importantly, the guidelines note that clinicians are also subject to the "professional virtues of competence and intellectual honesty." Specifically, clinicians should not claim to be experts in treating hypothyroidism without accredited training, and medical experts should not misuse medical knowledge to "personally profit, deceive patients, or purvey nonstandard, risky innovative therapies."

The principles of beneficence and non-maleficence apply to all aspects of healthcare and give rise to the most serious concern about non-physician care: the issue of social justice.

CHAPTER 11

AND JUSTICE FOR ALL?

The replacement of physicians by non-physician practitioners inevitably gives rise to questions about social justice: Which patients will receive care from which type of clinician? Will patients of limited means lose access to fully trained physicians?

There is already evidence of the development of two-tiered healthcare, especially in states that allow nurse practitioners to work independently of physician involvement. In these 'full practice authority' states, Medicare patients are two-and-a-half times more likely to receive primary care from a nurse practitioner rather than from a physician.[377] Low-income Medicaid patients, those from racial-ethnic minority groups, and patients with mental illness and substance abuse are also less likely to receive care from a physician in independent practice states.[378]

A 2020 study showed that liberalizing independent practice for nurse practitioners led to decreased physician access to patients of community health centers, even though these patients have much higher mental health needs than patients in other low-income U.S. populations.[379] The reason for decreased access to physician care is not necessarily because doctors don't want to work in these settings. Rather, health centers are preferentially hiring non-physicians, in part because of government policy. Since 1977, rural health clinics have been required to maintain a staffing ratio of at least 50% nurse practitioners and physician assistants to receive federal funding.[380]

It's not just underserved patients that are being restricted access to physician-led care. Doctors, even those working in large and prestigious healthcare organizations, are routinely being relegated to care by non-physician practitioners, even when they push back. This is one reason that many doctors are expressing concern about the corporate replacement of physicians by non-physician practitioners: If even doctors are unable to receive care from a physician, then what chance does the average patient have?

LOSING CHOICES IN EMERGENCY CARE

In 2019, psychiatrist Patrick Horn, MD experienced treatment by a nurse practitioner that he believes could have left him paralyzed or even cost him his life. While driving in icy conditions, Horn's truck lost contact with the road and crashed into a ravine. Horn said that the impact was so great that both front wheels cracked off and the airbags deployed as the vehicle rolled onto its side. "After seeing my vehicle, everyone at the scene said I was lucky to be alive, much less that I crawled out under my own power."

Horn was taken to an emergency department, but rather than being treated by a physician, a family nurse practitioner evaluated him. Horn said he was experiencing severe spinal back pain and abdominal pain, but the nurse practitioner ordered only a thoracic x-ray and prescribed the anti-nausea medication Zofran (ondansetron) for his abdominal pain. "She almost sent me out the door with an over-the-counter anti-inflammatory after misreading the x-ray as normal," he said. Horn insisted on having a radiologist review his x-ray before he was released. "The radiologist found that my x-ray was not normal—I had several fractured vertebrae in my mid-back."

As a physician, Horn knew that the nurse practitioner's care was inadequate, but because he was in so much pain and shock, he found it difficult to advocate for himself. "What's scary is that I'm a physician and knew some of what to ask for. What does the general public do when they don't know any better?"[381]

Neha Patel, MD said she was unable to receive care from a physician during an emergency room visit for abdominal pain and excessive bleeding while 8 weeks pregnant. "The ER was empty, but I was given a PA," she said. "She ordered an ultrasound which didn't show the cause of bleeding and did not perform a pelvic exam because she said I was bleeding too much for her to see anything," although Patel notes that emergency physicians have told her that pelvic exams are standard of care in this situation and routinely done despite vaginal bleeding. After five hours, the PA discharged Patel, telling her, "I don't know why you haven't miscarried yet, but you probably will."

Patel and her husband, also a physician, were upset and scared. "It is a vulnerable position to be in, never being seen by a physician." Fortunately, Patel was able to be evaluated by her obstetrician the next day. "My OB immediately found that I had a large subchorionic bleed. Thankfully, I stabilized, and the baby and I are fine for now. That being said, I am not fine with being treated by someone without the knowledge to provide basic care that affects me and my unborn child." Patel reached out to the hospital's risk management team and learned that the emergency department staffs a 1:1 ratio of physician to PA. "They claim their PAs get one year of residency alongside with the ER residents." Patel believes that it's important for physicians to speak out about the replacement of doctors. "For those of you on the fence about this battle, please remember we never know when we go from physician to patient."[382]

UNABLE TO RECEIVE CARE FOR THEIR CHILDREN

A particular concern to many physicians is the surprising difficulty that they face when advocating for their children to receive care from another doctor. A pediatric geneticist who cannot be identified for professional reasons said that she was restricted access to a neurosurgeon when her six-month-old baby was found to have an enlarged head circumference, a potential sign of excess brain fluid. "As a first-time mom, I was terrified," she said. "The pediatrician referred us to a neurosurgeon, but when I called to schedule, I was told that we would be seeing the PA." The physician pushed back, pointing out that she was a doctor herself, and that she worked at the same institution. "I was told, 'no, sorry, it's this or nothing.'"

Because she didn't want to see someone with less training than herself, the geneticist began to search for options. Fortunately, her husband, also a physician, shared space with a neurosurgeon. "Through his intervention, I was able to get an appointment within two days." The neurosurgeon ordered a non-sedating MRI scan on her child which revealed benign enlarged subarachnoid spaces. "He read it himself and explained the pathophysiology—that it was a normal variant that resolves by age two, and that there should be no developmental delay and nothing to worry about."

The geneticist had the opportunity to experience the alternate scenario vicariously when she received a referral to her genetic clinic from the same neurosurgery PA her baby was originally scheduled to see. "The PA had ordered two MRIs and unnecessarily referred the baby to me. They had to wait three months to see me for no reason," she noted. "It was very interesting to see the dichotomy of care; the contrast between care from a physician and care from a PA, especially since the baby was the same age as mine was, with a nearly identical head circumference growth chart and normal development." The experience truly drove home the difficulties that patients face when they are not permitted to see a physician. "The other mom went through this whole process. The emotional involvement, time, money, trauma to the child including double imaging."[383]

Dermatologist Katherine Nolan Lu, MD was unable to gain access to a pediatric dermatologist for her young daughter during a flare-up of eczema. "We had just moved to Cleveland for my husband to complete his fellowship training," she said. "This was the first time my daughter had been exposed to cold weather, and she was covered from head to toe and bleeding."

Lu's pediatrician suggested a pediatric dermatologist, so Lu called the Cleveland Clinic, known as a mecca for top-quality medical care. Rather than getting to see a physician, she was told that her daughter could only see a nurse practitioner, that the wait to see a physician was 3–4 months.[384]

Chandani Patel DeZure, MD, is a pediatrician who struggled to get her child evaluated after surgery at an Ivy League academic hospital. Although the surgeon specifically asked her to schedule a follow-up so that he could see how the wound was healing, she said that clinic administration refused to schedule it. "I went back and forth with the administrator on the online portal. They kept telling me that the NP was capable and fine. I finally said, 'No. I will wait for an appointment with the surgeon.' At that point, there was no further response." DeZure said that she ended up texting a photo to the surgeon. "When the chair of the surgery department tells me that he wants to see my son's surgical incisions himself, I'm going to listen," she said. "If it's a routine post-op incision evaluation, then I am probably better qualified and trained as a pediatrician to do the evaluation myself than a nurse practitioner, saving me time and money."[385]

UC Davis, known as a 'Public Ivy League' institution, refused to allow physician Navreet Mann's son to see an otolaryngologist. Mann's husband, also a physician, accompanied their child to the visit. "He was seen by the nurse practitioner, and when my husband asked to speak to the physician, the NP was surprised." When Mann learned that her son's follow-up visit was scheduled with the nurse practitioner again, she called the office to change to a physician. "The schedulers seemed very surprised by this request," she said, noting her disappointment. "We will be moving to a physician-only private practice."[386]

Elizabeth Kara, a surgeon, experienced a frightening situation when her son required a sedated dental procedure. "Because he was having nasotracheal intubation, I asked for an anesthesiologist to perform the procedure," she said. When Kara entered the operating room, she saw a student nurse anesthetist preparing to begin the procedure. "I didn't want to be disruptive in the OR. I am a surgeon and am used to commanding the room, but on the other side, I was at a loss for words."[387] Kara notes that it is doubtful that a non-medical member of the public would have been able to perceive the difference in training of clinicians, and questions whether patients are truly giving informed consent if they don't understand who is providing their medical care.

Meghan Scears, MD, a family physician, battled to ensure that her son Andre received physician-led care. Born with congenital heart disease, Andre initially had a duct stent placed to buy time to allow his heart to grow before definitive surgery. "We were assigned a physician assistant for monthly echocardiograms and follow-up visits, but were told that we could not see a cardiology physician until after the full repair," said Scears.

While she was concerned about a lack of physician involvement, Scears didn't want to overstep. "I figured; this is how they do it; this is a good place; they say the surgeon is really good." When complications arose that Scears suspected could have been avoided by better cardiology oversight, she decided to transfer Andre's care to Children's Hospital of Philadelphia. There Scears encountered the same issue—rather than being treated by physicians, much of her son's care was being managed by nurse practitioners.[388]

Scears recalls times in which she asked to speak with an attending physician, and was told no. Moreover, when she questioned the nurse practitioner's care plan, she was told by the medical director of the intensive care unit that if she had a problem with a member of the team, she could seek care elsewhere. "He had this conversation with me while Andre was in the catheterization lab having a procedure done," said Scears, who felt powerless. "What was I supposed to do? My baby was sick in the ICU." Sadly, Andre later died of complications from heart disease. While Scears has been reticent to tell her story, she thinks it's important for the public to know that in many cases, patients are not being permitted access to physicians, even at the most esteemed medical facilities.

FIGHTING FOR PHYSICIAN-LED CANCER CARE

Texas dermatologist Jessica Parsons, MD chose MD Anderson Cancer Center for her breast cancer treatment. Parsons says she chose this facility specifically because her mother, an inflammatory breast cancer survivor, was also treated there. "I feel that my mother is a survivor because of the recommendations made by the oncologist at MD Anderson, so when I had to choose for myself, years later, I chose to go there as well."

Parsons would return to MD Anderson for yearly follow-up mammograms and ultrasounds, but when she arrived at a recent appointment, she found herself assigned to a nurse practitioner. "Their excuse was that they were short-staffed, but as a physician myself, I wanted to have my once-yearly evaluation at the High-Risk Breast Center done by someone who had also gone to medical school and was an expert in their specialty," said Parsons. She said she was very disappointed to find a top-tier cancer center replacing physicians with non-physician practitioners. "This is a referral hospital, for goodness' sake."[389]

NO PHYSICIAN FOR ROUTINE CARE

Corinne Sundar Rao, MD is an internal medicine physician. "I'm an easy patient," she said. "I show up once a year at the gynecologist for a well-woman check, I'm compliant with care, and I don't waste the doctor's time. However, I want only physician care." Rao said that for the last four years, each time that she has called to schedule her annual appointment, the clinic staff has offered a visit with the nurse practitioner. "I always decline politely and ask for an appointment with the physician." This year, the staff refused. "They would not give me an appointment and told me that I had to see the NP." Rao said that she left the practice that day. "I had questions regarding personal decisions on hormone replacement therapy for post-menopausal symptoms, and this is something that I want to discuss with a physician, not an NP. Although I'm an internist, I know more than an NP on this topic." Rao also says that she would never trust her pelvic exam and gynecologic health in the hands of a non-physician. "I left the practice and found a wonderful GYN physician who sees me and answers my questions," she says. "How reassuring to be taken care of by a physician and how sad that this is even a question."[390]

NO PHYSICIAN FOR CHRONIC DISEASE

"I was diagnosed with a pituitary tumor in 2013 and referred to an endocrinologist for management," said family physician Brenda Hampton, MD. "The endocrinology office refused to book me with anyone except the NP." Hampton declined and transferred her care to a local medical school, where she was seen by an endocrinologist and properly diagnosed with acromegaly, a hormonal condition that can cause abnormal tissue growth. "I'm glad I refused to see a nurse practitioner, but it seems ridiculous that I had to work so hard to see a physician—I'm a doctor with a tumor dangling at the base of my brain. Why would I want to see someone with less education than myself?"[391]

Physician Rebecca Lundquist canceled an afternoon's worth of patients and fought traffic to keep her follow up with a neurosurgeon for an abnormality on an MRI. "I deliberately chose a neurosurgeon not at my institution because of his expertise," said Lundquist. Rather than seeing the neurosurgeon, Lundquist was assigned a nurse practitioner, who entered her exam room with a nurse practitioner student. "The NP pulled up my MRI and told me that the finding was so small that she couldn't find it." Lundquist said she had to "pull the physician card" to insist that the neurosurgeon talk to her.[392]

MK Farmer, MD is an Atlanta-based rheumatologist with a history of type 1 diabetes diagnosed at four years old. Her health has been complicated by dermatomyositis and congestive heart failure, and she has been hospitalized several times. "I've had my care relinquished to nurse practitioners both at academic teaching institutions and at private facilities," said Farmer, who nearly died during one of the experiences. "I was short of breath, and my oxygen level dropped to 46%," she recalled. "It was confusing because I wasn't in a good state of mind or position to advocate for myself." Fortunately, Farmer's friend, also a rheumatologist, was visiting her in the hospital at the time. She demanded a doctor immediately, telling the nursing staff, "Either call a Code Blue or I'll call it myself." Farmer said that when the intensive care physician evaluated her, he found that she had 7–8 liters of fluid in her lungs. "This physician saved my life," said Farmer, noting that her nurse practitioner team never even checked a chest x-ray despite her symptoms of shortness of breath.

In Farmer's experience, academics are increasingly utilizing non-physician practitioners. "I was supposed to be evaluated by a physician expert in POTS [postural orthostatic tachycardia syndrome] at a major teaching institution," she said, "but instead, a physician assistant was in charge of my testing." Farmer said that she asked if the physician would be present, and was told that he would be, but at the time of the test, only the PA was present. "The physician was actually in the operating room—it felt like a bait and switch."

A physician with inflammatory bowel disease said that the gastroenterology clinic she visits only allows appointments with a nurse practitioner. "They claim it's their policy—I have no choice. It's maddening because my case is complicated, I have asked questions of the nurse practitioner and gotten nothing," said the physician, who fears being dismissed from the only specialty clinic in town if she reveals her name. She also noted that she pays $400 for a 15-minute appointment and $200 for a telehealth visit with the nurse practitioner. "At this point, I would even take an alternating schedule so I can see a physician at every other visit, but nope. A [physician's] head popped in before a procedure and that's it." She said she has reached out to physicians in the group with her concerns. "I have been told that if I don't like it, I can go elsewhere."[393]

OBSTETRICAL CARE

Dermatologist Katherine Nolan Lu was refused physician care during her high-risk pregnancy. Her previous pregnancy was complicated by peripartum cardiomyopathy (inflammation of the heart muscle), so she requested that an obstetrician oversee her care. "When I got to the appointment, I was assigned a nurse practitioner instead." Lu explained again that her pregnancy was considered high-risk. "I was told that the obstetrician would deliver the baby, but that all my prenatal care would be provided by a nurse." Lu said she had to call over ten offices before she finally found a solo obstetrician who agreed to take her on. "I was already 20 weeks pregnant, and I had to wait another six weeks to be seen. I was really worried." Lu noted that during her previous pregnancy, she always saw a physician. "It seems like this difficulty in seeing a doctor is new."

Lu notes that she lives in a part of California that is not considered underserved or medically needy. "This is an area that is saturated with large hospital systems." She believes that the problem stems from the system, rather than the physicians themselves. "It is difficult to get past the triage desk when you try to schedule with a physician." While she hated to have to pull the 'doctor card,' Lu found that the only way to see another physician was to reach out to doctors directly, bypassing the main office.[384]

Psychiatrist Krystle Graham, DO experienced a similar situation during her pregnancy. Because she was 38 years old (pregnancy over the age of 35 is automatically considered high risk), and had experienced two previous miscarriages, Graham requested an early appointment with her regular obstetrician. "The nurse reviewed my chart and said that she did not feel that I needed to be seen before 8 weeks. Instead, she scheduled me for an ultrasound and a visit with the nurse practitioner."

Graham pushed back. "I explained my request to see a physician on my first visit because I wanted to discuss the potential need for workup by a maternal-fetal medicine specialist. I was told that NPs do all of the initial evaluations and are 'more familiar with the process.'" Graham decided to proceed with the appointment, and her ultrasound revealed a healthy 8-week fetus. Due to a previous miscarriage at 10 weeks, Graham and her husband, a cardiac anesthesiologist, asked for a referral to a specialist. "The nurse practitioner minimized our concerns. She quoted some studies from journal articles and gave us some handouts." As physicians, it was clear to the Grahams that the nurse practitioner didn't fully understand the scientific literature that she was sharing with them. They scheduled a follow-up visit but began to investigate establishing with a different obstetric group. Unfortunately, at 11 weeks, Graham's baby no longer had a detectable heartbeat.

Graham subsequently was evaluated by a maternal-fetal medicine specialist and was diagnosed with antiphospholipid antibody syndrome, a condition that causes miscarriages but can be treated with baby aspirin and low-dose heparin during pregnancy. "I'm unsure if our baby would have survived if our concerns had been heard, and I was able to discuss with an experienced physician, but I will always wonder. A simple workup may have identified these treatable risk factors," said Graham.[394]

OBSTETRICAL ANESTHESIA BY A CRNA STUDENT

Family physician Mareena Hanna, DO experienced an adverse outcome when a CRNA student placed her epidural when she was in labor with her second baby.[395] "I was a high-risk pregnancy, and my care was managed by a maternal-fetal medicine perinatology specialist." Hanna said she expected that an anesthesiologist would place her epidural when she was admitted to a Tampa, FL hospital for induction in May 2022.

"I specifically asked for an anesthesiologist, but I was told that there were none available and that CRNAs were in charge of placing epidurals in the facility," said Hanna. Since the hospital had a busy Labor and Delivery floor, she decided not to press the issue.

Two women from the anesthesia team entered Hanna's delivery room, identifying themselves by first name only. One of the women, who Hanna later learned was a CRNA student, began to prepare to place the epidural, palpating landmarks on her back. The first attempt failed. Hanna heard the CRNA student say, "I'm hitting bone." The student then made a second attempt, which also failed. At that point, Hanna suddenly felt a wave of nausea.

"I began to insist that I wanted an anesthesiologist," she recalled, only to be denied. As Hanna continued to ask for a physician, the CRNA told her, "Well, we'll call but they won't come." The CRNA tried to reassure her. "I do more epidurals than the anesthesiologist. It was the student that tried before, I'll be placing the epidural myself this time." Shocked at learning that it had been a student who had made the failed attempts, but feeling pressured, Hanna allowed the CRNA to continue. By the time the epidural was finally placed, Hanna's nausea increased, and she started to vomit. Then, her blood pressure dropped precipitously. "I began to feel out of it, but I could hear voices say, 'She's 70/30; get ephedrine!'"

Ephedrine, the medication used to increase Hanna's blood pressure back to normal had a secondary effect of accelerating her unborn baby's heart rate. The medical team had to wait until the baby's heart rate lowered to the range at which it would be safe to administer pitocin, a medication given to induce labor. Because of these complications, Hanna's labor continued for 22 hours until the baby was finally safely delivered.

Hanna's medical saga wasn't over. After her delivery, she developed a spinal headache, a known complication of epidural anesthesia caused by leakage of spinal fluid during the procedure. Due to the nature of these headaches, patients only feel relief by laying down in a flat position. "Because I had to stay laying down, I couldn't hold or nurse my baby," said Hanna, noting that nurses had to hand-express her breasts to feed the baby. Without being able to nurse, Hanna didn't produce enough milk, and her baby developed low blood sugar and had to be taken to the nursery to receive supplemental formula.

Hanna's headache persisted, and the anesthesia team was called to provide a treatment called a blood patch. In this procedure, a small amount of blood is drawn from the patient and injected into the epidural space to clot off the leak. "Once again, a CRNA came in and introduced himself by his first name only," Hanna said. He was joined by another student CRNA who was tasked with drawing Hanna's blood for the procedure. The student CRNA attempted and failed three times to draw Hanna's blood. Finally, an anesthesiologist was called to draw her blood under ultrasound guidance. Afterward, the CRNA injected a small amount of blood into Hanna's spine. "I immediately felt terrible back pain," said Hanna, who says that the CRNA scolded her, "You're supposed to tell us if you feel pressure."

The next day, Hanna still had a headache. She was told that sometimes the blood patch had to be repeated, but she declined another attempt. While her headache finally abated with medication, the trauma she experienced in the hospital persists.

FAIR PAY

While patients are being deprived access to the training and expertise of a physician, they are charged nearly the same amount for care, with non-physician practitioners billing patients at 85% of physician rates when practicing independently and 100% when working under physician supervision following a doctor's care plan. Now, non-physician advocates are promoting legislation that would require patients and insurers to pay the same amount for care, whether or not physicians are involved. In fact, pay parity is listed as part of the American Association of Nurse Practitioners' strategic plan,[396] and in 2017, Oregon became the first state to mandate pay parity by state Medicaid and commercial payers.[397] There have been multiple other political efforts to expand pay parity to other states. In 2019, nurse-midwives in Connecticut sought pay parity with obstetricians.[398] That same year, President Donald Trump called for pay parity in a proposed executive order,[399] and in 2020, Washington State Senator Emily Randall introduced legislation to mandate equal pay for nurse practitioners, physician assistants, and physicians.

While pay parity is sometimes seen as an issue of justice— equal pay for equal work—others note the unfairness of charging the same for labor performed by two groups with entirely different training. In a *Patients at Risk* podcast, Washington State Radiological Society past-president Pooja Voria, MD explained that while nurse practitioners and physician assistants are valued members of the healthcare team, "their skill set is not interchangeable with physicians, and they are not doing equal work."[400]

Consider the difference in training between a handyman and an electrician, Voria said. "If you have an electrical problem, you might call a handyman to come to fix it, or you could call an electrician. So why do we pay an electrician who's licensed, bonded, and insured significantly more money than a handyman? It's easy. It's because of their training, it's because of their education, it's because we expect more out of them. It's the same thing with healthcare. When we have nurse practitioners say that they do the same work as a physician, it's not the case."

Washington physician Niran Al-Agba also participated in the podcast. Having talked with Senator Randall about healthcare legislation in the past, she believes that the bill began with good intentions. "I think what happened was that someone said to Randall, 'Look, we're nurse practitioners and PAs working in the same urgent care as doctors, so why aren't we being paid the same?' She may be viewing it as an injustice, but I don't think she realizes that there is clear data showing nurse practitioner care costs more; they need more tests, they need more labs, they need more visits to do the job of physicians."[400]

Al-Agba notes that an unintended consequence of this type of legislation is rather than increasing pay for non-physician practitioners, pay parity may simply lower the pay for physicians. "You've got primary care, which is already a real headache, and now you're going to pay them less?" said Al-Agba, who points out the phenomenon that salaries decline as professions become more female-dominated.[401] "Women are more likely to work in primary care fields like pediatrics. When women take over a profession, whatever it is, the pay drops. It's not right; it's stupid, but what's going to happen when non-physicians get pay parity is they're going to pay all of us less."

In addition, Al-Agba argued that decreased pay is unlikely to motivate a student to choose medicine, a profession with a longer course of study. "Electricians are highly in demand, they're making six figures. They're earning that money because they're working in a high-risk job. So, getting full training as an electrician being licensed and bonded is worthwhile, because you do get paid more than the handyman. If you're going to take that away, eventually we aren't going to have doctors." She believes that pay parity will decrease access to physicians, noting that in her area, patients are already driving six hours to see a pediatrician rather than a nurse practitioner. "How is this pay parity going to improve access to physicians in Washington State? It's simply not going to. If pay parity passes, it's the last nail in the coffin. I think we're going to lose physicians."[400]

Pooja Voria worries that pay parity will lead to the development of a two-tiered health system, in which patients with money and education will seek out and pay for care from a physician. "I didn't grow up with a silver spoon in my mouth. I endured hardships, too, but I don't think healthcare should be the place where people have to cut corners."[400]

While advocates for pay parity argue that non-physicians can serve a role in providing rural healthcare, Al-Agba believes that this is one of the most dangerous places for them to work. "In a medically underserved area, there are a lot of decisions we make that are different," she said. "For example, we get a [complete blood count] a little bit earlier, so if a kid is septic, we have time to get them to a tertiary care center, which takes some time. We just have to be on guard. What happens is, now you have people with less training, who are less on guard, because they don't know any differently."

As an example, Al-Agba referred to the case of one-year-old Kyler, who died just three hours after being seen by a physician assistant at an urgent care. The PA diagnosed Kyler with a simple ear infection and sent him home, despite the child being "pale, cold, clammy, and acting lethargic." Kyler's real diagnosis was heart failure.[402] Al-Agba noted that during his deposition, the physician assistant testified that he had received just a four-week pediatric rotation in school, and then worked for two months at an urgent care, averaging one to two children per day. "What can go wrong? How can you spend just four weeks working with children and expect to call it the same care as a physician?"[400]

Al-Agba is tired of hearing the argument that doctors are just protecting their pocketbooks. "It's not because of ego. It's not because we stand to lose money as doctors. It's because it is actually safer for patients. One dead child is too many. How many more children are going to die unnecessarily for us to stop doing this experiment?"[400]

ACCOUNTABILITY

While non-physician advocates are calling for payment at the same level as physicians, there has been little attention given to the vast difference in liability between the professions. Historically, case law has held that nurse practitioners and physician assistants cannot be held to the same legal standards as physicians in malpractice cases, making them difficult to litigate.***

Further, because non-physicians have traditionally worked under physician supervision, attorneys have overwhelmingly sought damages from

*** While Byrd v. Marion General Hospital (1932) has exempted nurses practicing under physician direction from legal liability, some courts are reconsidering. In 2022, the North Carolina Supreme Court overturned legal precedent by allowing testimony implicating a CRNA involved in the care of a 3-year-old girl who developed permanent brain damage after heart surgery. In Connette v. Charlotte-Mecklenburg Hospital (2010), Justice Michael Morgan ruled that the increased independence of nurses in treating patients requires an updated view of malpractice law, especially since "the law-making body has been silent" despite changes in nursing practice autonomy. Morgan wrote that even when working under a physician supervision, "a nurse may be held liable for negligence and for medical malpractice in the event that the registered nurse is found to have breached the applicable professional standard of care."

doctors, keeping non-physician malpractice premiums artificially low. In some cases, physicians have been held vicariously liable for damages from harm done to patients that they had no contact with, simply based on a collaborative arrangement with a non-physician practitioner. For example, a self-employed nurse practitioner with her own clinic prescribed multiple controlled substances to a patient who later died from a drug reaction. Although the nurse practitioner never discussed the patient's care with her collaborating physician, the doctor was required to pay a judgment because he had failed to adequately monitor her practice standards.[403]

In cases of supervision, physicians must rely on the observations of the non-physician practitioner reporting to them. For example, pediatrician Abigail Kamishlian was held responsible for a penile injury to a newborn baby during his circumcision, even though the nurse midwife provided her with inaccurate information about the extent of the baby's condition.[404] According to reports, after certified nurse midwife Melissa Jones amputated the tip of baby DJ's penis, she contacted Kamishlian, who was the baby's pediatrician, telling her that the damage was just a "tiny sliver," "very, very small," just a "little, small piece of tissue, as thin as 2–3 sheets of paper." At a deposition, Jones testified, "I'm not a pediatrician, but I would think two millimeters, three millimeters, or four millimeters ... if you tried to make a stitch through it, it would just pull through and dissolve."

A handwritten note from Kamishlian documented the phone call, stating, "small piece of glans severed," and noting her advice to go to the emergency department if any bleeding that night, otherwise to follow up the next day. Jones seems to have underestimated the damage when speaking with Kamishlian, with testimony showing that Jones had to apply ten minutes of pressure and several sticks of silver nitrate to stop the bleeding.

Despite inaccurate information provided to Kamishlian, she was still held responsible for DJ's outcome. Attorneys alleged that if Kamishlian had advised Jones to take immediate action in referring the baby to a pediatric urologist, emergency reattachment surgery may have salvaged the child's penis. Instead, baby DJ required four surgeries over four years to repair the damage. A Clayton County jury found in favor of the plaintiff, awarding $31 million in damages.[405]

In 2019, a new legal precedent was set when a physician was found liable for malpractice for a patient he had never treated based on a telephone consultation with a nurse practitioner. Richard Dinter, MD, a hospitalist, was contacted by a nurse practitioner regarding the possible admission of a woman with abdominal pain, fever, and an elevated white blood cell count. While the information shared between the two is in dispute, Dinter recommended not to hospitalize the patient. When she died three days later of infection, her family sued. While a lower court initially found that hospitalist Dinter owed no duty to the patient since he had no established relationship with her, the Minnesota Supreme Court reversed that decision, allowing the suit to proceed.[406] While the facts of the case are hotly debated, the bottom line is clear: physicians can and will be held responsible for patients based on the information and assessment provided by a non-physician practitioner.

Meghan Galer, who worked as an emergency physician in a military system, says that physicians must personally verify information provided by non-physicians, and that she has learned to distrust information received from them by phone. "The reports were so unreliable that once I realized it was a nurse practitioner on the phone, I just wanted them to send their patient to me. I would just rather start over than take the word of one of these practitioners."[99]

Family physician Nancy Berley, MD experienced vicarious liability after she discussed a case with a nurse practitioner and signed off on the chart. The patient was subsequently hospitalized with a bad outcome, and Berley was sued, along with several other physicians who had collaborated with the nurse practitioner. While the visit that Berley consulted on was ultimately determined to be irrelevant to the patient's outcome, Berley still suffered repercussions from the suit, including being named in the settlement. "There is still some trauma associated with it for me," she said. "I went through a deposition, I was preparing for trial, I was dealing with lawyer visits while trying to maintain a practice and also have a family and a life." Berley notes that she is still required to explain the situation every time she applies for medical licensure. "It's been six years and sometimes I still have to text or email the lawyer to ask a question."[407]

Shenary Cotter, MD, a family physician who was a nurse before attending medical school, was sued when a nurse practitioner treated one of her patients in a nursing home. "I had a stable patient that I saw every 30 days, but in between our visits, the patient was started on Coumadin [a powerful blood thinner] by a nurse practitioner hired by the nursing home without my knowledge." Cotter said that nursing home staff called her to report that the patient was having a headache. Cotter advised that the patient be sent to the emergency room, but before the patient could be treated, she developed a massive brain bleed from excessive amounts of blood thinner medication and ultimately died. "This was not even a nurse practitioner I was supervising," said Cotter. "This was a lawsuit by association."[407]

Even worse, the company that hired the nurse practitioner abruptly closed, voiding his malpractice insurance. Plaintiff's attorneys dropped the nurse practitioner from the case and sought payment from Cotter, whose attorney advised her to settle because of anticipated jury sympathy for the patient's family. "They settled at $20,000 under my policy limits, and now I have a wrongful death suit which for physicians, those don't go away. They're on your record forever." Cotter said that even talking about her story is traumatic. "Even though this happened 14 years ago, it is still hard to talk about."

Emergency physician and attorney William Sullivan, DO, JD believes that the risk of vicarious or associated liability makes it all the more important that physicians exercise caution when working with non-physician practitioners. When reviewing their contracts, Sullivan advises his physician clients that if supervision is a term of their employment, they should add an addendum that the nurse practitioner or physician assistant must be adequately insured and properly trained in their field. He recommends that physicians refuse to supervise new non-physician graduates or those with on-the-job learning rather than formal certification. If companies push back, Sullivan tells his clients that they have to decide. "Either they will make the changes, or you accept the liability, but at least you go in knowing what your potential liability is when you sign the contract, as opposed to all of a sudden, getting named in lawsuits a year from now, and having no idea what you're liable for," he said. "I've got a list of cases where docs have gotten sued, or they've gotten judgments against them for multiple millions of dollars just for signing off on a non-physician chart. So, it's not a risk-free venture."[408]

Shenary Cotter says she is unlikely to ever collaborate with a nurse practitioner again. "It would have to be a very specific and controlled situation," said Cotter, who notes that the nurse practitioner who cared for her patient was a skilled clinician, "but they aren't physicians, and you're relying on somebody that has so much less training and experience." Cotter said that she would only feel comfortable in a situation in which she directly evaluated each patient after the nurse practitioner.[407]

Nancy Berley agrees. "I don't see a place where I could ever supervise a nurse practitioner again." However, Berley notes that just sharing a patient could put a physician at risk. "You have to remember that it becomes a matter of who touched the chart. So, if I saw a patient, and then they saw the patient, I could still be [sued] anyway."[407]

CHAPTER 12

DIVERTING THE TITANIC

The difference between imposter doctors and fully trained physicians can mean the difference between life and limb, but this story has a happy ending. Small town farming community veterinarian Karen Saintsing was making her rounds when she developed sudden and unexpected pain in her arm. "I couldn't imagine what I had done to cause the pain," she said, noting that while she had been working with goats in a shed the day before her symptoms started, there was no injury that she could recall. When the pain increased, she went to her local urgent care, where a nurse practitioner evaluated her. Not noting any remarkable physical findings other than Saintsing's pain, the nurse practitioner diagnosed her with a sprain.[409]

This diagnosis didn't seem to fit, and Saintsing racked her brain for an alternate explanation. She recalled a condition she had seen in animals, a medical emergency called compartment syndrome, which occurs when an encapsulated body part swells internally, usually after trauma or an injury. These structures are enclosed by a layer of fascia, a thin casing of connective tissue. Swelling within the compartment causes severe pain, and over time, internal pressure can strangulate tissue, leading to the loss of a limb without emergency surgery. "I asked the nurse practitioner if this could be compartment syndrome," said Saintsing. "She said, 'Absolutely not,' gave me a sling and an anti-inflammatory, and sent me out the door."

Over the next few hours, Saintsing's pain increased, bringing the usually stoic vet to tears. "I'm pretty tough. I've been kicked by all sorts of animals, but I finally went to the emergency department because I just wanted something to take away the pain." Fortunately, the small-town emergency physician immediately suspected the correct diagnosis. "He looked at my hand and noticed that I couldn't open it because it was too excruciating. It was kind of all scrunched up, and as soon as he looked at it, I could tell that this light bulb just went off in his mind," she said.

Stephanie Markle, DO, MPH, a trauma surgeon with extensive experience managing compartment syndrome discussed Saintsing's case on a *Patients at Risk* podcast. She noted that there are few physical findings in the condition, and that clinicians must have a low threshold for considering the diagnosis. "The first symptom is generally pain, followed by numbness and tingling. Later, you will see decreased skin color and the limb will be cool to the touch, followed by the loss of a pulse." Markle said that by the time the pulse is no longer present, the patient is at risk for irreversible damage including paralysis and gangrene.[409]

Fortunately for Saintsing, the emergency physician not only recognized the condition but immediately sprang into action. "He got on the phone with the referral university hospital, and in the meantime, he started ordering bloodwork, X-rays—things that weren't to make the diagnosis, but to reduce the amount of time needed to prepare me for being transferred," she said. "Once he got all that done, that's when he came to talk to me and said, 'this is compartment syndrome, you need to go. There's nothing we can do for you here. You need a hand specialist, and you need it now.'"

Trauma surgeon Stephanie Markle said that this was the right move. "When you suspect compartment syndrome, you move straight to treatment, which is opening the compartments surgically with a knife. This releases the pressure and allows blood flow to return." The procedure is performed in an operating room by an orthopedic or trauma surgeon.

Having treated animals with compartment syndrome, Karen Saintsing was immediately terrified. "I knew that there was a good chance that I might lose my arm. My biggest thought process was, 'what am I going to do? How am I going to deliver a calf with just one arm?' I love what I do, and I was trying to think of jobs I could do as a veterinarian in a farming community with just one arm."

Although the university hospital was a two-hour drive away, Saintsing was able to be treated in time. With a previous warning from the referring emergency doctor, the orthopedic team was standing by awaiting her arrival. "They pushed me right into the operating room," she recalled.

Stephanie Markle says that this is where the training of a physician comes into play. "The hardest thing to teach, and the part that comes with experience is being able to look into a room and know, 'is this person sick, or are they not sick?' You can have a person with a bone sticking out who is bleeding, but they are not in as much danger as the person with compartment syndrome who has no obvious signs." Markle notes that understanding the disease process and the rationale for intervening helps physicians to know how urgently they need to act. "Knowing what is time-sensitive and who needs attention first—That can truly only come from experience. There's no [substitute] other than just doing it and seeing thousands of patients over a course of seven years of training."

Training and education gave Karen Saintsing's emergency physician the advantage over her urgent care nurse practitioner. "That's why there are no shortcuts to becoming a physician," said Stephanie Markle, "because it just takes that amount of time and that volume until you've seen enough of these or to even just think about something that you may have never seen before, but it's in the back of your mind because at some point you learned about it."

Although Saintsing had to have several additional surgeries, she made a full recovery. "I was out of work for about a month and a half, and when I went back, it was hard because I still had to do a lot of physical therapy. The first time I delivered a calf again I was so happy. I took pictures and sent them to the hand surgeons because I was so excited."

Saintsing feels extremely fortunate that a physician was available to treat her in the emergency department. "If he wasn't there, I don't know if I would still have an arm today," she said. It is for that reason that she wants to share her story. "I'm so appreciative, and I want to make sure that patients don't lose access to a physician."

Patients like Karen Saintsing are becoming increasingly aware of the importance of physician-led care. A 2019 report on consumer preferences for primary care found a significant rise in patient demand for physicians. In 2014, seeing a physician instead of a nurse practitioner or physician assistant was ranked just 11th in importance to patients. By 2019, survey respondents ranked seeing a physician as the 5th most important aspect of care for basic urgent care and 6th most important when choosing a new primary care clinic. The survey noted that "this represents one of the largest and most impactful changes in consumer preferences that we observed over the past five years."[410] While the survey authors expressed their surprise at this change in consumer preference, by now, readers of this book are likely to be unsurprised. When it comes to your health, the experience and training of a physician make a difference.

HATTIESBURG CLINIC AND THE COST OF NON-PHYSICIAN CARE

Physician-led organizations are also becoming more aware of the risks involved in replacing physicians, including the impact on revenue. With an increasing emphasis on value-based care and rising costs in healthcare, Medicare is investing in accountable care organizations (ACOs), groups that emphasize cost-effective, high-quality care. The use of non-physician practitioners by ACOs steadily grew between 2013 and 2018, increasing from 18% to 39% (with a drop in primary care physicians from 60% to 42%).[411] However, a study published in 2022 by the Hattiesburg Clinic, one of the largest ACOs in the nation, may reverse that trend.

"The Hattiesburg Clinic is one of the top primary care clinics in the nation, especially in terms of accountable care," said Niran Al-Agba, who interviewed the authors of the clinic's study. "The whole point of these organizations is to provide appropriate primary care and preventive care to the largest number of patients at the lowest cost."[400]

Like many hospitals and clinics across the country, the Hattiesburg Clinic, which serves rural Mississippi, has been facing a shortage of primary care physicians. To supplement its staff of 300 doctors, the clinic hired 150 nurse practitioners and physician assistants. "They invested in their non-physicians as much as their physicians," said Al-Agba. "They wanted this to work."

The clinic's model involved allowing nurse practitioners and physician assistants to manage their own patient panels. Physicians were available for consultation and oversight, but not directly involved in day-to-day patient care. "The physicians had higher acuity or more risky patients," said Al-Agba. "They gave the more basic, healthy, what we would call 'easy' patients to the non-physician practitioners."

As a physician-led organization, Hattiesburg Clinic initiated a study of the quality of care provided by clinicians, using the extensive financial and outcome data collected by the accountable care organization. After analyzing the care of 33,000 Medicare-enrolled patients, the team was surprised to find that despite carrying panels of lower-risk patients, non-physician practitioners working independently had poorer outcomes and higher costs of care than physicians. Doctors performed better on 9 out of 10 quality measures, with areas like influenza vaccination rates showing double-digit differences. Non-physician practitioners had higher emergency room referrals (2%) and specialty referrals (8%). Ultimately, non-physician practitioners cost the clinic $119 more per patient per month, translating into $28.5 million annually.[412]

Niran Al-Agba says that these study results are meaningful. "This is the first large-scale study of independent nurse practitioners and physician assistants compared with physicians, and it found that doctors provided the highest quality care at the lower cost," she said. "When I read this study, it took me right back to the original Burlington study from 1974, one of the first studies on nurse practitioner care, where they found that costs were twice as high to provide similar quality to physicians. So physician-led care is always going to be the answer."[400]

This data analysis led Hattiesburg Clinic to completely redesign its model, returning to a truly physician-led system in which non-physician practitioners now work side-by-side with physicians. Patients establish care with a doctor, who formulates the diagnoses and establishes a treatment plan. A nurse practitioner or physician assistant participates in patient care, providing follow-up visits. Patients check in with a physician regularly and any time there is a change in symptoms. The study's co-author encourages other organizations to evaluate their own data. "That's what this was all about: trying to improve the healthcare of our patients and for the system."[413]

Physician leadership matters. For example, there is evidence that physician-owned hospitals have better outcomes at a lower cost. Although physician-owned hospitals were banned in 2010 as part of the Affordable Care Act, grandfathered facilities show high scores for quality and cost of care, outranking non-physician owned hospitals.[414] A 2016 study showed that physician-owned surgical hospitals outperformed other hospitals in providing high-value care[415] and an analysis of the cost of joint replacement surgery found that physician-owned hospitals had lower Medicare costs, fewer complications, and higher patient satisfaction.[416] Despite concerns that physicians would cherry-pick or overtreat patients, a 2015 review found no evidence that physician-owned hospitals systematically select more profitable or socioeconomically advantaged patients.[417]

Why do physician-led medical facilities perform better? The main reason, according to John W. Dietz Jr, MD, chair of the board of managers for Indiana Orthopedic Hospital: "When physicians own and operate the hospital, there is a driving sense of responsibility for the outcomes." An even bigger reason: "We took an oath."[414]

Indeed, by swearing to 'do no harm,' physicians commit to practicing in a medically ethical way that benefits patients (beneficence), avoids or minimizes harm (non-maleficence), and respects patient autonomy. One aspect of non-maleficence includes the practice of warning third parties of imminent harm. It is for this reason that many physicians feel an ethical obligation to speak out about the independent practice of medicine by lesser-trained clinicians, sometimes to their detriment.

Steven Maron, MD, a pediatrician with 31 years of experience, was fired from his job after writing a newspaper article explaining the differences in training between a physician and a nurse practitioner. Calling nurse practitioners "well-trained, dedicated, popular with patients, and intelligent," Maron said that it was important for the public to understand who is caring for them and the differences in education and training. Despite having worked at his facility caring for socioeconomically depressed children for 10 years without any disciplinary actions, Maron was terminated just days after his op-ed was published for violating the organization's principle of 'mutual respect.'[418]

A SINKING SHIP: AD HOMINEM ATTACKS

Indeed, when physicians dare to caution against independent medical practice by non-physicians, they face repercussions. Efforts to inform the public about the differences in training are often portrayed as a turf war, with physicians accused of being elitist, poor team players, or worse.

For example, on January 7, 2022, the medical website *Medscape* published the article 'PA Name Change Bad for Patients and the Profession,' written by this author. The article opposed the announcement of a name change from physician assistant to physician associate, citing concerns over transparency for patients. It further urged physician assistant leaders to reject the nurse practitioner model of seeking autonomous practice and to return to their traditional roots of a true physician-PA relationship.[419]

The article created a furor, garnering over 1,400 comments, many from nurse practitioners and physician assistants calling the author arrogant, egotistical, and money-grubbing. There were multiple demands that the piece be retracted and threats to cancel *Medscape* subscriptions.[420] The author was deluged with obscenity-laced emails and negative practice reviews. A meme was even circulated on social media in which the author's name was added to a list of infamous physicians, including sex offenders and Nazi war criminals.[421]

Nurse practitioner and physician assistant leaders were also outraged, and the American Association of Nurse Practitioners (AANP) and American Association of PAs (AAPA) joined forces to pen a letter entitled 'NPs, PAs say stop attacks and support healthcare colleagues.' Calling the article an attack on their professions, the letter stated that the commentary "divides healthcare providers and demeans the education, experience, and value of physician associates and nurse practitioners." It also stated, "The evidence is in, and it is irrefutable: PA- and NP-delivered care is associated with improved access to care, lower healthcare costs, and fewer avoidable emergency room visits."[422]

Despite multiple requests, *Medscape* declined an opportunity to respond to the so called irrefutable evidence, nor to answer the many factual challenges in the comments. Medscape Business of Medicine Editorial Director Keith Martin was clear: "We do not want to initiate a back-and-forth between your organization and the AAPA and AANP ... Both sides have said their peace [sic] and we plan to leave things where they are. Both perspectives were expressed and our comments section reflects the positions of the professions and what each side believes is misinformation about the other. With that said, we will decline to run the rebuttal."[423]

Medscape, a subsidiary of WebMD, was purchased by private equity company KKR in 2017 as part of a $2.8 billion deal.[424] KKR also owns healthcare conglomerate Envision Healthcare, one of the nation's largest hospital staffing companies and surgery center owners. While it's likely just a coincidence, the first hit of a Google search for 'Medscape' and 'Nurse Practitioner' is an ad from *Medscape* entitled, 'Nurse Practitioner Practice: Full Scope, Better Outcomes.'

Physicians afraid to speak out

While some doctors are vocal about their concerns, many others are afraid to speak out, and for good reason. In 2019, Sean Hampton, DO was cyber-bullied for a post that he wrote on Facebook commenting on the current education of nurse practitioners. "I simply wrote about the changes that I've seen in nurse practitioner education since I graduated medical school in 2008," said Hampton, who pointed out that many nurse practitioners now attend online school with minimal patient contact. Hampton said that after posting this on his personal business page, he was labeled a bully. "I was harassed online, attacked, and the Google ratings that I spent the last nine months building up were immediately destroyed."

Hampton also said that he received hate emails from nurse practitioners from all across the country. "It turns out they shared my post on one of their sites and encouraged each other to bash me into oblivion." Hampton deleted his post and said he understands why many physicians don't speak out. "The current landscape is becoming scary."[425]

Allergist Purvi Parikh, MD reported being doxxed (her personal information was exposed online) after she spoke out about the importance of physician-led care. "Someone posted my photo and office information and encouraged others to leave me negative reviews," she said. In another instance after a media interview, she was reported to New York University, where she has staff privileges and serves as faculty. "They said that I was denigrating NPs and PAs and was very unprofessional," said Parikh, who had recordings to prove that her remarks were nothing of the sort. "I got spoken to by the Chairman and media department," she said, "and while nothing came of it, it added stress to my day."[426]

A psychiatrist who works at a state hospital had a similar situation when she posted a comment on a public forum noting that nurse practitioners had less education and training than a physician. "Someone reported me to my employer, and I started receiving negative messages and bad reviews," she said. Because she lives and works in a small community and has children, she doesn't want to use her name here, and in fact, she has been using an alias on social media since this incident occurred. "I'm afraid," she said. "I've never been bullied before, and this has taken away my ability to speak freely."[427]

Another physician who must remain anonymous due to fear of losing her job faced repercussions after giving a lecture to medical students. "This was an informal lecture about why I chose radiology, and what I love about interventional radiology," said the physician, who gave up her free time to talk with medical students. "I told the students that I felt safer in my career as a radiologist because I felt that PAs and NPs could not easily replace us."

The physician later received a reprimand by email from the Dean of the PA school, who wrote, "Perhaps you were not aware that there were PA students in the audience. I received feedback from PA students who attended that they were very discouraged at the disparaging comments you made about PAs and NPs." The email continued, "Since APPs are growing in numbers as members of the healthcare team, it would be professional of you to keep your personal opinions to yourself, and not share in a presentation where your opinions impact future healthcare providers."[428]

In 2020, critics bullied a medical student and threatened to report him for tweeting a graph showing the difference in training hours between clinicians. In a since-deleted tweet, the third-year medical student wrote, "I'm baffled by the mid-level encroachment happening during a CRISIS. Remember, a medical student has more hours of training than an NP or PA. Everyone has a role in medicine and everyone is valuable, but we need to put patients and not profits first!"

The medical student faced numerous criticisms, with one user re-tweeting the post and tagging the student's medical school: "Is this one of your attending MS3 students?? He's disrespectful to his medical colleagues that function as a team across the board. If this is the future of medicine you're training, then God help us all. #Disgraceful #BadMedicine."[429]

Another user wrote, "I just screenshot this post with your name, and I'm sending post cards to all medical schools in the U.S. Good luck matching! 4 years of school for nothing."[430]

Emergency physician Natalie Newman defended the student's right to post his opinion on Twitter. "I don't tolerate bullying of medical students, and I made it clear that interfering with that student's matriculation will not be tolerated," she said. However, she warns medical students and residents to temper their comments while still in training. "If they get kicked out of school for a faux pas, that's one less doctor we have in our community. They have to be careful of what they say. It isn't necessarily wrong, but it can be inflammatory."[431]

More AANP criticisms

Other physicians have faced similar criticisms for voicing concerns, including neuropsychiatrist Alyson Maloy. In a 2021 interview about the effects of COVID-19 on medical staffing, Maloy stated that healthcare organizations were using the physician shortage as an excuse to install non-physicians in inappropriate roles, noting that nurse practitioners and physician assistants sought an expansion of independent practice rights during the public health emergency.[432] "In March of 2020, the same week that the state shut down for the pandemic and all medical personnel were converting our practices to telemedicine to continue to care for patients safely, physician assistants were able to get a bill that had been languishing in committee for two years pushed through in five days," Maloy said in a podcast interview. "This bill allowed them to function as a physician after about two years of practicing with some supervision." Maloy also pointed out that while physician assistant practice expansion was requested to facilitate care during the public health emergency, the legislation had no end date.[433]

Non-physician leaders took offense to Maloy's comments. April Kapu, the president of the AANP, criticized Maloy and a group that she represented, Physicians for Patient Protection (PPP), writing,

> It is unfortunate that … the author opted to interview a representative of an advocacy group that exists on the far fringes of organized medicine. Maloy and PPP would have physicians and medical students believe that their profession and indeed patients are somehow undermined by the outstanding care nurse practitioners deliver … Unfortunately, PPP is an outlier organization working to divide NPs and physicians rather than unite us to better serve patients and our nation's health care system.[434]

According to Maloy, there was nothing in her interview that indicated a low opinion of nurse practitioners, nor opposition to team-based care. "These conversations often devolve into calling physicians who take our position arrogant," she said. "It's just very difficult because we don't get down to the heart of the matter, which is the evidence showing that physician-led care is better."[433]

Phil Shaffer, who serves on the Physicians for Patient Protection board with Maloy, said that he had a visceral reaction to the AANP's response. "Honestly, I got through the first paragraph and had to stop; it was just too upsetting," he said. "Portraying your opponents as somehow unhinged marks the article as a propaganda piece, as opposed to a sober piece of scientific analysis of the issues." Shaffer rejected the view that his group is trying to damage team-based care. "The AANP is the one trying to remove the leader of the healthcare team. The person who is the most educated, and most qualified to lead the team is being pushed to the side so that their members can lead the team without proper education. Instead of PPP getting in the way of team-based care, the AANP is trying to destroy it."[433]

Alyson Maloy agreed, pointing to the AANP 2019 strategic plan, which included making nurse practitioners the chosen healthcare provider by patients. "Why on earth is this important?" she asked. "Wouldn't you think that what's important is advancing your education, staying up to date, standardizing the training, and stopping 100% online school? None of that is in their strategic plan."

Maloy said that her passion for this issue stems from patient safety concerns. She described a recent patient who was treated by a primary care nurse practitioner for a finger lesion. "The patient was treated for a presumed fungal infection for six months. Lo and behold, it's melanoma, the fastest metastasizing cancer we have, and that was a death sentence to this patient." No primary care physician and definitely no dermatologist would misdiagnose cancer as a fungal infection, Maloy argued, because physicians are trained to create a differential diagnosis, a list of possible causes of a patient's symptoms. "Some people may argue that maybe a nurse only needs 500 hours to do easy things like high blood pressure, or something simple," she said. "But the problem is that to know that something simple, you need to be so broadly trained that you can spot the zebra when you see it. That one person with a zebra illness doesn't care that it occurs in one in 100,000 people if they're the patient who has it." For non-physician practitioners, Maloy said that if it's not in the top few common diagnoses, it's going to be missed.[433]

Regarding non-physician advocate insistence that they can provide the same care as physicians, Phil Shaffer said that this needs to be definitively proven. "Carl Sagan said, 'Extraordinary claims require extraordinary proof.' He was talking about UFOs," Shaffer said, "but the hypothesis that a non-physician can practice to the same level as a physician with just a fraction of the training is on the level of UFOs. And they have done nothing to give us extraordinary proof."[433]

In April Kapu's editorial, she wrote, "Fulfilling the promise of nursing means speaking truth to the medical establishment and making it acknowledge an ethical obligation to reform professional hierarchies. The laws and norms that constrain nurses' ability to practice to the full extent of their skills and training were put in place by physicians to protect their privileges, independence, and income."[433]

Alyson Maloy notes that physician privileges and independence are earned through years of study and training. "When you average out the $300,000 of debt we go into for education, the 10–15 years of lost earning potential, the interest rates on the loans, the fact that we don't get overtime even though we routinely work 60, 70, 80-hour weeks in residency … People who argue about protecting our income just don't know anything about the practice of medicine and what we go through."

Maloy says that she speaks out not because she wants to repress non-physicians, but because she is frightened by the current situation. "When we find ourselves [or our children] in an ICU, losing access to doctors is really on the table here in the United States, [but] I really don't believe that the average American sees it happening."[429]

While April Kapu insisted in her editorial that, "it's time to break the glass ceiling," Alyson Maloy and Phil Shaffer argue that there is no glass ceiling because the study of medicine is not restricted to any certain group. "The glass ceiling invokes images of social injustice in medicine, but the profession is open to anyone, particularly in the last 20 years," said Shaffer.[433]

While the path to becoming a physician is rigorous, it is open to all. For example, Carl Allamby made headline news when he became a fully trained emergency physician at age 51. Allamby, a Black man who grew up in a rough East Cleveland neighborhood, worked his way through community college, attending night school while earning a living as a mechanic on his journey to become a physician. Despite overcoming incredible adversity, Allamby told reporters that he doesn't consider himself to be special. Rather, he says he followed a stepwise approach that he recommends to others: planning, sacrifice, and true dedication to an area of study, including "the conviction to stay the course, even when things become difficult."[435]

Rather than using training shortcuts, Alyson Maloy believes that the physician shortage must be solved by increasing funding for physician training slots. "I have never seen such heroic, creative gymnastics to solve a simple problem," she said. "In 1910, the Flexner Report established what it takes to practice medicine, but there seems to be a bizarre movement in this country right now where anybody can practice medicine and call it whatever they want, call it advanced nursing, call it physician associate, call it healthcare." Maloy says that patients need to know that it doesn't have to be this way. "It's as if people assume, 'Well, we don't have enough doctors; it's just the way it is. We have to get by with these complicated, bizarre solutions.' We're here, in the United States of America. We're one of the richest countries in the world. If we need to produce more doctors, that should not be a problem."[433]

PA criticisms

Christin Giordano McAuliffe, MD is another physician who faced criticism for an article that she wrote about the role of non-physicians in nephrology. A physician assistant before she returned to medical school to become a doctor, McAuliffe completed a three-year internal medicine residency and an additional two-year fellowship program to become a nephrologist, caring for patients with kidney disease. Having worked in both roles, McAuliffe is acutely aware of the differences in education and training between the professions, and she is concerned about the increasing use of non-physicians in nephrology, a field that involves the care of very complex and often seriously ill patients. McAuliffe shared her views in an article for the *American Society of Nephrology News*. She explained the differences in training between clinicians and urged the appropriate use of NPs and

PAs, ideally to assist fully trained nephrologists rather than performing independent patient evaluations.[436]

In response, physician assistant leaders Becky Ness, PA, the Chair of the National Kidney Foundation Council of Advanced Practice Providers, and Peter Juergensen, PA, the President of the American Academy of Nephrology PAs criticized McAuliffe, writing that her article lacked evidence-based data. They argued that her recommendation that non-physicians practice under direct physician supervision "is contrary to standard practice in any setting, and counters most state and federal laws regarding APP practice." Citing a shortage of nephrologists, the two wrote that research demonstrates that the inclusion of non-physician practitioners "increases access to care and provides high-quality care to the increasing number of patients with [kidney disease]."

Indeed, research shows that adding clinicians to physician-led care teams benefits patients with kidney disease. However, there are no studies evaluating the safety or efficacy of care when non-physician practitioners are used in place of nephrologists.[437] McAuliffe says that the practice is evidence of the disconnect between what is legally permitted and the ethical practice of medicine. "To maximize profits, corporations are increasingly employing non-physician providers with supervision models created by executives, and scope-of-practice guidelines created through lobbying rather than clinical evidence." Rather than allowing the criticism to silence her, McAuliffe responded with a call to action: "I invite all non-physician providers to join me in advocating for the highest quality and safest care for patients, rather than the interests of any healthcare professional or corporation."

PUSHING BACK

Many physicians are working together to pressure organizations to reprioritize physician-led care. For example, doctors used social media to publicize concerns about quality care at Memorial University Medical Center, a hospital owned by HCA Healthcare in Savannah, GA. In July 2021, Sound Physicians, a contract management group owned by UnitedHealth and private equity firm Summit Partners, announced a restructuring of the hospital's practice model. A memo from Sound Chief Hospitalist Dwayne Gard, MD, read,

> Starting August 3, 2021, Sound will be utilizing our Advanced Practice Providers (APPs) as day rounding providers. They will be working in a collaborative Dyad team with a Physician; however, the APP will be the

> primary provider taking care of a subset of our patients. Any communications regarding the patients assigned to these APPs should be directed to the PA or NP, rather than the physician.

After a social media backlash from doctors, including an article publicizing the change in *MedPage Today*, Sound reversed the decision. The company released an updated memo stating, "After a discussion with the Memorial Health University Medical Center leadership team, I want to communicate that we are not moving forward with this approach. We understand the critical role our physicians play in the care of their patients."[438]

In February 2023, a physician reported a similar policy reversal at her critical access hospital due to pressure from emergency physicians, sharing a screenshot of an email in which senior hospital leaders announced a decision to transition from nurse practitioner hospitalists back to physician hospitalists. The email cited feedback from emergency physicians as a deciding factor. "Ultimately we felt it was better for our patients given ... higher ER volumes, sicker patients ... difficulty securing transport and other issues."[468]

Pediatric emergency physician Mercy Hylton, MD was successful in revoking policy allowing nurse practitioners to treat newborns at her organization after a baby with herpes infection of the eye was misdiagnosed as having poison ivy. In a letter to the chief medical officer, Hylton wrote, "I find it unimaginable that any person responsible for diagnosing patients of any age could not be suspicious for herpes after seeing these pathognomonic lesions. It is also quite difficult to understand how a clinician could rationalize poison ivy in a newborn, especially when there was no history of any possible exposure." Hylton pointed out that this missed diagnosis could have been a fatal mistake.[439]

Perhaps one of the most effective ways that physicians can push back is by entering into politics directly. OB/GYN physician Rita Fleming worked as a nurse and then as a nurse practitioner before attending medical school. She was elected to the Indiana House of Representatives in 2018 and was instrumental in passing legislation in 2022 requiring truth in medical advertising in the state, including clear identification of clinician licensure. Fleming told reporters, "I just think it's important that the public knows who's caring for them, and I think it's important for each of us who have worked so hard to get our degrees to be proud of who we are and to educate the public about our unique contribution to their care."[440]

Leah Davis cited this law in a communication with the advertising editor of the Indiana Star-Tribune, which awarded a nurse practitioner the "Best Family Physician" Readers' Choice Award. Explaining the differences in the professions, Davis wrote that "it is essential that journalists understand the differences in healthcare training and include the appropriate titles/training in articles. Aside from the need to do so for journalistic integrity, it is now a legal obligation in Indiana." The editor responded favorably, noting that the award had been changed.[216]

Not all media outlets are as eager to adopt clarity in medical titles. On January 25, 2023, National Public Radio affiliate WGCU reported on a new doctorate program for certified registered nurse anesthetists (CRNAs) at Florida Gulf Coast University (FGCU) in a segment entitled "FGCU nurse anesthesiologists will be doctors for the first time." FGCU Professor Robert Bland was identified in writing and in a photograph as "Dr." without clearly labeling his degree as that of a non-physician, and the report quoted Bland as saying that "nurse anesthesiology is basically the same as medical anesthesiology."[469]

By now, readers know that nurse anesthetist training and anesthesiology training are not the same, and that having an anesthesiologist at the helm during a surgical complication saves lives—but the average patient may not. Further, the term 'nurse anesthesiologist,' a new title being promoted by some nursing advocates, may further blur the lines between who is a physician, and who is not. When listeners expressed concern about this reporting, WGCU was unapologetic, noting that Florida's Board of Nursing allowed a petitioner to use the term 'nurse anesthesiologist' in 2019, and that nothing in Florida statute forbids the practice. The Editor's note summarized: "WGCU stands by the use of 'nurse anesthesiologist.'"[469]

Implying (or in this case, frankly stating) that nurse and physician training are equivalent is inaccurate and deceptive to the public, who deserve to understand the education of those providing their medical care. Unfortunately, it seems that legislation is required to ensure such transparency, and in 2023, Florida Representative Ralph E. Massullo MD introduced a bill that would strengthen Florida's current Truth in Advertising laws, requiring accurate disclosure of the educational background of clinicians, and protecting medical titles.[470]

Physicians across the country are meeting with legislators to protect physician-led care, although the results are sometimes ironic. Pediatrician Cheryl Ferguson, MD joined several physicians to give testimony during an Indiana legislative committee hearing on independent nurse practice. "After the vote, one of the Representatives who was a staunch supporter of the bill came out to our group of physicians in the hallway," said Ferguson. "He told us that there was a medical emergency, and asked if any of us were serving as 'Doctor of the Day' (the volunteer physician that provides medical care during the legislative session)." Ferguson said she looked him squarely in the eye and asked, "Are you sure you don't want the 'Nurse Practitioner of the Day?'" Of course, the entire group went to help, because, as Ferguson says, that's what doctors do.[58]

RETHINKING PHYSICIAN SUPERVISION

While some doctors are working within the system to advocate for physician-led care, others are proposing more radical solutions. William P. Sullivan believes that the only way to move the needle is to completely remove physician supervision, and hold non-physicians to the same legal standard as doctors.[408]

Traditionally, case law in medical malpractice has limited the standard of care for nurse practitioners, instructing juries that advanced practice nurses cannot be held to the same standards as physicians.[441–443] This has made it difficult for plaintiff's attorneys to receive compensation for patients harmed by nurse practitioners, since they are not expected to perform to the level of a physician and therefore often released of legal and financial responsibility.

"Scope of practice for nurse practitioners and physician assistants is determined by state legislatures, not by physicians or medical organizations," said Sullivan in a *Patients at Risk* podcast, noting that each profession has its own legal standards. "You have the Medical Practice Act, the Nursing Practice Act, the PA Practice Act. The scope of practice contained within those different laws determines how much or how little a practitioner can perform."

Using his home state as an example, Sullivan points out that while the Illinois Medical Practice Act includes several different definitions, it does not define the practice of medicine. "The Illinois Nurse Practice Act states that the scope of practice of a nurse practitioner can include 'diagnosis, ordering tests, procedures, providing palliative end of life care, providing counseling'—those are all things that amount to the practice of medicine," he said. "So, when you talk about, 'should nurse practitioners be able to practice medicine?' to some degree, the state legislatures are already allowing them to practice medicine whether they want to call it that or not."

Sullivan says that non-physician advocates have long claimed adequate training and similar outcomes to physicians. "Why should a doctor supervise them if they are legally allowed to practice medicine and they claim to practice as well as a physician?" Sullivan notes that while advocates are quick to claim equivalence to physicians, when it comes to a lawsuit, "everybody backs off and says, 'I'm just a PA, sorry,' or 'I'm just an NP.' It can't work that way; you can't have two separate standards."[408]

Indeed, some plaintiff's attorneys are successfully challenging the court's definition of this standard of care. In the case of Alexus Ochoa, Travis Dunn and his associates argued that since Mercy Health Systems decided to hire nurse practitioners to function as the sole emergency department clinician, they should be held to the standard expected of that role. "As a technical matter, the law requires a nurse practitioner to testify to the standard of care of another nurse practitioner," said Dunn. "So, we called a nurse practitioner to testify to the standard of care, but we also called a physician because it was our philosophy that the healthcare corporation doesn't get to adjust the standard of care. The standard of care that a patient should expect going into an emergency room is the standard of care, period. It doesn't matter whether you attempt to meet that standard with a nurse practitioner, or you actually have a physician."[143]

Dunn notes that this approach put the defense in a difficult position. "If their nurse practitioner [expert witness] testified to a different standard of care, it proves our point. If the nurse practitioner testifies, 'Well, I didn't know to do that, because I'm just a nurse practitioner,' then that shows, [she] shouldn't have been in that position." The legal team argued this exact point, noting that a family nurse practitioner should never have been hired and credentialed to provide emergency care. "Even though this nurse practitioner made a lot of mistakes, she should never have been in that position. She was credentialed. She was given assignments. She was scheduled to be the only provider in the entire building at the time."

In the Ochoa case, the defense retained nurse practitioner expert witness Wendy Wright, a family nurse practitioner. According to Travis Dunn, Wright's expert opinion was that a nurse practitioner certification entitled the practice of virtually any aspect of medicine, "as long as you are educated and have experience." Dunn said that while Wright acknowledged that nurse practitioner Antoinette Thompson was trained in primary care and not acute care, she was qualified because she had previously worked as an emergency room nurse.

Dunn finds this argument disingenuous. "Nurse practitioners are asked to basically perform some of the functions of physicians—to diagnose, to order and interpret tests, and to prescribe medications, but those are not functions that you learn how to do as an ER nurse." Dunn said that Wright knew that as a family nurse practitioner, Thompson was not trained in acute care. "She was never trained on how to diagnose a pulmonary embolism, or which tests to order. But Wright said, 'Well, she knew all that from being an ER nurse.'"

Nurse practitioner advocates often use this argument, insisting that years of experience working as a bedside nurse allows them to function as well as a physician—or better. Dunn merely pointed out the logical fallacies. "Did [Thompson] ever order a test as an ER nurse? Was she ever required to interpret a test? Did she ever form a differential diagnosis? Did she ever diagnose a pulmonary embolus as an RN? No, because those aren't functions that are performed at the RN level, and so there is a gap there. [Wright] just basically ignored the fact that experience at the RN level does not translate to experience at the APRN level."

Like Travis Dunn, William Sullivan believes that if a non-physician is practicing independently without input from any physician, they are practicing medicine and should be held to the same standard. He notes that there is legal precedent for this type of argument. "I'm an emergency physician. If all of a sudden, I decide I want to do neurosurgery and I operate on a patient's brain, I'm not held to the standard of an emergency physician, I'm held to the standard of a neurosurgeon. [Further,] if the hospital credentials me as a neurosurgeon, then they can be liable for doing so. That's what the law says, if you are acting like a specialist, you're held to the standard of that specialist."[408]

Sullivan says that holding independent non-physicians to a lower standard than physicians is unfair. "I think it's unfair to patients and physicians to say [that they're] going to practice just like [physicians] do, but when something inevitably goes wrong, [they] suddenly say, 'we [have to be] held to a lesser standard.' Patients shouldn't have a higher hurdle to get over to prove that a non-physician was negligent." He also believes that equalizing liability will raise non-physician malpractice insurance rates to levels more commensurate with their actual risk.

IMPACT ON MALPRACTICE RATES

While malpractice insurance has historically been much less expensive for non-physicians due to lower overall rates of malpractice, that trend is beginning to change. Malpractice companies attribute the increase in malpractice risk to the utilization of non-physicians for more complex cases than in the past, with most nurse practitioner professional liability claims involving failure to properly diagnose, with death and cancer representing the two most common injuries.[444,445] According to the National Practitioner Database, claims against non-physicians have increased over the last ten years, while decreasing for physicians.[446] Claim payments are increasing for nurse practitioners, as is the cost to defend them against complaints to state boards of nursing.[447]

William Sullivan believes that these claims will continue to rise, increasing malpractice premiums for non-physicians and those who employ them. "If you're an insurer providing malpractice for an independent practitioner and you see that the claims are trending upwards, I would think you're going to price that into the premium both for that individual and for the hospital or the group that wants to hire them," said Sullivan. "Maybe it's still a few years off, but I think there's going to be an impact on insurance."[408]

Sullivan believes that insurers will raise rates much higher if malpractice risk becomes similar. "Eventually it will impact on hospital and group liability," said Sullivan, "making it less desirable for hospitals and clinics to hire non-physicians." Indeed, an analysis of closed malpractice claims showed that hospitals that employ or contract with non-physicians may already be at risk, with malpractice claims naming nurse practitioners and physician assistants more likely to be paid on behalf of the hospital (32% and 38%) compared to claims naming just physicians (8%).[447] Malpractice attorneys note that hospitals are being held liable for the care rendered by non-physician employees, even when they are not employed directly, and argue that the cost savings of non-physician practitioners may be offset by higher malpractice verdicts.[445]

Sullivan advises hospitals to pay more attention to this risk, especially as staffing companies advertise that nurse practitioners can see a third of patients safely at a third of physician cost. "The problem is, you don't know which third they can take care of," said Sullivan. "There can be a very innocuous finding, which I find when I work with NPs and PAs in my emergency department." Sullivan says that he is fortunate that he is usually able to evaluate every patient seen by the non-physicians he supervises. "I have caught a lot of little subtle things that if missed would have led to very bad patient outcomes. So, yes, NPs and PAs can see 33% of the cases independently, but figuring out which 33% is a little more difficult than it sounds."[408]

Niran Al-Agba works in Washington, one of the first states to authorize full nurse practitioner independence. Based on what she has seen, she is wary of the liability risks of non-physician practitioners. While she shares space with a pediatric nurse practitioner, she does not provide supervision. "She has her own shop, and I have my own shop, and we are very clear with patients. You can see the nurse practitioner, or you can see the pediatrician. Patients choose whom they want to see." Al-Agba says that she doesn't want to supervise because she fears the liability associated with independent practice by non-physicians. "I don't want to have a problem, and sometimes it's just amazing that the littlest finding that you get back ends up being something that matters. If you don't know how to read labs, like so many non-physicians—well, I wouldn't want to be responsible for someone else's decision. I can't live with that."[408]

INFORMED CONSENT

William Sullivan argues that removing physician supervision will have an ultimately beneficial downstream effect. "I think that there has to be that cornerstone, and this whole idea that the doctor still has to be liable for supervision, you've got to remove all that," he says. However, Sullivan admits that one factor gives him pause: the issue of informed consent.[408]

For patients to be educated consumers, they must know the difference between clinicians. In an article about non-physician malpractice, insurance company CEO Mark Spiro said that in many cases, patients are not informed of the clinician's credentials, or they don't understand and assume that a physician is treating them. Insurance attorney Amy Evans, JD, added that some patients, especially those who are older, complain to attorneys that they were never informed that they were being treated by non-physician practitioners. She says that non-physicians must ensure that patients are aware of their role.[445]

William Sullivan believes that if patients are adequately informed, they will make the right decision for themselves. "If you have a brain tumor and you need surgery for it, you're not just going to look in the Yellow Pages," he said. "You're going to do your research [to find] who is the best brain surgeon out there. I think it's going to be the same with patients if they know that they have a choice—someone who's got 11 or 12 years of medical education versus someone who has much less. Patients have to be able to decide based on the full amount of information. That's what informed consent is all about."[408]

Niran Al-Agba agrees that patients must learn the difference between clinicians. "That's why we wrote the book, *Patients at Risk*. It was about the evidence—there is no evidence that NPs and PAs practice the same as physicians—all the studies were supervised. I think once people know and ask, and understand who they are seeing, they can be better advocates for themselves." Unfortunately, she thinks that patients may have to learn the hard way. "In independent states, we just have to kind of move forward. If NPs and PAs want to be the same, let's let them be the same. Let's let them provide the same standard of care. If they can't, then that's something they'll have to let out in the wash."[408]

Case study: lack of informed consent

While informed consent is a hallmark of quality medical care, it is not always forthcoming regarding the replacement of physicians. Paul Armbruster experienced a lack of informed consent regarding his anesthesia care when he underwent a total hip replacement in Arizona in 2022, which he discussed in a *Patients at Risk* podcast. "I remember going to sleep, and then waking up in the recovery room with a breathing tube down my throat—which is not a very pleasant experience at all," Armbruster said, adding dryly, "If you've never had CPR before, I don't recommend it."[448]

According to medical records, Armbruster immediately developed respiratory failure and cardiac arrest upon arriving in the recovery room. A note from the post-anesthesia care unit (PACU) nurse read:

> Patient arrived to PACU around 0930. Upon arrived [sic] I noticed patients [sic] color was blue and notified anesthesiologist who was with patient my concern of patient not breathing adequately. I began to feel for a pulse and notice the patient was pulseless. I began compressions while the anesthesiologist was managing the patient's airway. I then called out for help and a code blue was called and in a timely manner all staff needed arrived. [Return of spontaneous breathing] was achieved at 0938. Emergency medical services arrived shortly after and patient was transferred to a higher level of care.[448]

Armbruster was taken to a university hospital, where he spent three days in the emergency department under observation. It was there that he learned that his anesthesia had been provided by a nurse anesthetist, with no supervising anesthesiologist on site. "No one reached out to me to tell me what had happened or to check on me," said Ambruster. "The only thing I heard from an orthopedic surgeon was [that I was] oversedated and [my] heart stopped."[448]

Armbruster said that before his surgery, he had no knowledge or understanding of the role of a CRNA. "The concept is totally foreign to me," he said. "If this event hadn't happened, I wouldn't have even known what a CRNA was." While the CRNA introduced himself during the preoperative evaluation, Ambruster said that he assumed that this was an assistant to the anesthesiologist. "I thought, this is like a physician's assistant. This is the nurse anesthetist who's going to be helping the anesthesiologist. It was never disclosed to me that he was the only person who was going to be looking after my anesthesia care."

While his anesthesia was provided by a CRNA-only group, Armbruster learned that Arizona law requires that CRNAs function under physician direction. Without an anesthesiologist present, Armbruster said that his surgeon was held responsible for the CRNA's care. "I've had multiple conversations with my actual surgeon post this event, and he says he was always told that he is not responsible for anesthesia during his surgeries," said Armbruster, noting that this makes sense, since it is impossible to operate and supervise anesthesia at the same time. "After the fact, the hospital told him that he is responsible for anesthesia, which unfortunately resulted in a conflict and his termination just a few weeks ago." In fact, Armbruster was supposed to have surgery on his other hip, but it was canceled because the surgeon was fired. "He was terminated because he wouldn't put his hand up and say, 'Yeah, I was the responsible physician.'"

Although Arizona law requires that CRNAs be supervised by a physician, Armbruster said that the law exempts the physician from liability for any acts performed by the CRNA. "There's a safe harbor clause, so it's sort of toothless," he said. Due to the way the statute is written, Armbruster believes that the hospitals are comfortable telling surgeons that they aren't responsible, despite strict legal definitions. "They're relying on this safe harbor provision that says, [their physicians] can't get in trouble anyway. So, what they're doing is essentially staffing surgery rooms with unsupervised CRNAs."

Armbruster believes that surgery centers are doing this to save money. The center where he had his procedure performed is owned by Healthcare Outcomes Performance (HOPCo), a "vertically integrated provider of musculoskeletal care services." It may come as no surprise to learn that HOPCo is owned by $6 billion private equity company Audax.[449] Investing mostly in healthcare holdings, Audax has acquired 26 companies, invested in 5, and sold 26 in the last three years.[450]

What can be done to ensure that patients receive care from anesthesiologists rather than CRNAs? Armbruster isn't sure. "The only recourse seems to be [that] if you die, you get a lot of money from a malpractice suit," he said. "I think they've done the math and they're willing to take a couple of deaths a year to make more money."[448]

PUNITIVE DAMAGES

Indeed, some corporations seem to take the Ford Pinto view that it's less expensive to pay claims than to exclusively hire physicians. For example, when Alexus Ochoa's family won a $6 million wrongful death suit against Mercy Health Systems, attorney Glendall Nix expressed hope that the verdict would change the company's policies and prevent further patient harm. However, Nix's associate Travis Dunn is doubtful. "I go back and forth," he said, noting that since Mercy was self-insured, the judgment was paid out of the multi-billion-dollar system's operating self-retention budget, which factors in the possibility of paying malpractice suits, and may not have made a meaningful dent in the system's overall profitability.[143]

Dunn believes that obtaining much larger punitive damages against corporations is the only thing that can change this behavior. "There are two types of damages. There are compensatory damages that are designed to compensate the family for their loss, and that's what the jury awarded the Ochoa family," said Dunn. "If we can show that the corporation acted with reckless indifference or with malice, then we can get into what's called punitive damages which are intended to punish the defendant." Dunn believes that his legal team was very close to proving that argument. "I think if we could have told the jury how much money that Mercy was saving by doing this, the verdict would have been very different."

Dunn and his team showed that Mercy systematically worked to increase the number of nurse practitioners staffing their facilities. "Mercy wanted to use more and more nurse practitioners," said Dunn. "Since Oklahoma has a specific statute that says a physician can only supervise two nurse practitioners, they were recruiting physicians who had privileges at the hospital to sign off on paperwork as being supervising physicians for people they'd never met, who they had never worked with, or even heard of." Dunn's team found email chains asking staff physicians to participate in this scheme. "To a couple of folks' credit, when they got those emails, there were doctors that [refused] to sign off on being a supervisor for someone that [they'd] never met, but there were lots and lots of doctors that did."

Dunn's team had investigative documents to prove that Mercy continued to misuse nurse practitioners even after Alexus Ochoa's death. "We would have been able to show how much money they saved from using nurse practitioners instead of physicians and how much money they make from this practice. We would have been able to argue, 'if you want to change this behavior, you have to hit this billion-dollar corporation hard enough for them to change.'"

Dunn regrets that the team wasn't able to get to this point because the jury did not find that Mercy acted with reckless indifference. He believes that after two weeks of testimony, the jury was tired. "The defense counsel said, 'Well, if you check punitive damage, we're going to have to come back and do another trial.'" In retrospect, Dunn wishes that he had pushed the issue. "We had testimony from one of the higher-ups that Mercy was continuing the same hiring practices. Looking back, if I had just said, 'It's one witness; you've been here for two weeks. Give me another two hours,' I think they would have awarded punitive damages. I believe the jury was headed in that direction, but they're human beings, too. They have their own lives. They'd just spent two weeks in this trial. [Nevertheless], I think that was a key point that I wish that I could go back and do differently."

The amount of profit that Mercy made by replacing physicians with nurse practitioners was not entered into evidence, and therefore not a matter of public record, thus Dunn cannot reveal the figure, but he believes that it was significant enough that it would have swayed the jury to award punitive damages, which could force companies to rethink dangerous practices. "We have to take this next step, and we have to be successful in convincing juries that they need to. It's not just about compensating the family, which they did. It's about punishing the defendant; it is about changing behavior. Once you get past that hurdle, and you're able to admit evidence to show the jury [that] this is a $6 billion corporation, and … they're continuing to do the same thing today, then we have what we need to change behavior."[143]

ENSURING TRUTH AND TRANSPARENCY

In 2017, 27-year-old Carlos David Castro Rojas underwent surgery at Baylor University Medical Center in Dallas, TX to repair a broken leg. During general anesthesia with a CRNA, Carlos suffered a brain injury from a loss of oxygen that left him in a vegetative state. Plaintiff's attorneys argued that Rojas had received inadequate informed consent from U.S. Anesthesia Partners regarding the use of a CRNA, saying that "no one explained to Carlos that there was a difference between providers or their qualifications" and that CRNAs were used to make more money for the company. The jury agreed, awarding the victim $21 million. Carlos's attorneys urged other patients to ask for a physician, noting, "unless you know you have a choice, you don't ask."[451]

Indeed, many patients report finding it difficult to determine which members of the care team are licensed physicians. While patients overwhelmingly prefer to have a physician in charge of their care, only 55% said that it was easy to identify a physician based on advertising and marketing materials. Seventy-nine percent of patients said that they would support state legislation to require clear identification of the education, skills, and training of healthcare professionals.[452]

Some state legislative bodies have taken steps to ensure that patients receive proper information about the credentials of their clinicians, including whether a physician is involved in their care. The New Jersey Health Care Transparency Act, signed into law in 2020, requires that healthcare professionals wear a name tag that includes the profession in which they are licensed. Clinics or medical offices must also post the clinicians' licensure, as well as identifying the name of the non-physician practitioner's supervising physician and the hours that the physician is present in the office.[453] Similar legislation passed in Indiana in 2022.

When passing independent practice for nurse practitioners in 2020, the state of California attempted to place safeguards and rules for transparency. For example, nurse practitioners are required to verbally inform new patients that they are not a physician and must post a notice advising patients that they are regulated by the Board of Registered Nursing, with contact information for the Board. Nurse practitioners are required to carry malpractice insurance and must not practice outside of their scope of training. In addition, they must establish a plan to refer patients to a physician for the following reasons:

- Emergent conditions requiring prompt medical intervention after initial stabilizing care has been started
- Acute decompensation of patient situation

- Problem which is not resolving as anticipated
- History, physical, or lab findings inconsistent with the clinical perspective
- Upon request of the patient.

While critics of the law worry that these referral rules will increase liability for physicians, others praise efforts to ensure truth and transparency for patients and to make it clear that patients have the right to request care from a physician.

On October 22, 2022, the law was applied when California Superior Court ordered nurse practitioner Sarah Erny to pay a nearly $20,000 fine for using the title 'doctor.' According to a court petition from San Luis Obispo District Attorney Dan Dow, Erny, who earned a Doctor of Nursing Practice from Vanderbilt University, misled the public by implying that she was a medical doctor and failed to clarify to patients that she was working under a collaborative arrangement with a physician. The document argued that the nurse practitioner owed a duty to accurately promote her credentials, noting that "elevating her doctorate by encouraging patients to call her 'Dr. Sarah' improperly shifts the burden of understanding the scope of services a registered nurse can perform."

In addition to paying a fine, Erny was ordered to correct her title on all online websites, prohibit others from calling her 'doctor,' and to correct patients who call her doctor by advising them that she is not a medical doctor but is a registered nurse or nurse practitioner."[454]

On a GoFundMe page that Erny created to raise money to pay for the fine, the nurse practitioner argued that she did nothing wrong, writing that "there is absolutely no danger in using the title I earned to patients." She also wrote that not being allowed to use the title doctor is 'very demoralizing,' because, "I worked very hard for this degree while I was working at [Community Health Centers] seeing 25 patients a day."[455]

While Sarah Erny disagreed with the Court's decision, District Attorney Dan Dow said, "Providing patients upfront with the proper title of our health care professionals aids consumers in making a more informed decision about their health care."[454]

Will other states follow California's lead in enforcing laws for non-physician practitioners? In 2020, Florida legalized independent practice exclusively for nurse practitioners practicing primary care, defined as family medicine, general pediatrics, and general internal medicine. Legislators justified the move by insisting that allowing independent practice would increase access to primary care for Floridians. Leah Michel, APRN was one of the first nurse practitioners to obtain an autonomous license in the state. But rather than working in primary care, Michel operates My Skin, a dermatology clinic in St. Petersburg, the fifth most populous city in Florida.

Despite her training as a Family nurse practitioner, Michel's website states that she specializes in 'medical dermatology,' and also promotes "the latest in anti-aging treatments," such as botox injections, fillers, and microneedling. The website's home page implies that Michel is a dermatologist, stating: 'Welcome to My Skin Dermatology | Dermatologist St. Petersburg, FL.' No supervising physician—dermatologist or otherwise—is listed on the website.[471] Whether state officials will take any action regarding this practice remains to be seen.

BUYER BEWARE

Not all states have initiated medical transparency laws, and non-physician advocates are working to oppose them. Noting that he was unaware that a nurse practitioner had treated his daughter Betty, who subsequently died, Jeremy Wattenbarger worked with Texas State Senator Jared Patterson to create legislation requiring that clinical staff properly identify themselves. Modeled after New Jersey's medical truth and transparency law, the legislation would have required credentials to be clearly stated, and that clinics without physicians onsite publicly notify patients and identify the supervising physician for any non-physician practitioners working at the facility.

But Betty's Law, as it was called, didn't even make it to the floor for a public hearing. "It was squashed by the Legislature pretty quick," said Jeremy. "I think the real sticking point was that they had to have the credentials. A lot of people don't want the credentials on the badge because they want to call themselves 'provider' which a consumer or patient assumes to be a physician. If they have to put their qualifications, then they have to identify themselves as a nurse and not just a provider. They didn't like that."[12]

When asked about Betty's Law, Cindy Zolnierek, the CEO of the Texas Nurse Association dismissed the need for such legislation, saying, "any patient loss is a tragedy, and while we do not know the details of this particular case, the evidence demonstrates that the care provided by advanced practice registered nurses is generally as safe, or safer than physicians. You will find anecdotes of misdiagnosis with unfortunate outcomes for both [nurse practitioners] and physicians. However, if you look at the statistics, patients have no greater risk when treated by APRNs."[456]

Physician Amy Townsend disagrees. "This a repetitive statement that we hear over and over from nursing leadership. It's almost like if they say it enough times, they think that it's going to make it reality," she said. "The truth is that there are no studies out there evaluating unsupervised medical practice by nurse practitioners. All the studies that they cite have been done under physician supervision. Most of the time, they're looking at very simple pre-diagnosed problems like high blood pressure or diabetes. Those type of scenarios are much different than trying to independently diagnose a random person that walks in off the street, and Betty is a great example." Townsend says that because there is such a discrepancy between the quality and quantity of training, "the burden really is on them to give proof of the statements that they're making, but they just have not done it."[12]

While Betty's Law failed to progress in the legislature, Jeremy Wattenbarger did help to stop a law intended to allow nurse practitioners independent practice in Texas. "House Bill 2029 was written and sponsored by Stephanie Klick, a nurse and committee chair," said Amy Townsend. "We had physicians show up to give testimony against the bill, but the biggest impact came from Jeremy's testimony about the death of his daughter, Betty."

Other states have also resisted efforts to rein in non-physician practitioners. Some critics call Arizona the wild west based on the state's loose oversight of medical practitioners like CRNA Tory Richmond. Richmond was not disciplined by the Arizona Board of Nursing, despite being named in two wrongful death lawsuits of dental patients who died under his care, including one patient whose mouth erupted in fire during a procedure.[457]

Arizona also allows naturopathic physicians, alternative care practitioners who are not medical doctors, to perform surgeries, including Brazilian butt lifts, a cosmetic procedure known for a high risk for complications, including a 3–4% mortality rate. In 2022, an Arizona judge dismissed multiple claims against Jose Ortiz, a naturopath who performed liposuction surgery on a patient. While a plaintiff's attorney had a naturopath and a plastic surgeon ready to testify against Ortiz, the judge did not allow them to act as expert witnesses, noting that Arizona law requires that only another naturopath with a similar practice performing liposuction may testify to the standard of care. Further, the Arizona Naturopathic Physicians Medical Board dismissed complaints against Ortiz, finding that he did not act outside the scope of his license.[458]

Bob Pegritz, a former physician assistant and malpractice expert witness says that it is essential that patients learn to identify clinician credentials and seek out physician-led care. "You shouldn't feel embarrassed when you're in a medical office to ask about credentials," he said. "It's just like purchasing other things in life—a smart consumer is a good consumer. Especially when it comes to a person's health. The more you know, the safer you are."[248]

PATIENTS NEED OPTIONS

It is not always easy to find a physician. After nearly dying during anesthesia managed by a CRNA, Paul Armbruster is seeking an anesthesiologist for his follow-up surgery. He says that finding a facility that utilizes physicians is more challenging than he expected. "The problem I'm having now is if you call up a surgery center—and this has happened to me twice in the past month—when I say, 'Hey, I had a bad experience with a CRNA, I went into cardiac arrest and I want to make sure that I get a physician for the procedure,' that is all too hard for them. I mean, they're not interested. It's a challenge for me to get health care because all of these hospitals are just pushing CRNAs in the operating room."[448]

To increase access to physicians, some companies are promoting physician-only care. Old Pueblo Anesthesia, a physician-owned and operated company, provides anesthesia across southern Arizona, and hires only anesthesiologists.[459] Nutex Health, a physician-led healthcare management company, has opened 21 micro-hospitals across eight states,[460] including Alexandria Emergency Hospital in Louisiana which staffs only board-certified emergency physicians.[461] More doctors must open and promote physician-led practices, and patients should seek them out (Appendix).

DIVERTING THE SHIP

When 18-year-old Libby Zion died in 1984, her bereaved father used his platform and political connections to force radical and lasting changes to graduate medical education. Likewise, in 1988, when Maryland freshman Senator Barbara Mikulski learned that a constituent's wife had died of cervical cancer after a misread Pap smear test, her tenacity led to the Clinical Laboratory Improvement Amendments (CLIA), a law enacted in 1992 that drastically improved clinical laboratory safety and quality.[462]

Will policymakers and legislators have the political will to return to common sense policies ensuring access to physician-led care for all Americans? Or will it take serious harm to a person of power or influence to divert this Titanic?

Natalie Newman believes that the ship can be saved. She compares the current state of medicine to the housing bubble of 2008: when stakeholders were making too much money to heed the warnings of an impending collapse. "The model of using non-physicians to replace doctors is unsustainable for one reason: non-physician practitioners are not physicians. It will be impossible to maintain the practice of medicine effectively and competently because they are unqualified to practice it." Newman says that with time, the market will correct, and the ship will right itself. Until then, patients face grave dangers.

"Diverting a ship is expensive, and not usually desired by the captain," says Newman, "but it's done in the best interest of the passengers—or in this case, the patients." Newman says that only the captain of a ship—physicians—can take the steps necessary to divert the path of the medical profession. This could involve rejecting employment by corporate groups, refusing to inappropriately supervise or to collaborate with non-physician practitioners, and a return to self-ownership through models like direct care.[431]

Physicians must unite to fight policies that restrict patient access to quality care, such as the right to own hospitals and the requirement for burdensome and unnecessary documentation to be paid for medical services. As Alyson Maloy notes, rather than having non-physicians 'practice at the top of their licenses,' physicians should be freed up from the burden of data entry and other administrative tasks. "I say, let physicians work to the top of our license. We don't need to be spending 20 hours a week hitting buttons on a computer to enter information into archaic electronic health systems. It's a waste of our talent, and that would free up a lot of physician hours to take care of patients."[246]

While patients are becoming more aware of the importance of ensuring care by a physician, they must act. Steps include reporting improper care if it occurs (see Appendix) and contacting legislators to demand truth and transparency among healthcare practitioners, as well as a concrete plan to increase the number of fully trained physicians. If a company replaces a patient's physician with a non-physician practitioner, they should consider seeking care elsewhere and explain to the administration why they are leaving.

Nurse practitioners and physician assistants who want to return to the traditional model of physician supervision must stand up to their leadership and insist that their voice be heard. They cannot allow corporations to place them in dangerous positions that compromise patient safety, and should insist on proper physician supervision.

If physicians, patients, nurse practitioners, and physician assistants work together, it's not too late to divert the Titanic.

ACKNOWLEDGEMENTS

This book was inspired by members of Physicians for Patient Protection, which began as a grassroots social media group of concerned physicians and developed into an official organization through the work of Carmen Kavali, MD, Chantel O'Shea, DO, Purvi Parikh, MD, Amy Townsend, MD, Ainel Sewell, MD, Roy Stoller, DO, Phil Shaffer, MD, Alyson Maloy, MD, Brian Wilhelmi, MD, JD, Sharon D'Souza, MD, MPH, Marsha Haley, MD, and me. We would not exist without the dedication and work of our founding executive director Linda Lambert, and current executive director Babette Atkins. We urge other physicians to join our organization at physiciansforpatientprotection.org.

Niran Al-Agba, MD, the co-author of the original *Patients at Risk* book, founded the *Patients at Risk* podcast with me, and her words continue to ring throughout this volume. She inspires me every day, along with the many other brave physicians who have faced personal attacks and professional repercussions to join us in advocating for patient safety. Responding to such criticism (or choosing not to respond) is not an easy task, and I thank my friend Steven Cohen, PsyD, who has had to put his psychology skills to work on me many times throughout this experience. I am also blessed and so grateful for the love and support of my husband Juan Mendoza.

I sincerely appreciate the contributions of the many physicians, patients, nurse practitioners, physician assistants, attorneys, and other experts who allowed me to share their stories and wisdom throughout this book. I encourage anyone who wants to share their experience in a podcast episode or otherwise to contact me through the website, PatientsAtRisk.com.

I cannot express my appreciation enough to Publisher Jeff Young, PhD at academic press Universal Publishers and to Editor Barbara Dalberry, whose work has been invaluable to ensure accuracy, clarity, and the removal of bias. Many thanks to Sean Wilkes, MD, for creating the graphics of physician training for various medical specialties. I also thank Teresa Camp-Rogers, MD, MS, Mehrdad Saririan, MD, and Phil Shaffer, MD for feedback and advice on early versions of the book and Cheryl Ferguson, MD for assistance with proofreading.

APPENDIX

NURSE PRACTITIONER PRACTICE AUTHORITY BY STATE (2022)[463]

Unsupervised practice immediately after certification	Unsupervised practice after a time period of supervised practice	Physician supervision or a collaborative practice agreement
Alaska	California—3 years/ 4600 hours*	Alabama
Arizona	Connecticut—3 years and 2,000 hours	Florida (non-primary care)
Arkansas	Delaware—2 years and 4,000 hours	Georgia
Colorado	Florida—primary care after 3,000 hours	Indiana
Hawaii	Illinois—4,000 hours	Kansas
Idaho	Maine—2 years	Louisiana
Iowa	Maryland—18 months	Mississippi
Kentucky	Minnesota—2,080 hours	Missouri
Massachusetts	Nebraska—2,000 hours	New York
Michigan	Nevada—2 years or 2,000 hours	North Carolina
Montana	South Dakota—1,040 hours	Ohio
New Hampshire	Vermont—2 years and 2,400 hours	Pennsylvania
New Jersey	Virginia—5 years	South Carolina
New Mexico	West Virginia—3 years	Tennessee
North Dakota		Texas
Oklahoma		Virginia
Oregon		Wisconsin
Rhode Island		Washington DC
Utah		
Washington		
Wyoming		
ALL Veterans Administration facilities		

Note: *Law passed in 2020—takes effect 2023.

HOW TO REPORT CONCERNS ABOUT IMPROPER CARE

Outpatient facility (office, clinic, urgent care center)

1. Send written communication (email or letter) to the Office Manager/Operations Director.
2. Copy that same written communication to the physicians in the practice, particularly any physician contractually connected to the non-physician practitioner (collaborating or supervising physician).
3. If the non-physician mismanagement is related to care by a nurse practitioner, report to your State Board of Nursing. If the mismanagement is related to care by a Physician Assistant, report to your state Board of Medicine. Some states have Joint Boards that oversee NPs or PAs. Use the search system at physiciansforpatientprotection.org to find out which Board to contact for your state. https://tinyurl.com/2ue3jzp4
4. If you used your insurance for the office visit related to the non-physician mismanagement, report it to your insurance company. Do an online search for the company's Grievance Hotline, then follow the instructions given. **Reporting to Medicare:** Contact Medicare (https://www.medicare.gov/talk-to-someone) to file a complaint with your Beneficiary and Family Centered Care-Quality Improvement Organization (BFCC-QIOs), which exists to manage all complaints and quality of care reviews for Medicare beneficiaries.
5. Report false advertising to your state Attorney General.
6. Tell your story. Discuss your concerns on social media, on review sites, and share it at https://www.physiciansforpatientprotection.org/physician-resources/tell-us-your-story/

Hospital or hospital-owned system, Veteran's Administration

1. Report to the Patient Advocate. This person might also be called a Patient Ombudsman, Patient Safety Liaison, or Patient Relations Representative. You can find out who this is by asking hospital staff or by looking at the posted or printed Patient Rights statement from the facility, or by calling the hospital operator.
2. Report to Risk Management at the facility. This is a department that handles any event that could lead to patient harm or liability. For the VA, report to the Office of the Inspector General—https://www.va.gov/oig/hotline/complainant-release-preference.asp
3. Report to the Chief Medical Officer of the facility or Associate Chief of Staff, usually a physician overseeing care in a particular specialty.

You'll want to report to the one in the specialty that concerns you (primary care, cardiology, nephrology, etc.).

4. If the non-physician mismanagement is related to care by a nurse practitioner, report to your State Board of Nursing. If the mismanagement is related to care by a Physician Assistant, report to your state Board of Medicine. Some states have Joint Boards that oversee NPs or PAs. Use our search system at physiciansforpatientprotection.org to find out which Board to contact for your state. https://tinyurl.com/2ue3jzp4
5. File a complaint with the State Board of Health. You can find that information using the search feature at the link above.
6. If you used your insurance for care related to the non-physician mismanagement, report it to your insurance company. Do an online search for the company's Grievance Hotline, then follow the instructions given. File a grievance with TriCare, if you used TriCare insurance.
7. Most importantly, file a Patient Safety Event with The Joint Commission, which is the body that accredits many hospitals in the U.S. You can file this report by going to www.jointcommission.org, and using the "Report a Patient Safety Event" link in the "Action Center" of the homepage. You can also file by fax to 630-792-5636. Or file by mail to Office of Quality and Patient Safety, The Joint Commission, One Renaissance Boulevard, Oakbrook Terrace, IL 60181.
8. Contact your Congressional representative. https://www.house.gov/representatives/find-your-representative. This will have the greatest impact and will inform our Congress when they consider scope of practice expansion in the future.

ADDITIONAL RESOURCES

American Medical Association—https://www.ama-assn.org/practice-management/scope-practice
Find a physician: https://yourphysicianfinder.com
Patients at Risk—PatientsatRisk.com
Physicians for Patient Protection—https://physiciansforpatientprotection.org

REFERENCES

1. Mundinger M. Opinion | quality health care with NPs and MDs. *The Wall Street Journal.* October 4, 2020. Retrieved October 24, 2021, from https://www.wsj.com/articles/quality-health-care-with-nps-and-m-d-s-11601819436
2. Patients at Risk. There's Something About Mary. November 12, 2020 [Video]. YouTube. https://youtu.be/PrmyfSSV4jk
3. McHugh, R. Families sound alarm on medical transparency after deaths of their children. *NewsNation Now.* December 18, 2020. Retrieved October 24, 2021, from https://www.newsnationnow.com/investigation/transparencyinhealthcare/
4. A Collaborative Work from Some of the Writers at Authentic Medicine. Sophia the worst: AANP statement on WGN's biased news story on nurse practitioner profession. *Authentic Medicine.* December 20, 2020. Retrieved October 24, 2021, from https://authenticmedicine.com/2020/12/sophia-the-worst-aanp-statement-on-wgns-biased-news-story-on-nurse-practitioner-profession/
5. National Task Force on Quality Nurse Practitioner Education. Criteria for Evaluation of Nurse Practitioner Programs, 5th Edition. *American Association of Colleges of Nursing.* 2016. Retrieved January 25, 2023, from https://cdn.ymaws.com/www.nonpf.org/resource/resmgr/Docs/EvalCriteria2016Final.pdf
6. Education and Training: Family Physicians versus Nurse Practitioners. American Academy of Family Physicians. Date unknown. Retrieved January 25, 2023 from https://www.aafp.org/dam/AAFP/documents/advocacy/workforce/scope/FPvsNP.pdf
7. AANP statement on WGN's biased news story on nurse practitioner profession. American Association of Nurse Practitioners. Date Unknown. Retrieved October 24, 2021, from https://www.aanp.org/news-feed/aanp-statement-on-wgns-biased-news-story-on-nurse-practitioner-profession
8. Bureau of Labor Statistics, U.S. Department of Labor, Occupational Outlook Handbook, Nurse Anesthetists, Nurse Midwives, and Nurse Practitioners 2021, at https://www.bls.gov/ooh/healthcare/nurse-anesthetists-nurse-midwives-and-nurse-practitioners.htm (visited September 08, 2022).
9. Bureau of Labor Statistics, U.S. Department of Labor, Occupational Outlook Handbook, Physician Assistants 2021, at https://www.bls.gov/ooh/healthcare/physician-assistants.htm (visited September 08, 2022).
10. Bureau of Labor Statistics, U.S. Department of Labor, Occupational Outlook Handbook, Physicians and Surgeons 2021, at https://www.bls.gov/ooh/healthcare/physicians-and-surgeons.htm (Reviewed September 08, 2022).
11. Quality of Nurse Practitioner practice. American Association of Nurse Practitioners. Date Unknown. Retrieved November 13, 2022, from https://www.aanp.org/advocacy/advocacy-resource/position-statements/quality-of-nurse-practitioner-practice

12. Patients at Risk. Betty's Story: 7-yr old dies just hours after evaluation by pediatric NP—Part 1. Sept 12, 2021. [Video] YouTube. https://www.youtube.com/watch?v=Su43DKxNZoY
13. Use of terms such as mid-level provider and physician extender. American Association of Nurse Practitioners. Retrieved October 28, 2022, from https://www.aanp.org/advocacy/advocacy-resource/position-statements/use-of-terms-such-as-mid-level-provider-and-physician-extender
14. Kendall, L. Graduate Medical Education has been threatened. *Am J Med.* 2020;133(9): 1017–1018. https://doi.org/10.1016/j.amjmed.2020.02.047
15. Zhang X, Lin D, Pforsich H, Lin VW. Physician workforce in the United States of America: forecasting nationwide shortages. Hum Resource Health. Feb 6, 2020; 18(1):8. doi: 10.1186/s12960-020-0448-3. PMID: 32029001; PMCID: PMC7006215.
16. Michas, F. Total active doctors in the U.S. by state 2022. *Statista.* June 8, 2022. Retrieved October 6, 2022, from https://www.statista.com/statistics/186269/
17. NP fact sheet. American Association of Nurse Practitioners. Retrieved October 6, 2022, from https://www.aanp.org/about/all-about-nps/np-fact-sheet
18. Statistical profile of Certified PAs. National Commission on Certification of Physician Assistants. 2021. Retrieved October 6, 2022, from https://www.nccpa.net/wp-content/uploads/2022/08/2021StatProfileofCertifiedPAs-A-3.2.pdf
19. Rich, S. Rx for physician glut: Pay hospitals not to train new ones. *The Washington Post*. March 9, 1997. Retrieved October 7, 2022, from https://www.washingtonpost.com/archive/politics/1997/03/09/rx-for-physician-glut-pay-hospitals-not-to-train-new-ones/f0514eed-3e43-4a19-8f09-6264acafd9a5/
20. Salsberg E, Grover A. Physician workforce shortages: Implications and issues for academic health centers and policymakers. *Acad Med.* 2006; 81: 782–787.
21. Auerbach, S. A bitter pill for the Health Industry. *The Washington Post*. November 17, 1995. Retrieved October 7, 2022, from https://www.washingtonpost.com/archive/politics/1995/11/17/a-bitter-pill-for-the-health-industry/9cd29ab5-eb29-4e39-bc70-2292905c9e2f/
22. American Association of Colleges of Osteopathic Medicine, American Medical Association, American Osteopathic Association, Association of Academic Health Centers, Association of American Medical Colleges, National Medical Association. Consensus Statement on Physician Workforce. Washington, DC; 1997.
23. AMA Association. 2020 compendium of Graduate Medical Education Initiatives Report. Retrieved October 9, 2022, from https://www.ama-assn.org/system/files/2020-08/2020-gme-compendium-report.pdf
24. U.S. Department of Health and Human Services, Office of Graduate Medical Education. Summary Report of the Graduate Medical Education National Advisory Committee, September 30, 1980. DHHS Publication No. (HRA) 81–651 April 1980. Retrieved October 6, 2022 from https://babel.hathitrust.org/cgi/pt?id=mdp.39015010022930&view=1up&seq=1
25. Dellabella, H. 50 years of the nurse practitioner profession. *Clinical Advisor.* December 20, 2018. Retrieved October 6, 2022, from https://www.clinicaladvisor.com/home/web-exclusives/50-years-of-the-nurse-practitioner-profession/
26. He XZ, Cyran E, Salling M. National trends in the United States of America physician assistant workforce from 1980 to 2007. Hum Resour Health. Nov 26, 2009;7:86. doi: 10.1186/1478-4491-7-86. PMID: 19941662; PMCID: PMC2788515.
27. Sharp, N. Graduate nursing education money and you. *Nursing Management*. May 1994; 25(5): 32. DOI:10.1097/00006247-199405000-00005

28. Carthon JM, Barnes H, Sarik DA. Federal Polices Influence Access to Primary Care and Nurse Practitioner Workforce. *J Nurse Pract*. 2015;11(5):526–530. doi: 10.1016/j.nurpra.2015.01.028. Epub 2015 Mar 4. PMID: 26457073; PMCID: PMC4596547.
29. Vestal, C. Nurse practitioners step in where doctors are scarce. The Pew Charitable Trusts. December 5, 2012. Retrieved October 9, 2022, from https://www.pewtrusts.org/en/research-and-analysis/blogs/stateline/2012/12/05/nurse-practitioners-step-in-where-doctors-are-scarce
30. Fulcher, R. Policy, Nursing Graduate Medical Education: Misdirected Funding. *Policy, Polit Nurs Pract.* Vol. 1 No. 2, May 2000; 1(2): 97–100, Sage Publications, Inc https://citeseerx.ist.psu.edu/viewdoc/download?doi=10.1.1.969.8857&rep=rep1&type=pdf
31. Eden J, Berwick D, Wilensky G, Committee on the Governance and Financing of Graduate Medical Education; Board on Health Care Services; Institute of Medicine, eds. Graduate Medical Education That Meets the Nation's Health Needs. Washington (DC): National Academies Press (US); September 30, 2014.
32. Robert Wood Johnson Foundation. Grant Number 65815. Grants Explorer. https://www.rwjf.org/content/rwjf/en/how-wework/grantsexplorer.html#start=2007&end=2009&amt=1000001&t=1926|1928|1924|1923|1929&s=15&sortBy=organization&ascending=true. Accessed June 12, 2020.
33. Institute of Medicine. *The Future of Nursing: Leading Change, Advancing Health.* Washington, DC: The National Academies Press; 2011.
34. US Government Accountability Office Health Care Workforce. *Views on Expanding Medicare Graduate Medical Education Funding to Nurse Practitioners and Physician Assistants*. US Government Printing Office, Washington, DC; 2019.
35. Cooper RA, Getzen TE, McKee HJ, Laud P. Economic and demographic trends signal an impending physician shortage. *Health Aff* (Millwood). 2002;21(1):140–54. doi: 10.1377/hlthaff.21.1.140. PMID: 11900066.
36. Schroeder SA. Western European Responses to Physician Oversupply: Lessons for the United States. *JAMA*. 1984;252(3):373–384. doi:10.1001/jama.1984.03350030041019
37. Shanosky, N., McDermott, D., & Kurani, N. (2020, September 17). *How do U.S. healthcare resources compare to other countries?* Peterson-KFF Health System Tracker. Retrieved October 6, 2022, from https://www.healthsystemtracker.org/chart-collection/u-s-health-care-resources-compare-countries/#Practicing%20physicians,%20density%20per%201,000%20population,%202018
38. Chan, B. From Perceived Surplus to Perceived Shortage: What Happened to Canada's Physician Workforce in the 1990s? *Canadian Institute for Healthcare Information*, June 2002. Retrieved October 6, 2022 from https://secure.cihi.ca/free_products/chanjun02.pdf
39. The Complexities of Physician Supply and Demand: Projections from 2019 to 2034. *AAMC*; 2021. Retrieved January 25, 2023, from https://www.aamc.org/media/54681/download
40. Kalter, L. U.S. medical school enrollment rises 30%. *AAMC*. July 5, 2019. Retrieved October 6, 2022, from https://www.aamc.org/news-insights/us-medical-school-enrollment-rises-30
41. National Resident Matching Program, Results and Data: 2022 Main Residency Match®. National Resident Matching Program, Washington, DC. 2022.
42. Grant, K. The Mental Health Toll of not matching. *Medical News.* July 7, 2021. Retrieved October 29, 2022, from https://www.medpagetoday.com/special-reports/exclusives/93454

43. Bernard, R. Match Day 2021 brings uncertain future for many graduating medical students. *Medical Economics.* April 14, 2021. Retrieved January 22, 2023, from https://www.medicaleconomics.com/view/match-day-2021-brings-uncertain-future-for-many-graduating-medical-students
44. Cade, T. The never-ending story of the Resident Physician Shortage Reduction Act. *Germane Solutions.* May 25, 2021. Retrieved October 26, 2022, from https://www.germane-solutions.com/Blog/359830/The-Never-ending-Story-of-the-Resident-Physician-Shortage-Reduction-Act
45. Robeznieks. A. 1,000 new GME slots are coming. CMS must not hamper their use. *American Medical Association.* March 16, 2022. Retrieved October 26, 2022, from https://www.ama-assn.org/education/gme-funding/1000-new-gme-slots-are-coming-cms-must-not-hamper-their-use
46. Menendez leads bipartisan call for Biden admin to increase Medicare GME positions: U.S. senator Bob Menendez of New Jersey. October 5, 2022. www.Senate.gov. Retrieved October 26, 2022, from https://www.menendez.senate.gov/newsroom/press/menendez-leads-bipartisan-call-for-biden-admin-to-increase-medicare-gme-positions
47. Raymond, R. California to require three years of GME for full physician licensure. The DO. September 16, 2021. Retrieved October 26, 2022, from https://thedo.osteopathic.org/2019/09/california-to-require-three-years-of-gme-for-full-physician-licensure/
48. *Assembly bill 890.* California Board of Registered Nursing. Retrieved October 26, 2022, from https://www.rn.ca.gov/practice/ab890.shtml
49. HB 1245 Nurse practitioners; practice without a practice agreement, repeals sunset provision. Legislative Information System. Date unknown. Retrieved October 26, 2022, from https://lis.virginia.gov/cgi-bin/legp604.exe?221%2Bsum%2BHB1245
50. HB 243 Medicine, osteopathy, chiropractic, and podiatric medicine; requirements for practitioners. Legislative Information System. Date Unknown. Retrieved October 26, 2022, from https://lis.virginia.gov/cgi-bin/legp604.exe?221+cab+HC10118HB0243+BREF
51. Al-Agba, N & Bernard, R (Hosts). If you need emergency medical care, will you be treated by a physician? (Episode 25). [Audio podcast]. In *Patients at Risk.* Buzzsprout. April 25, 2021. https://www.buzzsprout.com/1475923/episodes/8269851
52. Cook, T. After the Match: Corporations rush in to fill MD shortage. *Emergency Medicine News.* January 2017;39(1):1,32. doi: 10.1097/01.EEM.0000511940.27134.37
53. Tkacik, M. Private equity gloats over a doctor glut. *PNHP.* May 22, 2022. Retrieved November 20, 2022, from https://pnhp.org/news/private-equity-gloats-over-a-doctor-glut/
54. Statement on emergency medicine match 2022. *Takemedicineback.* March 3, 2022. Retrieved September 4, 2022, from https://www.takemedicineback.org/statement-on-emergency-medicine-match-2022
55. Middleton, L. Nurses to be trained to perform surgery to ease waiting times. *Metro.* February 24, 2020. Retrieved October 27, 2022. from https://metro.co.uk/2020/02/24/nurses-trained-perform-surgery-ease-waiting-times-12290393/
56. Boose, B. Pa grad holds lives in his hands—literally: *News: Des Moines University. Des Moines University—Medicine & Health Sciences.* May 21, 2020. Retrieved October 27, 2022, from https://www.dmu.edu/blog/2020/05/pa-grad-holds-lives-in-his-hands-literally/

57. Al-Agba, N & Bernard, R (Hosts). A nurse's journey to becoming a physician: From RN, BSN, MSN, CNS, CCNP to MD-MBA (Episode 21). [Audio podcast]. In *Patients at Risk*. Buzzsprout. Mar 28, 2021. https://www.buzzsprout.com/1475923/episodes/8147177
58. Ferguson C. Personal communication. November 5, 2022.
59. Al-Agba, N & Bernard, R (Hosts). NP-turned-physician discusses differences in training (Episode 6). [Audio podcast]. In *Patients at Risk*. Buzzsprout. December 13, 2020. https://www.buzzsprout.com/1475923/episodes/6776251
60. Kerr, E. Nursing Master's Programs with 100% Admit Rates. *U.S. News & World Report*. June 9, 2020. Retrieved January 24, 2023, from https://www.usnews.com/education/best-graduate-schools/the-short-list-grad-school/articles/nursing-masters-programs-with-the-highest-acceptance-rates
61. Medical School average GPA & MCAT, admissions statistics and acceptance rates (2021). *MedEdits*. June 29, 2021. Retrieved November 26, 2021, from https://mededits.com/medical-school-admissions/statistics/
62. Harvey PR, Trudgill NJ. The association between physician staff numbers and mortality in English hospitals. *EClinicalMedicine*. 2021;32:100709. doi: 10.1016/j.eclinm.2020.100709. PMID: 33681734; PMCID: PMC7910697.
63. Pronovost PJ, Angus DC, Dorman T, et al. Physician staffing patterns and clinical outcomes in critically ill patients. *Database of Abstracts of Reviews of Effects (DARE): Quality-assessed Reviews*. 2002. Available from: https://www.ncbi.nlm.nih.gov/books/NBK69457/
64. Ognjen G, Bekele A. Physician Staffing Models and Patient Safety in the ICU. *Chest*. 2009; 135(4): 1038–1044. ISSN 0012-3692, https://doi.org/10.1378/chest.08-1544
65. Patients at Risk. Nurse Practitioner speaks out against independent practice. Nov 23, 2020. [Video] YouTube. https://youtu.be/o5ySu6Q1E5Y
66. Patients at Risk. Nurse Practitioner describes gaps in education. April 12, 2021. [Video] YouTube. https://www.youtube.com/watch?v=up07M8ptEYM
67. Al-Agba N, Bernard R (Hosts). "Is it time for an NP/PA Flexner Report?" Patients at Risk. [Audio Podcast]. April 4, 2022. Buzzsprout. https://www.buzzsprout.com/1475923/episodes/10276149
68. Cook, T, Adler, J. After the Match: Boosting Profits Drives NP Diploma Mills. *Emergency Medicine News*: February 2021;43(2):1–35. doi: 10.1097/01.EEM.0000734568.43890.d0
69. Wilkes, S. adapted from Emergency nurse practitioner curriculum. *Emergency Nurse Practitioner, MSN School of Nursing*. Vanderbilt University. Date Unknown. Retrieved November 23, 2022, from https://nursing.vanderbilt.edu/msn/enp/enp_curriculum.php
70. Veenema T, Zare H, Proffit Lavin R, Schneider-Firestone S. Analysis of trends in nurse practitioner billing for emergency medical services: 2015–2018. *The American Journal of Emergency Medicine*. 2022. ISSN 0735-6757, https://doi.org/10.1016/j.ajem.2022.09.040
71. AAEM and AAEM/RSA position statement on emergency medicine training programs for Non-Physician Practitioners: AAEM—American Academy of Emergency Medicine. *AAEM*. Date Unknown. Retrieved December 22, 2021, from https://www.aaem.org/resources/statements/position/em-training-programs-for--pas-and-nps

72. Joint statement on the role of Advance Practice Registered Nurses. *Enaorg*. September 23, 2020. Retrieved December 22, 2021, from https://www.ena.org/press-room/2020/09/23/joint-statement-on-the-role-of-advance-practice-registered-nurses
73. Lavin, R, et al Analysis of Nurse Practitioners' Educational Preparation, Credentialing, and Scope of Practice in U.S. Emergency Departments. *Journal of Nursing Regulation*. 2022;12(4): 50–62. ISSN 2155-8256, https://doi.org/10.1016/S2155-8256(22)00010-2
74. The Productivity of Professions: Evidence from the Emergency Department David C. Chan Jr and Yiqun Chen NBER Working Paper No. 30608 October 2022 JEL No. I11,I18,J24,J44,M53.
75. Christensen EW, Liu CM, Duszak Jr R, Hirsch JA, Swan TL, Rula EY. Association of state share of non-physician practitioners with diagnostic imaging ordering among emergency department visits for Medicare beneficiaries. *JAMA Netw Open*. 2022;5(11):e2241297. doi: 10.1001/jamanetworkopen.2022.41297
76. Hemani A, Rastegar DA, Hill C, Al-Ibrahim MS. A comparison of resource utilization in nurse practitioners and physicians. *Effective Clinical Practice*. 1999;2(6):258–65. [PUBMED: 10788023].
77. Delaney KR, Vanderhoef D. The Psychiatric Mental Health Advanced Practice Registered Nurse Workforce: Charting the Future. *J Am Psychiatr Nurses Assoc*. 2019;25(1):11–18. doi:10.1177/1078390318806571
78. Patients at Risk. RN and former NP student exposes deficiencies in nurse practitioner education (Part 1). Feb 15, 2021[Video] YouTube. https://www.youtube.com/watch?v=bVe_MhgslHg
79. Al-Agba N, Bernard R (Hosts). Is this the end of the full-spectrum Family Physician? Discussing proposed ACGME changes to Family Medicine residency training [Audio podcast]. Feb 28, 2022. Retrieved from https://www.buzzsprout.com/1475923/episodes/9974588
80. Pei L, Wu H. Does online learning work better than offline learning in undergraduate medical education? A systematic review and meta-analysis. *Medical Education Online*. 2019; 24(1): 1666538. https://doi.org/10.1080/10872981.2019.1666538
81. Gross G, Ling R, Richardson B, Quan N. In-person or virtual training?: Comparing the effectiveness of community-based training. *Am J Distance Educ*. 2022;1–12. https://doi.org/10.1080/08923647.2022.2029090
82. NAEP long-term trend assessment results: Reading and Mathematics. *The Nation's Report Card*. (2022). Retrieved November 10, 2022, from https://www.nationsreportcard.gov/highlights/ltt/2022/
83. Fulton CR, Clark C, Dickinson S. Clinical hours in nurse practitioner programs equals clinical competence: Fact or misnomer? *Nurse Educator*. 2017; 42(4):195–198. https://doi.org/10.1097/ NNE.0000000000000346
84. McNelis A, Dreifuerst KT, Beebe S, Spurlock D. Types, Frequency, and Depth of Direct Patient Care Experiences of Family Nurse Practitioner Students in the United States. *J Nurs Regul*. 2021;12(1):19–27. https://doi.org/10.1016/S2155-8256(21)00021-1
85. Al-Agba, N & Bernard, R (Hosts). Why access to poor healthcare can be more dangerous than no care at all. [Audio podcast episode]. Patients at Risk. [Audio podcast]. March 7, 2021. Buzzsprout https://www.buzzsprout.com/1475923/episodes/8036649
86. Kumar A, Kearney A, Hoskins K, Iyengar A. The role of psychiatric mental health nurse practitioners in improving mental and behavioral health care delivery for children and adolescents in multiple settings. *Arch Psychiatr Nurs*. 2020;34(5):275–280. doi: 10.1016/j.apnu.2020.07.022. Epub 2020 Jul 18. PMID: 33032746; PMCID: PMC7547148.

87. @pppforpatients. Photo of smiley face with a zippered mouth "And sometimes the strongest NP voice is silent …" How can #NPsLead by censoring their nurses for speaking up? Nurses want physician supervision and #physicianled care for all their patients? [Twitter post]. Aug 9, 2019. Accessed June 12, 2020. https://twitter.com/pppforpatients/status/1159660324229922816
88. Dardy. Its official, the Psych NP profession is oversaturated. *Life of a Psych NP*. September 4, 2021. Retrieved August 30, 2022, from https://www.youtube.com/watch?v=OuPw-aABL60&t=730s
89. Human Resources and Services Administration. National projections of supply and demand for selected behavioral health practitioners: 2013–2025. *Bhw.HRSA.gov.* 2016. Retrieved from https://bhw.hrsa.gov/sites/default/files/bhw/health-workforce-analysis/research/projections/behavioral-health2013-2025.pdf
90. Patients at Risk. RN exposes deficiencies in NP education—and the growth of the NP 'cash' practice (Part 2). February 28, 2021 [Video] YouTube. https://www.youtube.com/watch?v=C_3ldnJILvw&t=1293s
91. Jeny Conrad-Rendon—owner—absolute health. *Linkedin*. Date Unknown. Retrieved November 28, 2021, from https://www.linkedin.com/in/jeny-conrad-rendon-2a483749
92. Taz. *This petty s**t just never ends. I'm going to do something I rarely do, which is show screenshots, unredacted, of bullying in action. Rayne Thoman is an RN who is against FPA. She is a seasoned psychiatric nurse who resigned from her psych NP program because it was substandard. pic.twitter.com/zhsewvvgw4. Twitter.* Posted March 5, 2021. Retrieved November 28, 2021, from https://twitter.com/Suburbanbella/status/1367988164955041796
93. Marquette University Nursing. Becoming a Nurse Practitioner with a Non-Nursing Bachelor's. Distance MSN Programs. https://mastersnursing.marquette.edu/blog/becoming-a-nurse-practitioner-with-a-non-nursing-bachelors-degree/. Published May 11, 2020. Accessed June 9, 2020.
94. Bal, D. The Best Online RN-to-MSN Programs of 2023. *Nurse Journal*. January 5, 2023. Retrieved January 26, 2023, from https://nursejournal.org/degrees/msn/best-online-rn-to-msn-programs/
95. Pezenik, S. Feds announce massive takedown of fraudulent nursing diploma scheme. January 25, 2023. *ABC News*. Retrieved January 26, 2023, from https://abcnews.go.com/US/feds-announce-massive-takedown-fraudulent-nursing-diploma-scheme/story
96. Robbins, R. Nursing Exam Failure Rates Spark Review of Test Results. December 29, 2022. *Medscape.* Retrieved January 26, 2023, from https://www.medscape.com/viewarticle/986303
97. Galer M. Personal communication. November 25, 2022.
98. Grinspoon P. *Why is it so challenging to find a primary care physician? Harvard Health*. September 28, 2022. Retrieved October 22, 2022, from https://www.health.harvard.edu/blog/why-is-it-so-challenging-to-find-a-primary-care-physician-202209282822#
99. Al-Agba, N, Bernard R (Hosts). Primary care: So easy anyone can do it? Patients at Risk. [Audio podcast] October 17, 2021. Buzzsprout. https://www.buzzsprout.com/1475923/episodes/9252747
100. Gray BM, Vandergrift JL, McCoy RG, et al. Association between primary care physician diagnostic knowledge and death, hospitalisation and emergency department visits following an outpatient visit at risk for diagnostic error: a retrospective cohort study using medicare claims. *BMJ Open* 2021;11:e041817. doi: 10.1136/bmjopen-2020-041817
101. Faza B. Personal communication. Nov 21, 2022.

102. Mary O'Neil Mundinger, DrPH. *Columbia School of Nursing*. June 29, 2021. Retrieved February 12, 2022 from https://www.nursing.columbia.edu/profile/mary-oneil-mundinger-drph
103. Poses R. To whom do "udidoos" owe a duty? *Health Care Renewal*. March 27, 2006. Retrieved February 12, 2022, from https://hcrenewal.blogspot.com/2006/03/to-whom-do-udidoos-owe-duty.html
104. Google scholar citations for Primary care outcomes in patients treated by nurse practitioners or physicians: a randomized trial. Google scholar citations. Retrieved November 10, 2022, from https://scholar.google.com/citations
105. Clarke PN, Ellenbecker CH. Nursing research and the impact on healthcare reform: dialogue with Carol Hall Ellenbecker. *Nurs Sci Q*. 2011;24(1):31–34. https://doi.org/10.1177/0894318410389063
106. Sox HC. Independent Primary Care Practice by Nurse Practitioners. *JAMA*. 2000;283: 106–107.
107. Bernard R. Opinion | MDs offer more than nurse practitioners. *The Wall Street Journal*. September 25, 2020. Retrieved October 24, 2021, from https://www.wsj.com/articles/m-d-s-offer-more-than-nurse-practitioners-11601068900.
108. Mundinger MO, Kane RL, Lenz ER, et al. Primary care outcomes in patients treated by nurse practitioners or physicians: a randomized trial. *JAMA*. 2000;283(1):59–68. doi:10.1001/jama.283.1.59
109. Bray CO, Olson KK. Family nurse practitioner clinical requirements: Is the best recommendation 500 hours? *J Am Acad Nurse Pract*. 2009;21(3): 135–139. https://doi.org/10.1111/j.1745-7599.2008.00384.x
110. Laurant M, van der Biezen M, Wijers N, Watananirun K, Kontopantelis E, van Vught AJAH. Nurses as substitutes for doctors in primary care. *Cochrane Database of Systematic Reviews*. 2018;7(Art): CD001271. doi: 10.1002/14651858.CD001271.pub3
111. InnovateMED Columbia University Medical Center (2014, Nov 15). *Mary Mundinger—Is Primary Care Dying?* [Video] YouTube. https://www.youtube.com/watch?v=0BUGdOs74Q8&t=746s
112. Mundinger MO, Carter MA. Potential Crisis in Nurse Practitioner Preparation in the United States. *Policy, Polit Nurs Pract*. 2019;20(2):57–63. doi:10.1177/1527154419838630
113. Lohr RH, West CP, Beliveau M, et al. Comparison of the quality of patient referrals from physicians, physician assistants, and nurse practitioners. *Mayo Clin Proc*. 2013;88(11):1266–1271. doi:10.1016/j.mayocp.2013.08.013
114. Poses, R. A more entangled web: The UnitedHealth case. *Health Care Renewal*. August 12, 2006. Retrieved February 12, 2022, from https://hcrenewal.blogspot.com/2006/08/more-entangled-web-unitedhealth-case.html
115. Davis M. UnitedHealth Board has generosity in its Blood. *TheStreet*. October 13, 2003. Retrieved February 12, 2022, from https://www.thestreet.com/investing/stocks/unitedhealth-board-has-generosity-in-its-blood-10118738
116. Nurse researcher. *ExploreHealthCareers.org*. July 14, 2017. Retrieved February 12, 2022, from https://explorehealthcareers.org/career/nursing/nurse-researcher/
117. Mary O. Mundinger Net Worth, bio and Unitedhealth Group Inc insider trades. *Benzinga*. June 9, 2008. Retrieved February 12, 2022, from https://www.benzinga.com/sec/insider-trades/unh/mary-o.-mundinger
118. Mundinger Mary Oneil Net Worth *GuruFocus.com*. February 12, 2022. Retrieved February 12, 2022, from https://www.gurufocus.com/insider/mundinger+mary+oneil/name

119. Demand for Jury Trial. *United States District Court* District of Minnesota. *Verified Derivative Complaint St Pauls Teachers Retirement Fund et al vs United Health Group.* [PDF]. May 18, 2006. Retrieved February 12, 2022, from https://static.blbglaw.com/docs/UnitedHealthCplt5.18.06.pdf
120. Hon. Kathleen A. Blatz and Hon. Edward C. Stringer. UnitedHealth Group Incorporated Report of the Special Litigation Committee. [PDF] December 6, 2007. Retrieved February 12, 2022, from http://cdn-ecomm.dreamingcode.com/public/188/documents/Version-20111207142033-United_Health_2-188-1408-1.pdf
121. Thew J. Nurse practitioner salaries on the rise. *HealthLeaders Media.* August 8, 2018. Retrieved February 12, 2022, from https://www.healthleadersmedia.com/nursing/nurse-practitioner-salaries-rise
122. Snowbeck, C. UnitedHealth Group projects more than $300 billion in revenue next year. *Star Tribune.* November 30, 2021. Retrieved February 12, 2022, from https://www.startribune.com/unitedhealth-group-forecasts-2022-revenue-will-hit-317-billion/600122190/
123. Nursing champion: UnitedHealth Group. *Campaign for Action.* April 22, 2015. Retrieved February 12, 2022, from https://campaignforaction.org/champion-nursing-unitedhealth-group/
124. Disclosure Updated. *JAMA.* 2022;327(2):185. doi:10.1001/jama.2021.23340
125. Robert Wood Johnson Foundation Gives AARP Foundation $10 Million for New Center to Address the Nursing Workforce Crisis Threatening Patient Care." Robert Wood Johnson Foundation Press Release December 6, 2007. Retrieved January 24, 2023, from https://philanthropynewsdigest.org/news/robert-wood-johnson-foundation-awards-10-million-to-aarp-foundation
126. Champion Nursing Council: Future of Nursing. *Campaign for Action.* December 16, 2021. Retrieved February 12, 2022, from https://campaignforaction.org/champion-nursing-council/
127. Advisory Committee and funders for the rand compare project. *RAND Corporation.* Date Unknown. Retrieved February 12, 2022, from https://www.rand.org/health-care/projects/compare/advisory-committee-and-funders.html
128. Primary care in high-income countries: How the United States compares. Primary Care in High-Income Countries: How United States Compares. *Commonwealth Fund.* March 15, 2022. Retrieved October 6, 2022, from https://www.commonwealthfund.org/publications/issue-briefs/2022/mar/primary-care-high-income-countries-how-united-states-compares
129. Starfield B, Shi L, Macinko J. Contribution of primary care to health systems and health. Milbank Q. 2005;83(3):457–502. doi: 10.1111/j.1468-0009.2005.00409.x. PMID: 16202000; PMCID: PMC2690145.
130. Gray DJP, Sidaway-Lee K, White E, Thorne A, Evans PH. Continuity of care with doctors-A matter of life and death? A systematic review of continuity of care and mortality. *BMJ Open.* June 1, 2018. Retrieved December 23, 2021, from https://bmjopen.bmj.com/content/8/6/e021161
131. Short MN, Ho V. Weighing the Effects of Vertical Integration Versus Market Concentration on Hospital Quality. *Medical Care Research and Review.* 2020;77(6):538–548. doi:10.1177/1077558719828938
132. Patients at Risk. The High Cost of Healthcare Part 1. September 6, 2021. [Video] YouTube. https://youtu.be/2J7LAV8CgdU
133. Ellenbogen, M., & Segal, J. Differences in Opioid Prescribing Among Generalist Physicians, Nurse Practitioners, and Physician Assistants. *Pain Medicine.* 2020;21(1): 76–83. https://doi.org/10.1093/pm/pnz005

134. Katersky, A. Cigna received millions of Medicare dollars based on invalid diagnoses, lawsuit claims. *ABC News*. October 22, 2022. Retrieved October 27, 2022, from https://abcnews.go.com/Health/cigna-received-millions-medicare-dollars-based-invalid-diagnoses/story?id=91632162
135. What Is the Difference Between a Medical Doctor and a Nurse Practitioner? *Minuteclinic*. Date Unknown. Retrieved October 26, 2022, from https://www.cvs.com/minuteclinic/why-choose-us/doctor-vs-nurse-practitioner
136. Minemyer P. Report: Visits to primary care doctors decline, but more patients with employer plans are seeing NPS, Pas. *Fierce Healthcare*. November 20, 2018. Retrieved October 27, 2022, from https://www.fiercehealthcare.com/practices/report-visits-to-primary-care-physicians-decline-among-patients-employer-insurance-but
137. Eskew, P, Klink, K. Direct Primary Care: Practice Distribution and Cost Across the Nation. *J Am Board Fam Med*. November 2015, 28 (6) 793–801; DOI: https://doi.org/10.3122/jabfm.2015.06.140337
138. Ellison A. 10 states with the most for-profit hospitals by percentage. *Becker's Hospital Review*. Date Unknown. Retrieved September 3, 2022, from https://www.beckershospitalreview.com/rankings-and-ratings/10-states-with-the-most-for-profit-hospitals-by-percentage.html
139. Nonprofit Hospital CEO Compensation: How Much Is Enough? *Health Affairs Forefront*, February 10, 2022. DOI: 10.1377/forefront.20220208.925255
140. Mercy quick facts. *Mercy*. October 17, 2022. Retrieved October 26, 2022, from https://www.mercy.net/newsroom/mercy-quick-facts/
141. Executive compensation at Mercy health (Chesterfield, MO). *Paddock Post*. August 22, 2020. Retrieved November 8, 2022, from https://paddockpost.com/2020/08/22/executive-compensation-at-mercy-health/
142. Staff Reports. On the job: Mercy signs lease to run El Reno's Parkview Hospital. *The Oklahoman*. June 23, 2010. Retrieved October 26, 2022, from https://www.oklahoman.com/story/business/2010/06/23/on-the-job-mercy-signs-lease-to-run-el-renos-parkview-hospital/61231207007/
143. Patients at Risk. What happens when hospitals replace physicians with NPs? [Video] YouTube. Nov 22, 2021. https://www.youtube.com/watch?v=nZ4c3MDy_1k
144. Allen S, Wingerter M. Mercy to close El Reno Hospital, open outpatient facility. *The Oklahoman*. November 6, 2018. Retrieved October 26, 2022, from https://www.oklahoman.com/story/news/columns/2018/11/06/mercy-to-close-el-reno-hospital-open-outpatient-facility/60490470007/
145. Bryant M. ACA is taking a toll on physician-owned hospitals. *Healthcare Dive*. July 11, 2017. Retrieved September 3, 2022, from https://www.healthcaredive.com/news/aca-is-taking-a-toll-on-physician-owned-hospitals/446761/
146. Al-Agba N, Bernard R. (Hosts). Patients at risk from private equity takeover of emergency departments [Audio Podcast]. May 30, 2021. Retrieved from buzzsprout.com/1475923/episodes/8522300
147. Marco, C, Courtney, M, Ling, L, et al. The Emergency Medicine Physician Workforce: Projections for 2030. *Ann Emerg Med*. 2021;S0196; DOI: https://doi.org/10.1016/j.annemergmed.2021.05.029
148. McNamara R: Conterpoint: Contract management groups—A detriment to the specialty and practitioners of emergency medicine. *Ann Emerg Med*. June 1994; 23:1350–1353.

149. McNamara R. Corporate practice: AAEM—American Academy of Emergency Medicine. *AAEM*. Date Unknown. Retrieved December 18, 2021, from https://www.aaem.org/get-involved/sections/yps/rules-of-the-road/corporate-practice?fbclid=IwAR3W750jqhRyivmXzijdSPmrcVLMiIx1tcMINb0ouJD2zRfJdaXsckPP89A
150. Ronald A Helstrom—Professor (profile). *eMedEvents*. Date Unknown. Retrieved December 12, 2021, from https://www.emedevents.com/speaker-profile/ronald-a-hellstern
151. Alpinism. ACEP Directors Academy faculty offers helpful advice on how to staff emergency departments. *Student Doctor Network*. April 10, 2021. Retrieved February 27, 2022, from https://forums.studentdoctor.net/threads/acep-directors-academy-faculty-offers-helpful-advice-on-how-to-staff-emergency-departments.1439263/. Slide Screenshot. (Original presentation no longer available https://www.envisionphysicianservices.com/campaigns/breakthrough-series/presentation-materials/presentations/09-staffing-your-ed-core-concepts.pdf).
152. Elkind P. Investors extracted $400 million from a hospital chain that sometimes couldn't pay for medical supplies or gas for ambulances. *ProPublica*. Date Unknown. Retrieved December 12, 2021, from https://www.propublica.org/article/investors-extracted-400-million-from-a-hospital-chain-that-sometimes-couldnt-pay-for-medical-supplies-or-gas-for-ambulances
153. Morgenson G. Some doctors say a focus on profits is hurting health care in U.S. ERS. *NBCNews.com*. March 28, 2022. Retrieved July 24, 2022, from https://www.nbcnews.com/health/health-care/doctor-fired-er-warns-effect-profit-firms-us-health-care-rcna19975
154. Clark C. TeamHealth will pay $15 million to emergency physicians. *Medical News*. March 15, 2022. Retrieved October 26, 2022, from https://www.medpagetoday.com/special-reports/exclusives/97666
155. Geographic variation in private equity penetration across physician specialties. *NIHCM*. 2022. Retrieved November 8, 2022, from https://nihcm.org/publications/geographic-variation-in-private-equity-penetration-across-physician-specialties
156. U.S. dermatology partners and the Corporate Practice of Medicine. *Dolcefino Consulting*. July 26, 2021. Retrieved February 27, 2022, from https://dolcefino.com/2021/07/23/u-s-dermatology-partners-and-the-corporate-practice-of-medicine/
157. Perlberg H. How private equity is ruining American Health Care (1). *Bloomberg Law*. May 20, 2020. Retrieved November 8, 2022, from https://news.bloomberglaw.com/health-law-and-business/how-private-equity-is-ruining-american-health-care
158. Why investors are pouring billions into primary care. February 24, 2022. *Advisory Board*. Retrieved November 10, 2022, from https://www.advisory.com/daily-briefing/2022/02/24/primary-care
159. Peebles A. Primary care: Health investors bet billions on Medicine's worst-paying specialty. *Bloomberg.com*. February 10, 2022. Retrieved November 10, 2022, from https://www.bloomberg.com/news/features/2022-02-10/primary-care-health-investors-bet-billions-on-medicine-s-worst-paying-specialty
160. Davis C. The good clinic primary care group staffs solely with Nurse Practitioners. 'The Good Clinic' is the First Primary Care Group Staffed Solely by Nurse Practitioners. *HealthLeaders Media*. August 22, 2022. Retrieved September 5, 2022, from https://www.healthleadersmedia.com/nursing/good-clinic-primary-care-group-staffs-solely-nurse-practitioners
161. Home. *Mitesco Inc*. March 10, 2022. Retrieved September 5, 2022, from https://www.mitescoinc.com/

162. Rahil CM, Sheikh SH. UK's biggest GP chain replacing doctors with less qualified staff. *BBC News*. June 13, 2022. Retrieved September 5, 2022, from https://www.bbc.com/news/health-61759643
163. Knight V. Private equity ownership of nursing homes triggers Capitol Hill questions—and a GAO probe. *Kaiser Health News*. July 27, 2022. Retrieved September 3, 2022, from https://khn.org/news/article/private-equity-ownership-of-nursing-homes-triggers-federal-probe/
164. Hawryluk M. Hospices have become big business for private equity firms, raising concerns about end-of-life care. *Kaiser Health News*. July 29, 2022. Retrieved September 3, 2022, from https://khn.org/news/article/hospices-private-equity-firms-end-of-life-care/
165. Starkman E. Starkman: Metro Detroit mourns passing of 'Gentle soul' Richard Curbelo. *Deadline Detroit*. February 22, 2021. Retrieved November 13, 2022, from https://www.deadlinedetroit.com/articles/27267/starkman_metro_detroit_mourns_passing_of_gentle_soul_richard_curbelo
166. Starkman E. Starkman: Beaumont Hospital staffers horrified after patient dies during routine colonoscopy. *Deadline Detroit*. January 25, 2021. Retrieved December 19, 2021, from https://deadlinedetroit.com/articles/27205/starkman_beaumont_hospital_staffers_horrified_after_patient_dies_during_routine_colonoscopy
167. Kirk B. Clear lake medical center rebrands to HCA Houston Healthcare. *Clear Lake, TX Patch*. February 6, 2019. Retrieved September 4, 2022, from https://patch.com/texas/clearlake/clear-lake-medical-center-rebrands-hca-houston-healthcare
168. Saba R. FAAEM. Confirmed. *Twitter*. March 31, 2021. Retrieved September 4, 2022 from https://twitter.com/sabarizvimd/status/1377444450474065921/photo/1
169. Personal communication. April 21, 2021. Screenshot of HCA Patient Consent Form. https://www.facebook.com/photo?fbid=10164879816500263&set=gm.2608328892806052
170. In the news. Watertown Regional Medical Center and LifePoint Health Finalize Joint Venture. Unknown Date. Retrieved September 4, 2022, from https://lifepointhealth.net/news/2015/09/02/watertown-regional-medical-center-and-lifepoint-health-finalize-joint-venture
171. Ready T. Wisconsin Hospital replaces all anesthesiologists with crnas. *Medscape*. April 15, 2021. Retrieved September 4, 2022, from https://www.medscape.com/viewarticle/948723#vp_1
172. Wilkes S. Adapted from DNP nurse anesthesia curriculum. *Curriculum—DNP-CRNA—School of Nursing, CSUF.* Date Unknown. Retrieved November 24, 2022, from https://nursing.fullerton.edu/programs/dnpcrna/curriculum.php
173. Taz. This is not good news for the residents of Watertown, WI. Watertown Regional Medical Center (courtesy of the private equity-backed, Contract Medical Group Envision) removed all of its anesthesiologists for a 100% Crna model. In a nutshell, they replaced physicians with nurses. *pic.twitter.com/73os9cajzf. Twitter*. March 28, 2021. Retrieved December 19, 2021, from https://twitter.com/Suburbanbella/status/1376227395640823808?fbclid=IwAR1zPtI8wBhsVNodqybPfXMGA-zByVT-sU_-b5u61xpgL9Y4dUA5_eDBt6c0
174. American Society of Anesthesiologists. Summary of research studies comparing anesthesia professionals [PDF]. Date Unknown. Retrieved June 10, 2020 from https://www.asahq.org/~/media/sites/asahq/files/public/advocacy/federal%20activities/researchcomparinganesthprofs-two-pages.pdf?la=en. Published 2016.
175. Silber JH, Kennedy SK, Even-Shoshan O, et al. Anesthesiologist direction and patient outcomes. *Anesthesiology*. 2000;93(1):152–163. doi:10.1097/00000542-200007000-00026

176. Ttuaj A. Wisconsin's Corporate Practice of Medicine Doctrine: Dead Letter, Trap for the Unwary, or Both? State Bar of Wisconsin. *Meissner Tierney Fisher & Nichols*. Milwaukee, Wisconsin. Date Unknown. Retrieved on December 19, 2021 from https://www.wisbar.org/AppFiles/HLE_2015/3_S4_MedicineDoctrine.pdf
177. Envision. The Facts about CRNA Care Models. Screenshot obtained April 31, 2021.
178. Watertown Regional Medical Center tapped to join New Health System, *ScionHealth*. Watertown Regional Medical Center. Date Unknown. Retrieved September 4, 2022, from https://www.watertownregional.com/news/watertown-regional-medical-center-tapped-to-join-new-health-system-scionhealth
179. Al-Agba N, Bernard R (Hosts). Patient dies during routine colonoscopy after cost-cutting 'private equity' anesthesia takeover [Audio Podcast]. Feb 14, 2021. Retrieved from https://www.buzzsprout.com/1475923/episodes/7591213
180. Burns ML, Saager L, Cassidy RB, Mentz G, Mashour GA, Kheterpal S. Association of Anesthesiologist Staffing Ratio With Surgical Patient Morbidity and Mortality. *JAMA Surg*. Published online July 20, 2022. doi:10.1001/jamasurg.2022.2804
181. Durr B. How many doctors have left mission? HCA won't say. *Asheville Watchdog*. March 23, 2022. Retrieved September 4, 2022, from https://avlwatchdog.org/how-many-doctors-have-left-mission-hca-wont-say/
182. Two Charlotte area hospitals among $260 million global settlement between hospital chain and the United States. The United States Department of Justice. September 25, 2018. Retrieved September 4, 2022, from https://www.justice.gov/usao-wdnc/pr/two-charlotte-area-hospitals-among-260-million-global-settlement-between-hospital-chain
183. Mecia T. The doctor won't see your newborn now. *North Carolina Health News*. June 19, 2021. Retrieved September 4, 2022, from https://www.northcarolinahealthnews.org/2021/06/19/the-doctor-wont-see-your-newborn-now/
184. Kaplan L. Characteristics and perceptions of the US nurse practitioner hospitalist workforce. *J Am Assoc Nurse Pract*. 2021; (33): 1173–1179.
185. Kleinpell RM, Grabenkort WR, Kapu AN, Constantine R, Sicoutris C. Nurse Practitioners and Physician Assistants in Acute and Critical Care: A Concise Review of the Literature and Data 2008–2018. *Crit Care Med*. 2019;47(10):1442–1449. doi: 10.1097/CCM.0000000000003925. PMID: 31414993; PMCID: PMC6750122.
186. Henkel, G. Nurse Practitioners, Physician Assistants Play Key Roles in Hospitalist Practice. *The Hospitalist*. July 1, 2013. Retrieved January 25, 2023, from https://www.the-hospitalist.org/hospitalist/article/125734/nurse-practitioners-physician-assistants-play-key-roles-hospitalist
187. Al-Agba N, Bernard R (Hosts). If you are hospitalized, will your care be overseen by a physician? *Patients at Risk*. [Audio Podcast]. May 09, 2021. https://www.buzzsprout.com/1475923/episodes/8396552
188. T. Alost. Personal communication. October 18, 2022.
189. Patients at Risk. Midlevel Malpractice [Video]. October 10, 2021. YouTube. https://youtu.be/CVIMnXItdnU
190. Butler M, Collins R, Drennan J, et al. Hospital nurse staffing models and patient and staff-related outcomes. *Cochrane Database Syst Rev*. 2011:CD007019.
191. Sabin J, Subbe CP, Vaughan L, Dowdle R. Safety in numbers: lack of evidence to indicate the number of physicians needed to provide safe acute medical care. *Clin Med* (Lond). 2014;14(5):462–7. doi: 10.7861/clinmedicine.14-5-462. PMID: 25301904; PMCID: PMC4951952.
192. Royal College of Physicians Guidance on safe medical staffing. Report of a working party London: RCP, 2018. Accessed October 26, 2022 at www.rcplondon.ac.uk/projects/outputs/safe-medical-staffing

193. Al-Agba N and Bernard R (Hosts). The headlines don't always match the data: an example of egregious methodology in NP literature. *Patients at Risk.* [Audio Podcast]. June 6, 2022. https://www.buzzsprout.com/1475923/episodes/10579558
194. Jacobs J. Increased number of inpatient NPs linked to improved patient outcomes. *Clinical Advisor*. February 4, 2022. Retrieved November 22, 2022, from https://www.clinicaladvisor.com/home/my-practice/nurse-practitioner-career-resources/nurse-practitioner-positive-inpatient-outcomes/
195. Reno, J. Nurse practitioner, no doctor at Your Urgent Care Clinic. *Healthline.* November 4, 2019. Retrieved October 27, 2022, from https://www.healthline.com/health-news/nurse-practitioner-no-doctor-urgent-care-center#The-nurse-practitioner-point-of-view
196. Ruegg T. A nurse practitioner-led urgent care center: Meeting the needs of the patient with cancer. Nurse Practitioners, Emergency Care, Emergency Department, Oncologic Emergency, Health Policy. *CJON.* 2013, 17(4), E52-E57. DOI: 10.1188/13.CJON.E52-E57
197. Sakr M, Kendall R, Angus J, Sanders A, Nicholl J, Wardrope J. Emergency nurse practitioners: a three part study in clinical and cost effectiveness. *Emerg Med J.* 2003;20(2):158–63. doi: 10.1136/emj.20.2.158. Erratum in: Emerg Med J. 2003 May;20(3):302. Saunders A [corrected to Sanders A]. PMID: 12642530; PMCID: PMC1726060.
198. Ryan K, Rahman A. Examining factors influencing patient satisfaction with nurse practitioners in rural urgent care centers. *Journal of the American Academy of Nurse Practitioners.* 2012;24:77–81. doi:10.1111/j.1745–7599.2011.00688.x
199. Al-Agba N. When your doctor isn't a doctor. *The New Republic.* October 23, 2022. Retrieved October 23, 2022, from https://newrepublic.com/article/165235/when-urgent-care-doctor-is-not-doctor
200. Ramm M. Urgent care told him he had the flu. It was really meningitis—and a jury awarded him $27m. *USA Today.* November 22, 2022. Retrieved November 22, 2022, from https://www.usatoday.com/story/news/nation/2022/11/22/iowa-man-27-million-meningitis-misdiagnosed/10754821002/
201. SDAPA's priority bill advances after passage in South Dakota Senate Committee. *AAPA.* February 9, 2022. Retrieved November 22, 2022, from https://www.aapa.org/news-central/2022/02/sdapas-priority-bill-advances-after-passage-in-south-dakota-senate-committee/
202. Al-Agba R, Bernard R (Hosts). Standardized exams: what it takes to become a physician—and the failure of the DNP USMLE experiment. *Patients at Risk.* [Audio Podcast]. Jan 25, 2021. Buzzsprout. https://www.buzzsprout.com/1475923/episodes/7471351
203. Al-Agba N, Bernard R (Hosts). Physician assistant and former-PA-turned-physician discuss the state of the profession. *Patients at Risk.* [Audio Podcast]. July 25, 2021. Buzzsprout. https://www.buzzsprout.com/1475923/episodes/8889586
204. Moote M, Krsek C, Kleinpell R, Todd B. Physician Assistant and Nurse Practitioner Utilization in Academic Medical Centers. *Am J Med Quality.* 2011;26(6):452–460. doi:10.1177/1062860611402984
205. Daugharty K. What is the EMR mandate. *Record Nations.* December 23, 2021. Retrieved October 26, 2022, from https://www.recordnations.com/2020/03/what-emr-mandate/

206. Carayon P, Wetterneck TB, Alyousef B, Brown RL, Cartmill RS, McGuire K, Hoonakker PL, Slagle J, Van Roy KS, Walker JM, Weinger MB, Xie A, Wood KE. Impact of electronic health record technology on the work and workflow of physicians in the intensive care unit. *Int J Med Inform.* 2015;84(8):578–94. doi: 10.1016/j.ijmedinf.2015.04.002. Epub 2015 Apr 15. PMID: 25910685; PMCID: PMC4490834.
207. Boetel R. Residents complained before loss of Accreditation, UNM says. *Albuquerque Journal.* December 15, 2019. Retrieved July 24, 2022, from https://www.abqjournal.com/1401413/residents-complained-before-loss-of-accreditation-unm-says.html
208. Carmody B. How much are resident physicians worth? *The Sheriff of Sodium.* February 25, 2022. Retrieved July 24, 2022, from https://thesheriffofsodium.com/2022/02/04/how-much-are-resident-physicians-worth/
209. Government Accountability Office. PHYSICIAN WORKFORCE: Caps on Medicare Funded Graduate Medical Education at Teaching Hospitals. May 2021. GAO 21-391. https://www.gao.gov/assets/gao-21-391.pdf
210. HCA Blog. HCA Healthcare welcomes record class of residents and fellows in 2021. *HCA Healthcare Today.* November 22, 2021. Retrieved November 20, 2022, from https://hcahealthcaretoday.com/2021/07/26/hca-healthcare-welcomes-record-class-of-residents-and-fellows-in-2021/
211. Robeznieks A. Fla. governor's proposed budget includes $80 million for GME. *Modern Healthcare.* February 1, 2013. Retrieved November 20, 2022, from https://www.modernhealthcare.com/node/408486/printable/print
212. Roberts LW. The Closure of Hahnemann University Hospital and the Experience of Moral Injury in Academic Medicine. *Academic Medicine:* April 2020; 95(4): 485–487. doi: 10.1097/ACM.0000000000003151
213. Kahane I. Personal communication. November 20, 2022.
214. Yale School of Medicine Physician Assistant Online Program. *Yale School of Medicine.* Retrieved November 20, 2022 from https://paonline.yale.edu/
215. Dean's Update 2021-11-22. MSU Osteopathic Medicine. November 22, 2021. Retrieved October 9, 2022, from https://com.msu.edu/news_overview/deans-update/deans-update-2021-11-22
216. Davis L. Personal communication. November 1, 2022.
217. AAEM and AAEM/RSA position statement on emergency medicine training programs for Non-Physician Practitioners: AAEM—American Academy of Emergency Medicine. *AAEM.* Date Unknown. Retrieved December 22, 2021, from https://www.aaem.org/resources/statements/position/em-training-programs-for--pas-and-nps
218. Kesten K et al. Educational characteristics and content of postgraduate nurse practitioner residency/fellowship programs. *J Am Assoc Nurse Pract*: February 2021;33(2):126–132. doi: 10.1097/JXX.0000000000000341
219. Al-Agba N and Bernard R. (Hosts). Psych NP patient affair ends tragically: The Case of Jay Baltz—Part 1. *Patients at Risk.* [Audio Podcast]. December 20, 2020. https://www.buzzsprout.com/1475923/episodes/6923366
220. Solberg, A. Interestingly, @JohnsHopkins medicine is only interested in being inclusive on doctor's day despite making claims otherwise. pic.twitter.com/jcap9rkehl. *Twitter.* April 1, 2021. Retrieved October 15, 2022, from https://twitter.com/AgnesSolberg/status/1377697079670153219

221. Colvin LS. Kevin W. Sowers, M.S.N., R.N., F.A.A.N. Retrieved October 15, 2022, from https://www.hopkinsmedicine.org/about/leadership/biographies/kevin-sowers.html
222. Al-Agba N, Bernard R. (Hosts). Addressing the Shortage of Bedside Nurses. *Patients at Risk*. [Audio Podcast]. February 28, 2021. Buzzsprout. https://www.buzzsprout.com/1475923/episodes/7730365
223. *Sarah Rebey, PA-C*—Indianapolis, Indiana, United States. *Linkedin*. Date Unknown. Retrieved November 28, 2021, from https://www.linkedin.com/in/sarah-rebey-pa-c-aaa644124
224. Interview invites 2020–21. Retrieved November 28, 2021, from http://neurosurgeryhub.org/showthread.php?tid=2064&page=34
225. PA-C, S. So disheartened to see this. Applicants, if you don't respect the entire healthcare team, and especially a program that so reliant on apps, maybe reconsider your path. pic.twitter.com/ivyg63dvcg. *Twitter*. December 5, 2020. Retrieved November 28, 2021, from https://twitter.com/sarahbellumPA/status/1335287218923966466
226. Escobar G. We have our vascular PA and NP regularly interview our future trainees. 100% part of the team! Their experiences on interviews have directly led to the removal of people from being ranked! My trainees will always respect, support and learn from everyone they work with. pic.twitter.com/eieselehn6. *Twitter*. December 6, 2020. Retrieved October 9, 2022, from https://twitter.com/GAEscobarMD/status/1335412325164191744
227. King E. For our faculty positions, we often have apps interview candidates because we value our apps' opinions on their future colleagues. Anyone who doesn't respect apps doesn't get through the door with US. *Twitter*. December 6, 2020. Retrieved October 9, 2022, from https://twitter.com/E_King_MD/status/1335419123388583936
228. Lamb C. I have friends applying for residency interviewed by a lone pa. I have nothing against PAS whatsoever, or collaborative care; in fact I'm a proponent of that—but how can you expect someone who didn't do residency to have insight into that experience for a resident-to-be? *Twitter*. December 6, 2020. Retrieved October 9, 2022, from https://twitter.com/lambchopsMD/status/1335725129041666051
229. Stanford Medicine. Richard Besser, Robert Wood Johnson Foundation CEO. Dean's lecture series. 2019. YouTube. March 28, 2019. Retrieved October 26, 2022, from https://www.youtube.com/watch?v=eGkyY4L7NCc
230. Jha S. Navigating the paradox of scarcity—the case for physician extenders. *J Am Coll Radiol*. 2021;18(1): 148–150. https://doi.org/10.1016/j.jacr.2020.09.040
231. Al-Agba N, Bernard R. (Hosts). Who will be reading your next x-ray? The replacement of radiologists by 'radiology assistants' (Part 1). *Patients at* Risk. [Audio Podcast]. January 28, 2022. Buzzsprout. https://www.buzzsprout.com/1475923/episodes/9971528
232. Borthakur A, Barbosa EM Jr, Katz S, Knollmann FD, Kahn CE Jr, Schnall MD, Litt H. WITHDRAWN: Radiology Extenders: Impact on Throughput and Accuracy for Routine Chest Radiographs. *J Am Coll Radiol*. 2020;S1546-1440(20)31004-8. doi: 10.1016/j.jacr.2020.09.044. Epub ahead of print. PMID: 33065074; PMCID: PMC7553053.
233. Al-Agba N, Bernard R. (Hosts). Who will be reading your next x-ray? The replacement of radiologists by 'radiology assistants' (Part 2). *Patients at* Risk. [Audio Podcast]. February 14, 2022. "https://www.buzzsprout.com/1475923/episodes/9974234

234. Riegert M, Nandwani M, Thul B, Chiu AC, Mathews SC, Khashab MA, Kalloo AN. Experience of nurse practitioners performing colonoscopy after endoscopic training in more than 1,000 patients. *Endosc Int Open*. 2020;8(10):E1423-E1428. doi: 10.1055/a-1221-4546. Epub 2020 Sep 22. PMID: 33015346; PMCID: PMC7508647.
235. Patients at Risk. Will an NP or PA perform your next colonoscopy? [Video] YouTube. August 22, 2022. https://youtu.be/u_Gfs6FW3dA
236. Ray JJ, Bowers KD, King-Mullins E, Dykes S, Fabrizio A, Friel C, Hayden D, Jenkins C, Justiniano CF, Laryea J, O'Connor L, Stapleton S, Tuckson W. *Endosc Int Open*. March 14 2022;10(3):E227-E228. doi: 10.1055/a-1672-3985. PMID: 35295240; PMCID: PMC8920597.
237. Fejleh MP, Shen C, Chen J, Bushong J, Dieckgraefe, B, Sayuk G. Quality metrics of screening colonoscopies performed by PAs. *JAAPA*. 2020;33(4):43–48.
238. Lampariello M. PAs and gastroenterologists prove equally capable of performing colonoscopies. *Clinical Advisor*. September 2, 2020. Retrieved September 5, 2022, from https://www.clinicaladvisor.com/home/topics/gastroenterology-information-center/pas-and-gastroenterologists-proven-equally-capable-of-performing-colonoscopies/
239. Stephens M, Hourigan LF, Appleyard M, Ostapowicz G, Schoeman M, Desmond PV, Andrews JM, Bourke M, Hewitt D, Margolin DA, Holtmann GJ. Non-physician endoscopists: A systematic review. *World J Gastroenterol*. 2015;21(16):5056–71. doi: 10.3748/wjg.v21.i16.5056. PMID: 25945022; PMCID: PMC4408481.
240. Carranza A, Munoz P, Nash A. Comparing quality of care in medical specialties between nurse practitioners and physicians. *J Am Assoc Nurse Pract*. 2021;33(3):184–193. doi: 10.1097/JXX.0000000000000394
241. Caine N, Sharples LD, Hollingworth W, French J, Keogan M, Exley A, Bilton D. A randomized controlled crossover trial of nurse practitioner versus doctor-led outpatient care in a bronchiectasis clinic. *Health Technology Assessment*. 2002; 6: 1–82.
242. Norton L, Tsiperfal A, Cook K, Bagdasarian A, Varady J, Shah M, Wang P. Effectiveness and Safety of an Independently Run Nurse Practitioner Outpatient Cardioversion Program (2009 to 2014). *Am J Cardiol*. 2016;118(12):1842–1846. doi: 10.1016/j.amjcard.2016.08.074. Epub 2016 Sep 15. PMID: 27771002.
243. Saririan M. Personal communication. October 27, 2022.
244. Berigan E. Personal communication. October 28, 2022.
245. Cook CL, Schwarz HB. Advanced practice clinicians—neurology's underused resource. *JAMA Neurology*, 2021;78(8):903. https://doi.org/10.1001/jamaneurol.2021.1416
246. Al-Agba N, Bernard R. (Hosts). JAMA Neurology's solution to neurologist shortage: Just substitute NPs/ Pas. *Patients at Risk*. [Audio Podcast]. June 27, 2021. https://www.buzzsprout.com/1475923/episodes/8765114
247. Wilkes S. Adapted from Family nurse practitioner. Curriculum, Family Nurse Practitioner. MSN School of Nursing, Vanderbilt University. 2022. Retrieved November 25, 2022, from https://nursing.vanderbilt.edu/msn/fnp/fnp_curriculum.php
248. Al-Agba N, Bernard R. (Hosts). Former PA and author of 'Hospital Confidential' discusses midlevel malpractice risk. *Patients at Risk*. [Audio Podcast]. March 14, 2022. Retrieved from https://www.buzzsprout.com/1475923/episodes/10099288
249. National Resident Matching Program, Results and Data: 2016 Main Residency Match®. National Resident Matching Program, Washington, DC. 2016.

250. Cai A, Mohrotra A, Germack H, Busch A, Huskamp H, Barnett, M. Trends In Mental Health Care Delivery By Psychiatrists And Nurse Practitioners In Medicare, 2011–19. *Health Affairs*. 2022;41(9): 1222–1230.
251. VH1 Renews Sketch Comedy Series 'Stevie TV' For A Second Season Of Hilarity And Mischief. *TV by the Numbers*. April 19, 2012. Retrieved on August 30, 2022, from https://web.archive.org/web/20120423094751/http://tvbythenumbers.zap2it.com/2012/04/19/vh1-renews-sketch-comedy-series-stevie-tv-for-a-second-season-of-hilarity-and-mischief/130009/
252. Al-Agba N, Bernard R. (Hosts). Friend of YouTube sensation Stevie Ryan speaks out about her care by psych NP. *Patients at Risk*. [Audio Podcast]. May 2, 2021. Buzzsprout. https://www.buzzsprout.com/1475923/episodes/8352853-friend-of-youtube-sensation-stevie-ryan-speaks-out-about-her-care-by-psych-np
253. Case No. 4002019001626. (Gerald M. Baltz) Accusation. Before the Board of Registered Nursing Department of Consumer Affairs State of California. June 15, 2020.
254. American Medical Association. Romantic or sexual relationships with patients. Code of Ethics Opinion 9.1.1. Retrieved October 16, 2022 from https://www.ama-assn.org/delivering-care/ethics/romantic-or-sexual-relationships-patients
255. Miller D. After YouTuber Stevie Ryan's death, a nurse practitioner faces scrutiny. *Los Angeles Times*. April 1, 2021. Retrieved November 27, 2021, from https://www.latimes.com/business/story/2021-04-01/stevie-ryan-death-nurse-practitioner
256. State of Washington Department of Health Amended Statement of Charges for Gerald Michael Baltz. April 21, 2022. Retrieved August 30, 2022 at https://fortress.wa.gov/doh/providercredentialsearch/PDF/1637120960.pdf
257. Dil C. Audit: California Nursing Board faked docs on investigations. *KCRA*. July 1, 2020. Retrieved November 27, 2021, from https://www.kcra.com/article/audit-california-nursing-board-faked-docs-on-investigations/33017471#
258. CBS Sacramento. Audit: California Nursing Board Faked Docs On Investigations. June 30, 2020. Retrieved August 07, 2020, from https://sacramento.cbslocal.com/2020/06/30/audit-california-nursing-board-faked-docs-on-investigations/
259. Miller D. Nurse practitioner who treated the late actress Stevie Ryan stripped of California licenses. *Los Angeles Times*. March 10, 2022. Retrieved July 23, 2022, from https://www.latimes.com/business/story/2022-03-10/la-nurse-pratictioner-stevie-ryan
260. Old Ballard Psych [Temporarily Closed]. *Google*. Retrieved November 9, 2022, from https://www.google.com/search?q=old%2Bballard%2Bpsych&oq=old%2Bballard%2Bpsych&aqs=chrome.0.69i59.2260j0j15&sourceid=chrome&ie=UTF-8
261. Casey C. Ground-breaking Nurse Practitioner Program turns 50. Date Unknown. *University of Colorado CU Anschutz Medical Campus*. Retrieved June 20, 2020, from https://www.cuanschutztoday.org/ground-breaking-nurse-practitioner-program-turns-50/
262. American Nurses Association, American Psychiatric Nurses Association & International Society of Psychiatric–Mental Health Nurses. *Psychiatric–Mental Health Nursing: Scope and Standards of Practice*. 2nd Edition. Silver Spring, MD: Nursesbooks.org. 2013
263. Psychiatric-Mental Health nurse practitioner (across the lifespan) certification (PMHNP-BC): ANCC. American Nurses Credentialing Center. Retrieved August 30, 2022, from https://www.nursingworld.org/our-certifications/psychiatric-mental-health-nurse-practitioner/

264. Wilkes S. Adapted from Psychiatric-Mental Health Nurse practitioner (lifespan). Curriculum. MSN School of Nursing, Vanderbilt University. Date Unknown. Retrieved November 24, 2022, from https://nursing.vanderbilt.edu/msn/pmhnp/pmhnp_curriculum.php
265. Clinical Hour Requirements for PMHNP Program. Midwestern State University Texas. Retrieved on August 30, 2022 from https://msutexas.edu/academics/hs2/nursing/msn/adaclinical-hour-requirements-for-pmhnp-program.pdf
266. ACGME Program Requirements for Graduate Medical Education in Psychiatry. February 7, 2022. Accreditation Council for Graduate Medical Education. https://www.acgme.org/globalassets/pfassets/programrequirements/400_psychiatry_2022_tcc.pdf
267. Al-Agba N, Bernard R. (Hosts). The Differences between Psychiatrists and Psych NPs: The Case of Jay Baltz—Part 2 [Audio Podcast]. *Patients at Risk*. December 27, 2020. Retrieved from https://www.buzzsprout.com/1475923/episodes/6922829
268. Dr. Jay Baltz, DNP: Los Angeles Psychiatric Nurse practitioner: Affordable. *MelrosePsych*. (2021, August 31). Retrieved November 27, 2021, from https://melrosepsych.com/los-angeles-psychiatric-nurse-practitioner-jay-baltz/
269. Jay Baltz profile page. *Facebook*. Date Unknown. Retrieved November 27, 2021, from https://www.facebook.com/jay.baltz.1 (no longer available).
270. Baltz GM, Lach H. Perceptions, Knowledge, and Use of Electronic Cigarettes: A Survey of Mental Health Patients, *Issues in Mental Health Nursing*. 2019;40(10):887–894. DOI: 10.1080/01612840.2019.1579281
271. Nursing practice, D.N.P. *SLU*. Date Unknown. Retrieved November 27, 2021, from https://www.slu.edu/nursing/degrees/graduate/nursing-dnp.php
272. Mundinger MO, Carter MA. Potential Crisis in Nurse Practitioner Preparation in the United States. *Policy Polit Nurs Pract*. 2019;20(2):57–63. doi: 10.1177/1527154419838630. Epub 2019 Apr 3. PMID: 30943837.
273. The Psych NP. Why you should start your own telepsychiatry practice now! *YouTube*. April 10, 2021. Retrieved August 30, 2022, from https://www.youtube.com/watch?v=BDD-kUapPjo&t=21s
274. About Samantha Heim, PMHNP. *Home*. Date Unknown. Retrieved October 30, 2022, from https://partnersinpsychiatry.org/about-samantha-heim-pmhnp
275. Alfes CM, Zimmermann EP. 11A: Introduction to the Role of the Psychiatric-Mental Health Nurse Practitioner. In *Clinical simulations for the advanced practice nurse: A comprehensive guide for faculty, students, and Simulation Staff*. Springer Publishing Company. 2020: 449–450). Essay.
276. Wheeler K, Haber, J. Development of Psychiatric–Mental Health Nurse Practitioner Competencies: Opportunities for the 21st Century. *J Am Psychiatr Nurses Assoc*. 2004; 10(3): 129–138. DOI: 10.1177/1078390304266218
277. Muench, U, Fraze, T. The Future of Behavioral Health—Harnessing the Potential of Psychiatric Mental Health Nurse Practitioners. *JAMA Netw Open*. 2022;5(7):e2224365. doi:10.1001/jamanetworkopen.2022.24365
278. Bo Kyum Yang, Mehmet Burcu, Daniel J. Safer, Alison M. Trinkoff, Zito J. Comparing Nurse Practitioner and Physician Prescribing of Psychotropic Medications for Medicaid-Insured Youths. *J Child Adolesc Psychopharmacol*. 2018:166–172. http://doi.org/10.1089/cap.2017.0112
279. Muench U, Jura M, Samson Z, Brown TT, Spetz J. Prescribing patterns of nursing home residents living with dementia by specialty and provider type. UCSF Health workforce Center on Long Term Care; 2022. https://healthworkforce.ucsf.edu/publication/prescribing-patterns-nursing-home-residents-living-dementia-specialty-and-provider-type

280. Phoenix, B, Hurd, M, Chapman, S. Experience of Psychiatric Mental Health Nurse Practitioners in Public Mental Health. *Nursing Administration Quarterly*: July/September 2016; 40(3):212–224. doi: 10.1097/NAQ.0000000000000171
281. Perry A. UCLA wants to boost supply of psych nurse practitioners by offering online training. *LAist*. January 31, 2020. Retrieved November 27, 2021, from https://laist.com/latest/post/20200131/mental_health_nurse_practitioners_UCLA_online_course
282. Safdar K. Cerebral treated a 17-year-old without his parents' consent. They found out the day he died. *The Wall Street Journal*. September 30, 2022. Retrieved October 16, 2022, from https://www.wsj.com/articles/cerebral-treated-a-17-year-old-with-out-his-parents-consent-they-found-out-the-day-he-died-11664416497?fbclid=IwAR0pUXFSIDzq8WM-XoOrkqPr4PWAmZgKsFvjUn9sFoc-CubvuLndoW3Taus
283. Reuter D. A former nurse at embattled telehealth startup cerebral said that in her experience, nurse practitioners were handing out antipsychotic medicines like 'candy'. *Business Insider*. June 30, 2022. Retrieved July 23, 2022, from https://www.businessinsider.com/telehealth-startup-cerebral-prescribed-psych-meds-2022-6
284. What is a cerebral care counselor? Expert help for your emotional health. *Cerebral*. Date Unknown. Retrieved August 31, 2022, from https://cerebral.com/blog/what-is-a-care-counselor
285. Tan G. SoftBank Vision Fund 2 Backs Cerebral at $4.8 Billion Valuation. *Bloomberg.com*. December 8, 2021. Retrieved July 23, 2022, from https://www.bloomberg.com/news/articles/2021-12-08/softbank-vision-fund-2-backs-cerebral-at-4-8-billion-valuation
286. Swetlitz I, Davalos, J. Does Done prescribe Adderall for ADHD? Yes, but some patients are frustrated. *Bloomberg.com*. July 25, 2022. Retrieved August 31, 2022, from https://www.bloomberg.com/news/articles/2022-07-25/does-done-prescribe-adderall-for-adhd-yes-but-some-patients-are-frustrated
287. Done. ADHD managed: ADHD treatment made just for you. *Done*. Date Unknown. Retrieved August 31, 2022, from https://www.donefirst.com/
288. Depression & Anxiety Medication Online. *For hers*. Retrieved August 31, 2022, from https://www.forhers.com/psychiatry
289. Cerebral, Sponsored Facebook post (advertisement). *Facebook*. Screenshots obtained August 17, 2020.
290. Cerebral. Prescribers, therapists and counselors near you. *Cerebral*. Date Unknown. Retrieved August 31, 2022, from https://cerebral.com/care-team/prescribers?fbclid=IwAR13CWYRv6ZshGSlkNWNV_yJE1QWsEuOE2s4OSaoY6YpB0bI-188wAsjpyNA
291. Livingston S. 2,000 leaked documents and employees say Silicon Valley healthcare startup cerebral harmed hundreds of patients and prescribed serious medication with abandon. *Business Insider*. June 28, 2022. Retrieved August 31, 2022, from https://www.businessinsider.com/cerebral-leaked-documents-suggest-patient-harm-2022-6
292. Mosendz P, Melby C. ADHD Drugs Are Convenient To Get Online. Maybe Too Convenient. *Bloomberg.com*. March 11, 2022. Retrieved July 23, 2022, from https://www.bloomberg.com/news/features/2022-03-11/cerebral-app-over-prescribed-adhd-meds-ex-employees-say
293. Werner A, Kegu J. Former cerebral employees say company's practices put patients at risk: It's chaotic. It's confusing. It could be extremely dangerous. *CBS News*. June 22, 2022. Retrieved August 30, 2022, from https://www.cbsnews.com/news/cerebral-ceo-mental-health-startup/?ftag=CNM-00-10aac3a

294. Landi H. Ex-cerebral executive files lawsuit claiming the startup overprescribed ADHD meds. *Fierce Healthcare*. April 29, 2022. Retrieved July 23, 2022, from https://www.fiercehealthcare.com/health-tech/former-cerebral-executive-files-lawsuit-alleging-unsafe-prescribing-practices
295. Winkler R. Harlan band's descent started with an easy online Adderall prescription. *The Wall Street Journal*. August 20, 2022. Retrieved August 31, 2022, from https://www.wsj.com/articles/harlan-bands-descent-started-with-an-easy-online-adderall-prescription-11660916158
296. Newman N. Cerebral: A mindless strategy. *Authentic Medicine*. July 5, 2022. Retrieved August 31, 2022, from https://authenticmedicine.com/2022/07/cerebral-a-mindless-strategy/?fbclid=IwAR1e_KzNewr9yYoLxJ7zZP0ocvnBFAXJ4Ye0PbJmOm8lvDocx6-xad66HXA
297. Become a buprenorphine waivered practitioner. *SAMHSA*. Retrieved September 1, 2022, from https://www.samhsa.gov/medication-assisted-treatment/become-buprenorphine-waivered-practitioner
298. Rinker B. Money flows into Addiction Tech, but will it curb soaring opioid overdose deaths? *Fierce Biotech*. March 21, 2002. Retrieved September 1, 2022, from https://www.fiercebiotech.com/medtech/money-flows-addiction-tech-will-it-curb-soaring-opioid-overdose-deaths
299. About Ophelia: Reinventing the drug rehab model: Who we are. *Ophelia*. Retrieved September 1, 2022, from https://ophelia.com/about-us
300. Sepulveda A, Vasile G, Lux K, Todd C. More than a Suboxone app. *Workit Health*. June 10, 2022. Retrieved September 1, 2022, from https://www.workithealth.com/blog/more-than-a-suboxone-app/
301. Barnett ML, Lee D, Frank RG. In rural areas, Buprenorphine Waiver adoption since 2017 driven by nurse practitioners and physician assistants. *Health Aff* (Millwood). 2019;38(12):2048–2056. doi: 10.1377/hlthaff.2019.00859. PMID: 31794302; PMCID: PMC6938159.
302. Abram M, Guilamo-Ramos V, Forbes M. Buprenorphine Induction Simulation: Focus on Patient Safety and Quality Care. *Clinical Simulation in Nursing*. 2020; 4:35–41. ISSN 1876-1399, https://doi.org/10.1016/j.ecns.2019.11.009
303. The Opioid Addiction Clinic Course. *The Elite Nurse Practitioner*. Date Unknown. Retrieved September 4, 2022, from https://courses.elitenp.com/p/the-opioid-addiction-clinic-course
304. Aron S. Personal communication. November 25, 2022.
305. Hoffman R, Weinhouse G. Management of moderate and severe alcohol withdrawal syndromes. In: *UpToDate*. UpToDate: Waltham, MA. 2021.
306. Fink P, Deyo R, Hallvik S, Hildebran C. Opioid Prescribing Patterns and Patient Outcomes by Prescriber Type in the Oregon Prescription Drug Monitoring Program, *Pain Medicine*, 2018;19(12): 2481–2486. https://doi.org/10.1093/pm/pnx283
307. Lozada MJ, Raji MA, Goodwin JS, Kuo YF. (2020). Opioid Prescribing by Primary Care Providers: a Cross-Sectional Analysis of Nurse Practitioner, Physician Assistant, and Physician Prescribing Patterns. *Journal of General Internal Medicine*. 2020;35(9): 2584–2592. https://doi.org/10.1007/s11606-020-05823-0
308. State of Tennessee v Endo Health Solutions and Endo Pharmaceuticals. Circuit Court of Knox County, Tennessee Sixth Judicial District at Knoxville. May 14, 2019. Accessed January 2, 2022 at https://www.tn.gov/content/dam/tn/attorneygeneral/documents/pr/2019/pr19-20-complaint.pdf

309. Kelman B. Pain clinic nurse who gave 'colossal' prescriptions kept license due to board error, state attorneys say. *The Tennessean.* June 10, 2018. Retrieved October 16, 2022, from https://www.tennessean.com/story/money/2018/12/24/opioid-epidemic-nurse-christina-collins-prescriptions-east-tennessee/2269886002/
310. Kelman B. 3 alarming scripts from a nurse practitioner who was one of Tennessee's biggest opioid prescribers. *WBIR.com.* October 17, 2018. Retrieved October 16, 2022, from https://www.wbir.com/article/news/local/od-epidemic/3-alarming-scripts-from-a-nurse-practitioner-who-was-one-of-tennessees-biggest-opioid-prescribers/51-605003866
311. Osdol PV. Action news investigates: Suspended nurse practitioner saw patients and prescribed drugs, former employees say. *WTAE.* January 31, 2019. Retrieved September 11, 2022, from https://www.wtae.com/article/pittsburgh-suspended-nurse-practitioner-saw-patients-prescribed-drugs-former-employees-say/26102311#
312. Boots MT. Anchorage nurse practitioner faces 18 felony charges, including manslaughter, in opioid case. *Anchorage Daily News.* March 12, 2020. Retrieved September11,2022,fromhttps://www.adn.com/alaska-news/crime-courts/2020/03/12/anchorage-nurse-practitioner-faces-18-felony-charges-including-manslaughter-in-opioid-case/
313. Kim V. "Rock doc" continues to prescribe addictive drugs despite indictment. *The Fix.* May 15, 2019. Retrieved January 2, 2022, from https://www.thefix.com/rock-doc-continues-prescribe-addictive-drugs-despite-indictment
314. Khazan O. The hard-partying, rock-obsessed nurse at the center of a massive opioid bust. *The Atlantic.* February 25, 2021. Retrieved January 2, 2022, from https://www.theatlantic.com/health/archive/2021/01/rock-doc-opioids/617405/
315. INDICTMENT—United States Department of Justice. April 15, 2019. Retrieved January 2, 2022, from https://www.justice.gov/criminal-vns/file/1155421/download
316. Al-Agba N, Bernard R. (Hosts). Board of Nursing vs Board of Medicine: A case study of nurse practitioner 'Rock Doc' Jeffrey Young. *Patients at Risk.* Audio Podcast]. June 13, 2021. Retrieved from https://www.buzzsprout.com/1475923/episodes/8572990
317. Department of Health and Human Services. Director of the Office of Inspector General. State Boards and Medical Discipline. Department of Health and Human Services. Director of the Office of Inspector General. Performance Indicators, Annual Reports, and State Medical Discipline: A State by State Review. 1990. https://oig.hhs.gov/oei/reports/oei-01-89-00563.pdf
318. Fast A. Nurses are waiting 6 months or more for licenses despite hospitals' need for nurses. *NPR.* March 9, 2022. Retrieved October 30, 2022, from https://www.npr.org/2022/03/09/1085544625/nurses-are-waiting-6-months-or-more-for-licenses-despite-hospitals-need-for-nurs
319. Testimony regarding House Bill 2066 Carol Moreland, MSN, R.N. Executive Administrator. Health and Human Services, Committees, Kansas State Legislature. February 11, 2019. Retrieved October 30, 2022, from http://kslegislature.org/li_2020/b2019_20/committees/ctte_h_hhs_1/
320. Al-Agba N, Bernard R. (Hosts). Independent nurse practice in California—what patients and physicians should know [Audio Podcast]. *Patients at Risk.* February 21, 2021. Retrieved from buzzsprout.com/1475923/episodes/7709509

321. Newsengine. Owner of Eagle River Medical Clinic arrested on Federal Drug Charges. *The Alaska Star*. October 10, 2019. Retrieved September 11, 2022, from https://www.alaskastar.com/2019-10-09/owner-eagle-river-medical-clinic-arrested-federal-drug-charges
322. Cunningham D. Opioid patient 'at a loss' after Prescriber's suspension. *FOX 17 West Michigan News (WXMI)*. May 10, 2019. Retrieved October 30, 2022, from https://www.fox17online.com/2019/05/10/opioid-patient-at-a-loss-with-prescribers-suspension
323. Moore LM. Nurse suspended over opioid prescriptions enters agreement to get license back. *mlive*. October 21, 2019. Retrieved October 16, 2022, from https://www.mlive.com/news/muskegon/2019/10/nurse-suspended-over-opioid-prescriptions-enters-agreement-to-get-license-back.html
324. Bernstein M. Former nurse practitioner who helped run 'Pill Mill' in Portland sentenced to 4 years. *Oregonlive*. March 27, 2019. Retrieved October 22, 2022, from https://www.oregonlive.com/crime/2019/03/former-nurse-practitioner-who-helped-run-pill-mill-in-portland-to-be-sentenced-in-federal-court.html
325. Wexler R. The primary care shortage, nurse practitioners, and the patient-centered medicalhome. *VirtualMentor*.2010;12(1):36–40.doi:10.1001/virtualmentor.2010.12.1.pfor1-1001
326. NP Fact Sheet. American Association of Nurse Practitioners. https://www.aanp.org/about/all-about-nps/np-fact-sheet. Accessed June 10, 2020.
327. U.S. Department of Health and Human Services, Health Resources and Services Administration, National Center for Health Workforce Analysis. Highlights From the 2012 National Sample Survey of Nurse Practitioners. Rockville, Maryland: U.S. Department of Health and Human Services. 2014. [PDF].Retrieved from https://bhw.hrsa.gov/sites/default/files/bhw/nchwa/npsurveyhighlights.pdf. Accessed June 10, 2020.
328. Oregon Center for Nursing. Primary care workforce crisis looming in Oregon: Nurse practitioners vital to filling the gap, but not enough to go around. *Oregon Center for Nursing*. 2020. Retrieved January 25, 2023, from https://oregoncenterfornursing.org/wp-content/uploads/2022/07/2020_PrimaryCareWorkforceCrisis_Report_Web-1.pdf
329. Agency for Health Care Research and Quality. Primary care workforce facts and stats no. 2: The number of nurse practitioners and physician assistants practicing primary care in the United States. Retrieved January 25, 2023, from https://www.ahrq.gov/sites/default/files/publications/files/pcwork2.pdf
330. Allan J. The elite nurse practitioner. *The Elite Nurse Practitioner.* February 16, 2021. Retrieved December 23, 2021, from https://elitenp.com/
331. Allan J. The NP market saturation. *The Elite Nurse Practitioner.* April 16, 2021. Retrieved October 22, 2022, from https://elitenp.com/the-np-market-saturation/
332. Allan J. Sharks of the NP world. *The Elite Nurse Practitioner.* April 6, 2021. Retrieved October 22, 2022, from https://elitenp.com/sharks-of-the-np-world/
333. Martin B. The Economic Burden and Practice Restrictions Associated With Collaborative Practice Agreements: A National Survey of Advanced Practice Registered Nurses. *J Nurs Regul*. 2019;9(4): 22–30. ISSN 2155-8256, https://doi.org/10.1016/S2155-8256(19)30012-2
334. Collaborating Physicians for Nurse Practitioners. *Collaborating Docs.* October 12, 2022. Retrieved October 22, 2022, from https://collaboratingdocs.com/

335. Allan J. How much should a physician collaborator cost? *The Elite Nurse Practitioner,* Retrieved from https://elitenp.com/how-much-should-a-physician-collaborator-cost/, on December 21, 2021. Now removed; screenshot.
336. Allan J. Courses & books. *The Elite Nurse Practitioner.* September 7, 2022. Retrieved December 21, 2021, from https://elitenp.com/products/
337. Rutledge CM, Kott K, Schweickert PA, Poston R, Fowler C, Haney TS. Telehealth and eHealth in nurse practitioner training: current perspectives. *Adv Med Educ Pract.* 2017 Jun 26;8:399–409. doi: 10.2147/AMEP.S116071. PMID: 28721113; PMCID: PMC5498674.
338. Zemlak JL, Wilson P, VanGraafeiland B, Rodney T. Telehealth and the Psychiatric Mental Health Nurse Practitioner: Beyond the COVID-19 Pandemic. Journal of the American Psychiatric Nurses Association. 2021;0(0). doi:10.1177/10783903211045119
339. Allan J. How to create a telemedicine practice. *The Elite Nurse Practitioner.* Retrieved December21,2021fromhttps://courses.elitenp.com/p/how-to-create-a-telemedicine-practice
340. The GLAM NP: IV therapy, Injectables and wellness. *The Glam NP™.* Date Unknown. Retrieved December 30, 2021, from https://www.theglamnp.com/
341. Allan J. The IV-infusion and injection course. *The Elite Nurse Practitioner.* Retrieved December 24, 2021 from https://courses.elitenp.com/p/the-iv-infusion-clinic-course
342. FDA warns about stem cell therapies. U.S. Food and Drug Administration. FDA.gov. September 3, 2019. Retrieved December 24, 2021, from https://www.fda.gov/consumers/consumer-updates/fda-warns-about-stem-cell-therapies
343. Allan J. The stem cell and Regenerative Injection Clinic Course. *The Elite Nurse Practitioner.* Date Unknown. Retrieved December 21, 2021, from https://courses.elitenp.com/p/the-stem-cell-and-regenerative-injection-clinic-course
344. Lade D C. A deeper look at stem cell clinic where 3 patients lost sight after treatment. *Sun.* April 3, 2017. Retrieved December 30, 2021, from https://www.sun-sentinel.com/health/fl-stem-cell-injections-court-complaint-20170322-story.html
345. Renehan AG, Zwahlen M, Minder C, O'Dwyer ST, Shalet SM, Egger M. Insulin-like growth factor (IGF)-I, IGF binding protein-3, and cancer risk: systematic review and meta-regression analysis. *Lancet (London, England).* 2004;*363*(9418): 1346–1353. https://doi.org/10.1016/S0140-6736(04)16044-3
346. Allan J. The Advanced Clinical Peptide Treatment Course. *The Elite Nurse Practitioner.* Date Unknown. Retrieved December 24, 2021, from https://courses.elitenp.com/p/the-advanced-clinical-peptide-treatment-course
347. Al-Agba N, Bernard R. (Hosts). Chiropractor-owned "neuropathy" clinic scams patient for $8000. *Patients at Risk.* [Audio Podcast]. April 11, 2021. https://www.buzzsprout.com/1475923/episodes/8235520
348. Rathner S. 5 things to know about the carecredit card. *NerdWallet.* October 26, 2021. Retrieved December 30, 2021, from https://www.nerdwallet.com/article/credit-cards/carecredit-card
349. Teitz L. Family sues Nederland Clinic in loved one's death. *Beaumont Enterprise.* May25,2018.RetrievedDecember30,2021fromhttps://www.beaumontenterprise.com/news/article/Family-sues-Nederland-clinic-in-loved-one-s-death-12944878.php
350. Center for Drug Evaluation and Research. FDA Drug Safety Communication: FDA cautions about using testosterone products for low testosterone due to aging; requires labeling change to inform of possible increased risk of heart attack and

stroke with use. U.S. Food and Drug Administration. February 26, 2018. Retrieved December 24, 2021, from https://www.fda.gov/drugs/drug-safety-and-availability/fda-drug-safety-communication-fda-cautions-about-using-testosterone-products-low-testosterone-due

351. Allan J. The men's health and Testosterone Clinic course. *The Elite Nurse Practitioner.* Date Unknown. Retrieved December 22, 2021, from https://courses.elitenp.com/p/the-men-s-health-and-testosterone-clinic-course
352. Elite Nurse Practitioner Group. *Facebook Group*. Screenshots. Date Unknown.
353. AllanJ.Thewomen'shealthandHormoneReplacementtherapycourse.*TheEliteNurse Practitioner.* Date Unknown. Retrieved December 22, 2021, from https://courses.elitenp.com/p/the-women-s-health-and-hormone-replacement-therapy-course
354. Al-Agba N, Bernard R. (Hosts). Hormone Pellet Therapy: Is it Worth the Risk? *Patients at Risk.* [Audio Podcast]. May 16, 2021. Buzzsprout. https://www.buzzsprout.com/1475923/episodes/8436913
355. Allan J. The Ketamine Infusion Clinic Course. *The Elite Nurse Practitioner.* Date Unknown. Retrieved December 22, 2021, from https://courses.elitenp.com/p/the-ketamine-infusion-clinic-course
356. Jason A. Duprat. *Facebook.* October 23, 2019. Retrieved October 22, 2022, from https://www.facebook.com/jasonaduprat/posts/pfbid02y7hDDsUSPkeqJDKC2TbMnYYVSPmWtMCTSqrvxuekBcnEmgeDh6G9C2VRS4Q5urvxl
357. One in three pain patients suffer side effects after ketamine infusion therapy, study finds. *American Society of Anesthesiologists (ASA).* October 21, 2019. Retrieved December 24, 2021, from https://www.asahq.org/about-asa/newsroom/news-releases/2019/10/9-ketamine-side-effects
358. Huetteman E. FDA overlooked red flags in Drugmaker's testing of New Depression Medicine. *Kaiser Health News.* July 8, 2019. Retrieved December 24, 2021, from https://khn.org/news/fdas-approval-of-new-depression-drug-overlooked-red-flags-in-its-testing/
359. Allan J. The dermatology and cosmetic skin care course. *The Elite Nurse Practitioner.* Date Unknown. Retrieved December 22, 2021, from https://courses.elitenp.com/p/the-dermatology-and-cosmetic-skin-care-course
360. Allan J. The aesthetics and botox clinic course. *The Elite Nurse Practitioner.* Date Unknown. Retrieved December 22, 2021, from https://courses.elitenp.com/p/the-aesthetics-and-botox-clinic-course
361. Venkataram J. Tumescent liposuction: a review. *J Cutan Aaesthet Surg.* 2008; 1(2), 49–57. https://doi.org/10.4103/0974-2077.44159
362. R/noctor. NP does liposuction but don't worry! It's not surgery because "the opening is skin deep." *Reddit.* July 24, 2021. Retrieved December 31, 2021, from https://www.reddit.com/r/Noctor/comments/oqxj78/np_does_liposuction_but_dont_worry_its_not/
363. MidlevelWTF. Nurse practitioners demonstrate sterile surgical technique in classy Instagram liposuction video. *Midlevel.WTF*. September 21, 2021. Retrieved December 31, 2021, from https://www.midlevel.wtf/nurse-practitioners-demonstrate-sterile-surgical-technique-in-classy-instagram-liposuction-video/
364. That One Guy in Your Class. I messaged them on Instagram and this was their reply. Any validity to this? pic.twitter.com/gvqpnqap97. *Twitter.* July 23, 2021. Retrieved December 31, 2021, from https://twitter.com/boredandquippy/status/1418721349669904384/
365. Shelley C, Founder/Owner of Ageless 360 Aesthetics, MSN FNP-BC. *Linkedin.* Date Unknown. Retrieved December 31, 2020 from https://www.linkedin.com/in/shelley-c-79146832/

366. MidlevelCare. For-profit NP Diploma Mill Chamberlain University has "No group work"! No wonder why many NPS are so anti-interdisciplinary/interprofessional and poor team players! Why are they lobbying politicians so desperately to dissolve the healthcare team? Selfish, lazy, dangerous. pic.twitter.com/jigickvywa. *Twitter*. July 23, 2020. Retrieved December 31, 2021, from https://twitter.com/MidlevelCare/status/1312540918055084032
367. Comprehensive liposuction & fat transfer basic training for beginners. *International Society of Cosmetology*. Date Unknown. Retrieved December 31, 2021, from https://www.iscgmedia.com/iscg-lipo-course.html
368. Welcome to the Free Webinar. *Elite Medical Workshops*. Date Unknown. Retrieved December 31, 2021, from https://liposuction.elitemedworkshopsacademy.com/broadcast-room
369. Dr. Abbie Bledsoe, DNP, RN, FNP-C—Family Nurse. *Linkedin*. Date Unknown. Retrieved December 31, 2021 from https://www.linkedin.com/in/dr-abbie-bledsoe-dnp-rn-fnp-c-23730584
370. Doctor of nursing practice. Indiana State University. August 3, 2121. Retrieved December 31, 2021, from https://www.indstate.edu/academics/online/graduate/doctorate/dnp
371. Medical training and workshops for physicians and nurses. *Empire Medical Training*. Date Unknown. Retrieved December 31, 2021, from https://www.empire-medicaltraining.com/
372. Home. Indianapolis, In. *Ageless Aesthetics*. Date Unknown. Retrieved October 22, 2022, from https://agelessindy.com/
373. Barbed suture lift: Thread facelift: Thread lift: Thread lift cost. *ISAPS*. February 2, 2021. Retrieved January 1, 2022, from https://www.isaps.org/procedures/facial-plastic-surgery/barbed-suture-lift/
374. Allan J. The thyroid optimization course. *The Elite Nurse Practitioner*. Date Unknown. Retrieved October 22, 2022, from https://courses.elitenp.com/p/the-thyroid-optimization-course
375. Jonklaas J, Bianco AC, Bauer AJ, Burman KD, Cappola AR, Celi FS, Cooper DS, Kim BW, Peeters RP, Rosenthal MS, Sawka AM; American Thyroid Association Task Force on Thyroid Hormone Replacement. Guidelines for the treatment of hypothyroidism: prepared by the American Thyroid Association Taskforce on thyroid hormone replacement. *Thyroid*. 2014 Dec;24(12):1670–751. doi: 10.1089/thy.2014.0028. PMID: 25266247; PMCID: PMC4267409.
376. Juan AS. Southeast Texas nurse practitioner surrenders license, Optimum Clinic evicted. *KFDM*. January 30, 2019. Retrieved October 22, 2022, from https://kfdm.com/news/local/southeast-texas-nurse-practitioner-surrenders-license-optimum-clinic-evicted
377. Kuo YF, Loresto FL Jr, Rounds LR, et al.: States with the least restrictive regulations experienced the largest increase in patients seen by nurse practitioners. *Health Affairs*. 2013;32:1236–1243.
378. Yang BK, Trinkoff AM, Zito JM, Burcu M, Safer DJ, Storr CL, Johantgen ME, Idzik S. Nurse practitioner Independent Practice Authority and mental health service delivery in U.S. Community Health Centers. *Psychiatric Services*. 2017;68(10):1032–1038. https://doi.org/10.1176/appi.ps.201600495
379. Park J, Han X, Pittman P. Does expanded state scope of practice for nurse practitioners and physician assistants increase primary care utilization in community health centers? *J Am Assoc Nurse Pract*. 2020;32(6):447–458. doi: 10.1097/JXX.0000000000000263. PMID: 31397738.

380. Brom HM, Salsberry PJ, Graham MC. Leveraging health care reform to accelerate nurse practitioner full practice authority. *J Am Assoc Nurse Pract*. 2018;30(3): 120–130. https://doi.org/10.1097/JXX.0000000000000023
381. Horn P. Personal communication. April 23, 2019.
382. Patel N. Personal communication. September 11, 2022.
383. Confidential personal communication. October 26, 2022.
384. Lu K. Personal communication. August 21, 2021.
385. DeZure C. Personal communication. September 11, 2022.
386. Mann N. Personal communication. September 12, 2022.
387. Kara E. Personal communication. September 11, 2022.
388. Scears M. Personal communication. September 11, 2022.
389. Parsons J. Personal communication. August 23, 2021.
390. Rao C. Personal communication. September 11, 2022.
391. Hampton B. Personal communication. September 11, 2022.
392. Lundquist R. Personal communication. September 11, 2022.
393. Confidential Personal communication. October 27, 2022.
394. Graham K. Personal communication. August 23, 2021.
395. Hanna M. Personal communication. November 1, 2022.
396. American Association of Nurse Practitioners. Strategic Plan Accordion [Screenshot].
397. OregonLaws.org. 2017 ORS 743A.036. Services provided by certified nurse practitioner or licensed physician assistant. 2017. www.oregonlaws.org/ors/743A.036.
398. Altimari D. Nurse-midwives seek pay parity with OB-GYNs. *Courant.com* Retrieved June 20, 2020 from https://www.courant.com/politics/capitol-watch/hc-pol-nurse-midwives-pay-equity-20190228-ojopek4yd5ah5kvifqshhsdej4-.story.html?fbclid=IwAR3S07T7uNmGnltgAYRhrFL0WwyxG0WefrBf_3GPzx-02KXlY4yVymJEC30M. Published February 28, 2019.
399. Executive Order on Protecting and Improving Medicare for Our Nation's Seniors. Date Unknown. Retrieved June 20, 2020 from https://www.whitehouse.gov/presidential-actions/executive-order-protecting-improving-medicare-nations-seniors/
400. Al-Agba, N, Bernard, R (Hosts). Equal pay for 'equal' work: Inside the NP fight to be paid the same as physicians [Audio Podcast]. Patients at Risk. March 28, 2022. Retrieved from buzzsprout.com/1475923/episodes/7709509
401. Miller CC. As women take over a male-dominated field, the pay drops. *The New York Times*. March 18, 2016. Retrieved October 31, 2022, from https://www.nytimes.com/2016/03/20/upshot/as-women-take-over-a-male-dominated-field-the-pay-drops.html
402. Koop C. Boy died hours after he was diagnosed with earache. His Missouri mom is awarded $1.8M. *The Kansas City Star*. June 21, 2021. Retrieved October 27, 2022, from https://www.kansascity.com/news/nation-world/national/article252446403.html
403. COLLIP v. RATTS LLP No. 49A05–1501–CT–1 (Indiana 2015).
404. Waters V. Chilling testimony underway in case of botched Clayton County Circumcision. *95.5 WSB*. September 18, 2018. Retrieved October 27, 2022, from https://www.wsbradio.com/news/local/chilling-testimony-underway-case-botched-clayton-county-circumcision/cnkNGSxcdaMMNVfrYehtOK/
405. Sharpe J. Clayton jury awards boy $31M for botched circumcision. *AJC*. September 2218. Retrieved October 27, 2022, from https://www.ajc.com/news/local/breaking-clayton-jury-awards-boy-million-for-botched-circumcision/6iCLX0geH4UIiCLC2iwHJL/

406. Warren v. Dinter, 926 N.W.2d 370 (Minn. 2019).
407. Patients at Risk. Vicarious liability: Family physicians discuss malpractice suits due to NP association [Video]. January 15, 2023. YouTube. https://youtu.be/GlfPSnHgC1A
408. Al-Agba, N & Bernard, R (Hosts). Point of view: Let NPs and PAs practice independently—but hold them to the same standard as a physician [Audio podcast]. Patients at Risk. June 20, 2022. Buzzsprout. https://www.buzzsprout.com/1475923/episodes/10736605
409. Patients at Risk. Compartment syndrome: Physician training saves Vet's arm [Video]. December 23, 2022. YouTube. https://youtu.be/x7OXE1BaVxU
410. Market Innovation Center. 2019 updates in Primary Care Consumer Preferences—Advisory Board. 2019. Retrieved October 27, 2022, from https://www.advisory.com/-/media/Project/AdvisoryBoard/shared/Research/MIC/Executive-Research-Briefings/2019/2019-Updates-in-Primary-Care-Consumer-Preferences_MIC.pdf
411. Nyweide DJ, Lee W, Colla CH. Accountable care organizations increase in non-physician practitioners may signal shift for health care workforce. *Health Aff* (Millwood). 2020 Jun;39(6):1080–1086. doi: 10.1377/hlthaff.2019.01144. PMID: 32479221.
412. Batson B, Crosby, S, Fitzpatrick J. Targeting Value-Based Care with Physician-Led Care Teams. *Journal of the Mississippi State Medical Association*. 2022 January;63(1):18–21. Retrieved September 5, 2022, from https://ejournal.msmaonline.com/publication/?m=63060&i=735364&p=20&ver=html5
413. Robeznieks A. Amid doctor shortage, NPs and PAs seemed like a fix. Data's in: Nope. *American Medical Association*. March 17, 2022. Retrieved March 27, 2022, from https://www.ama-assn.org/practice-management/scope-practice/amid-doctor-shortage-nps-and-pas-seemed-fix-data-s-nope
414. Henry TA. Physician-owned hospitals seize their moment. *Mo Med*. 2013 Jul-Aug;110(4):282–4. PMID: 24003640; PMCID: PMC6179879.
415. Ramirez AG, Tracci MC, Stukenborg GJ, Turrentine FE, Kozower BD, Jones RS. Physician-owned surgical hospitals outperform other hospitals in medicare value-based purchasing program. *J Am Coll Surg*. 2016 Oct;223(4):559–67. doi: 10.1016/j.jamcollsurg.2016.07.014. Epub 2016 Aug 5. PMID: 27502368; PMCID: PMC5045811.
416. Courtney P. Maxwell A, Darrith B, Bohl D, Frisch NB, Valle D, Craig J. Reconsidering the Affordable Care Act's restrictions on physician-owned hospitals: Analysis of CMS data on total hip and knee arthroplasty. *Bone Jt Open*. 2017;99(22):1888–1894 doi: 10.2106/JBJS.17.00203
417. Blumenthal, D, Orav, E, Jena A, et al. Access, quality, and costs of care at physician owned hospitals in the United States: observational study. *BMJ* 2015;351:h4466 doi: 10.1136/bmj.h4466
418. Bernard R. Physicians face punishment for speaking out about non-physician care. *Medical Economics*. Date Unknown. March 31, 2018Retrieved from https://www.medicaleconomics.com/med-ec-blog/physicians-face-punishment-speaking-out-about-non-physician-care. Accessed May 19, 2020.
419. Bernard R. PA name change bad for patients and the profession. *Medscape*. January 7, 2022. Retrieved September 5, 2022, from https://www.medscape.com/viewarticle/966059
420. MidlevelWTF. Butthurt physician assistants can't handle the truth. *Midlevel.WTF*. January 13, 2022. Retrieved October 28, 2022, from https://www.midlevel.wtf/butthurt-physician-assistants-cant-handle-the-truth/

421. MidlevelWTF. Physician assistant compares PPP president to a Nazi war criminal. *Midlevel.WTF*. September 2, 2022. Retrieved November 1, 2022, from https://www.midlevel.wtf/physician-assistant-compares-ppp-president-to-a-nazi-war-criminal/
422. Kapu A, Orozco J. NPS, PAS say stop attacks and Support Healthcare colleagues. *Medscape*. January 14, 2022. Retrieved September 5, 2022, from https://www.medscape.com/viewarticle/966589?src=
423. Confidential personal communication. April 18, 2022.
424. Corp WM. WebMD to be acquired by KKR's internet brands. *PR Newswire*. June 26, 2018. Retrieved November 10, 2022 from https://www.prnewswire.com/news-releases/webmd-to-be-acquired-by-kkrs-internet-brands-300492704.html
425. Hampton S. Personal communication, October 30, 2022.
426. Parikh P. Personal communication, November 20, 2022.
427. Confidential personal communication. November 4, 2022.
428. Confidential personal communication. October 27, 2022.
429. Michelle. @UCRSoM @itsmadmedicine is one of your aspiring MS3 students?? He's disrespectful to his medical colleagues that function as a team across the board. If this is the future of medicine, your training, then god help us all. #disgraceful #badmedicine pic.twitter.com/qrtyd4tsot. *Twitter*. April 1, 2020. Retrieved October 27, 2022, from https://twitter.com/Michell48520357/status/1245417710126862337
430. MD DC. PSA #MedTwitter-Don't do this. And if you're an anonymous account doxing med students, you seriously need a life. Better yet, go volunteer in NY. Also LOL @Bpace8136 if you think any residency cares about your tweet @purviparikhmd @Reese_Tassey @drdanchoi @amychomd @LeahHoustonMD PIC. TWITTER.COM/GIST9YS6GO. *Twitter*. April 8, 2020. Retrieved October 27, 2022, from https://twitter.com/813jaferd/status/1247926832730693632
431. Newman, N. Personal communication. October 27, 2022.
432. Shryock, T. Covid exacerbates physician shortage. *Medical Economics*. September 29, 2021. Retrieved January 25, 2023, from https://www.medicaleconomics.com/view/covid-exacerbates-physician-shortage
433. Patients at Risk. Is PPP a 'fringe' group? Responding to the AANP's accusations in Medical Economics [Video]. December 20, 2021. YouTube. https://youtu.be/EDXn7RAomTM
434. Kapu, A. Response: Full practice authority for nurse practitioners needed to address physician shortage. *Medical Economics*. October 5, 2021. Retrieved January 25, 2023, from https://www.medicaleconomics.com/view/response-full-practice-authority-for-nurse-practitioners-needed-to-address-shortage
435. Romo V. What's it take to go from mechanic to physician at 51? Patience, an Ohio doctor says. *NPR*. October 5, 2022. Retrieved November 2, 2022, from https://www.npr.org/2022/10/05/1126661330/carl-allamby-mechanic-to-physician
436. McAuliffe C. Use of non-physician providers in the Nephrology workforce needs careful consideration and urgent attention. *ASN Kidney Care News*. September 2022.
437. McCrory G, Patton D, Moore Z, O'Connor T, Nugent L. The impact of advanced nurse practitioners on patient outcomes in chronic kidney disease: A systematic review. *Journal of Renal Care*. 2018;44(4), 197–209. https://doi.org/10.1111/jorc.12245
438. Taz. Whether it was due to bad pr, the article in MedPage or backlash by whomever, the unsound decision made by sound physicians to have a "dyad" model using npps has been cancelled. This is the kind of cancel culture I like. One in which CPOM keeps its nose out of medicine so pic.twitter.com/r7flyykboc. *Twitter*. July

24, 2021. Retrieved October 27, 2022, from https://twitter.com/Suburbanbella/status/1419031762026467329

439. Hylton M. Personal conversation. November 20, 2022.
440. Hall M, Suddeath D. Indiana law to require more transparency in medical provider advertising. *News and Tribune*. June 16, 2022. Retrieved November 2, 2022, from https://www.newsandtribune.com/news/indiana-law-to-require-more-transparency-in-medical-provider-advertising/article_94276afc-ed8d-11ec-bfc9-5398978a9128.html
441. Fein v. Permanente Medical Group S.F. No. 24336. Retrieved June 10, 2020 from https://law.justia.com/cases/california/supreme-court/3d/38/137.html. 1985
442. Simonson v. Keppard. 225 S.W.3d 868 (Tex. App. 2007).
443. Lattimore vs Dickey. Retrieved June 10, 2020 from https://law.justia.com/cases/california/court-of-appeal/2015/h040126.html. 2015.
444. Myers LC, Sawicki D, Heard L, Camargo CA Jr, Mort E. A description of medical malpractice claims involving advanced practice providers. *J Healthc Risk Manag*. 2021 Jan;40(3):8–16. doi: 10.1002/jhrm.21412. Epub 2020 May 3. PMID: 32362078.
445. Advanced practice providers see more complex patients, sued more. Online Continuing Medical Education. *Relias Media—Continuing Medical Education Publishing*. December 1, 2020. Retrieved October 25, 2022, from https://www.reliasmedia.com/articles/147133-advanced-practice-providers-see-more-complex-patients-sued-more-often
446. Data Analysis Tool. The NPDB—Data Analysis Tool. Date Unknown. Retrieved October 25, 2022, from https://www.npdb.hrsa.gov/analysistool/
447. Staff Writers. Nurse practitioner liability report reveals malpractice claim costs are on the rise. *Daily Nurse*. September 14, 2022. Retrieved October 25, 2022, from https://dailynurse.com/nurse-practitioner-malpractice-liability-report
448. Bernard R (Host). Lack of informed consent: Patient nearly dies after CRNA mishap [Audio Podcast]. November 21, 2022. Retrieved from https://www.buzzsprout.com/1475923/episodes/11607643
449. Audax. Portfolio factsheet. Audax Private Equity | Hopco | Portfolio. Retrieved October 25, 2022, from https://www.audaxprivateequity.com/system/uploads/fae/file/asset/275/Audax_PE_Firm-Profile-Website.pdf
450. Audax private equity mergers and acquisitions summary. *Mergr*. Retrieved October 25, 2022, from https://mergr.com/audax-private-equity-mergers-acquisitions
451. Smith M. Dallas jury awards $21M to patient who was put under anesthesia and suffered brain injury. *WFAA.com*. October 31, 2022. Retrieved November 1, 2022 from https://www.wfaa.com/article/news/local/investigates/dallas-jury-awards-21m-to-patient-who-suffered-brain-injury/287-9f1c5fab-fb69-40c4-bc64-17b5f59a789a
452. American Medical Association. Truth in Advertising Survey Results. 2018. https://www.ama-assn.org/sites/ama-assn.org/files/corp/media-browser/premium/arc/tia-survey_0.pdf
453. New Jersey Health Care Transparency Act. S2465. Date Unknown. Retrieved November 2, 2022, from https://trackbill.com/bill/new-jersey-senate-bill-2465-new-jersey-health-care-transparency-act/1923061/
454. Jones C. SLO County DA: Nurse fined for falsely advertising as doctor. *San Luis Obispo News*. November 14, 2022. Retrieved November 18, 2022, from https://www.sanluisobispo.com/news/local/crime/article268743042.html
455. Legal fees, organized by Sarah Erny. *Gofundme.com*. Retrieved November 18, 2022, from https://www.gofundme.com/f/94gpwr-legal-fees?fbclid=IwAR153u2-PcTBN9hzUEXiz9UXCj69vrTOzMp3qGGsSx1C8N2gafCuP2wqBrI